Transnational Dynamics of

Civil wars are the dominant form of violence in the contemporary international system, yet they are anything but local affairs. This book explores the border-crossing features of such wars by bringing together insights from international relations theory, sociology, and transnational politics with a rich comparative-quantitative literature. It highlights the causal mechanisms – framing, resource mobilization, socialization, among others – that link the international and transnational to the local, emphasizing the methods required to measure them. Contributors examine specific mechanisms leading to particular outcomes in civil conflicts ranging from Chechnya, to Afghanistan, to Sudan, to Turkey. *Transnational Dynamics of Civil War* thus provides a significant contribution to debates motivating the broader move to mechanism-based forms of explanation, and will engage students and researchers of international relations, comparative politics, and conflict processes.

JEFFREY T. CHECKEL is Professor of International Studies and Simons Chair in International Law and Human Security at Simon Fraser University, and Research Professor in the Centre for the Study of Civil War at the Peace Research Institute Oslo (PRIO). He has published extensively in leading European and North American journals, and is the author of *Ideas and International Political Change: Soviet/Russian Behavior and the End of the Cold War* (1997), editor of *International Institutions and Socialization in Europe* (Cambridge University Press, 2007), and co-editor (with Peter J. Katzenstein) of *European Identity* (Cambridge University Press, 2009).

Transnational Dynamics of Civil War

Edited by

JEFFREY T. CHECKEL
Simon Fraser University
Peace Research Institute Oslo

CAMBRIDGE
UNIVERSITY PRESS

University Printing House, Cambridge CB2 8BS, United Kingdom

Published in the United States of America by Cambridge University Press, New York

Cambridge University Press is part of the University of Cambridge.

It furthers the University's mission by disseminating knowledge in the pursuit of
education, learning and research at the highest international levels of excellence.

www.cambridge.org
Information on this title: www.cambridge.org/9781107643253

© Cambridge University Press 2013

First published 2013
First paperback edition 2014

A catalogue record for this publication is available from the British Library

Library of Congress Cataloguing in Publication data

Transnational dynamics of civil war / edited by Jeffrey T. Checkel, Simon Fraser
University, Peace Research Institute Oslo.
    pages cm
Includes bibliographical references and index.
ISBN 978-1-107-02553-0
    1. Civil War.   2. International relations.   I. Checkel, Jeffrey T., 1959– editor
of compilation.
    JC328.5.T73 2013
    303.6′4–dc23

2012028899

ISBN 978-1-107-02553-0 Hardback
ISBN 978-1-107-64325-3 Paperback

For Bullers

Contents

Figures

Tables

Contributors

FIONA B. ADAMSON – Associate Professor, Department of Politics and International Studies, SOAS, University of London

KRISTIN M. BAKKE – Lecturer in Politics and International Relations, School of Public Policy, University College London

ANDREW BENNETT – Professor, Department of Government, Georgetown University

JEFFREY T. CHECKEL – Professor and Simons Chair, School for International Studies, Simon Fraser University, and Research Professor, Centre for the Study of Civil War, Peace Research Institute Oslo

STEPHAN HAMBERG – Ph.D. Candidate, Department of Political Science, University of Washington

KRISTIAN BERG HARPVIKEN – Director, Peace Research Institute Oslo

SARAH KENYON LISCHER – Associate Professor, Department of Politics and International Affairs, Wake Forest University

MARTIN AUSTVOLL NOME – Post-doctoral Research Associate, Centre for the Study of Civil War, Peace Research Institute Oslo

HANS PETER SCHMITZ – Associate Professor, Maxwell School of Citizenship and Public Affairs, Syracuse University

NILS B. WEIDMANN – Marie Curie Post-Doctoral Fellow, Centre for the Study of Civil War, Peace Research Institute Oslo

ELISABETH JEAN WOOD – Professor, Department of Political Science, Yale University

Preface

Our iconic images of civil war emphasize its local and localized nature. From village-level atrocities during the Greek civil conflict, to bombed-out buildings in Grozny, the capital of Chechnya, to child soldiers cradling AK-47s in Uganda, the focus is on failed or failing states. The very term civil war is meant to mark such conflict as something quite different from inter-state wars. Indeed, the word civil implies that such wars play out in some reasonably well-defined space, typically within the borders of a state.

We now know, however, this is rarely in fact the case. Rebel groups fighting civil wars often operate and recruit across borders; in many instances, neighboring states intervene in an ongoing civil conflict; diaspora communities – transnational in nature by their very essence – play key roles in many civil wars. Such wars thus have border-crossing and transnational dimensions; these need to be explored – theoretically and empirically – if we are to understand fully the complex dynamics behind what has become the dominant mode of organized violence in the international system.

This book addresses such challenges and does so by bringing together insights and arguments from two distinct research programs: work in international relations and sociology on peaceful transnationalism; and a rich and growing comparative-quantitative literature on civil war. The latter has documented in a sophisticated and rigorous manner the importance of transnationalism in civil conflict; the former provides a set of theoretical arguments and methods to explain the nature of these transnational dynamics. Put more colloquially, ours is an endeavor where transnationalism meets the dark side of global politics.

This meeting is captured through the articulation of several causal mechanisms linking the international and transnational to the local and particular. However, the analysis is anything but abstract, as we examine specific mechanisms leading to particular outcomes in a given civil conflict. This operational focus puts a premium on method, on how we actually measure mechanisms in action. And here, we join with many others in arguing that a key measurement tool is process tracing. Thus, beyond literatures on transnationalism and civil war, our approach and findings speak directly to key conceptual and methodological debates motivating the broader move to mechanism-based forms of explanation.

All chapters have benefitted from several rounds of discussion and revision. Chapter 1 started as a conceptual memo for a first project workshop, a brainstorming meeting held at the Peace Research Institute Oslo (PRIO) in December 2007. This was followed by three workshops – Washington DC (October 2008), Simon Fraser University (October 2009), PRIO (August 2010) – where the other chapter drafts were discussed and debated.

I owe thanks to many people and institutions, most importantly to the Centre for the Study of Civil War (CSCW) at PRIO. Scott Gates, Andrew Feltham, and others created a welcoming and intellectually exciting environment for a civil-war "newbie" – one who had spent the previous decade studying a slightly different topic (European integration and identity). I would like especially to thank and acknowledge Kristian Berg Harpviken, both for inviting me to join the CSCW and for his key role at early stages of this project.

Matthew Evangelista and Scott Gates gave indispensable help at a crucial later stage. At our last workshop, they acted as discussants not only of individual chapters, but also of the project as a whole. Their differing areas of expertise (Evangelista – transnationalism; Gates – civil war), trenchant criticisms, and constructive suggestions have made this a much better book. Shortly after this final meeting, when the manuscript was under review at Cambridge, two anonymous reviewers did a brilliant job reminding me that ours is a volume with important things to say about civil war – and not just about method and mechanisms!

For helpful comments on various parts of the manuscript, I thank – in addition to those already named – Andy Bennett, Lars-Erik Cederman, Marty Finnemore, Stephan Hamberg, Anna Holzscheiter, Andy Mack, Martin Austvoll Nome, Martha Snodgrass, and Elisabeth Wood, as well as the students of my May 2011 Ph.D. seminar, "Qualitative Methods and the Study of Civil War," and seminar audiences at the Peace Studies Program, Cornell University; the Mershon Center for International Security Studies, Ohio State University; the Swiss Federal

Institute of Technology (ETH Zürich); the University of Washington International Security Colloquium; the Otto Suhr Institute of Political Science, Free University Berlin; and the Liu Institute for Global Issues, University of British Columbia.

Last and certainly not least, I owe a debt of gratitude to Damian Penfold, who carefully – and cheerfully – edited and formatted the entire manuscript in-between conducting stints, and to Eileen Doherty-Sil for preparation of the index. At Cambridge University Press, I thank John Haslam for organizing an efficient, rigorous but fair review process, and Carrie Parkinson for overseeing the production of the book.

For administrative and logistical assistance, I thank Andrew Feltham at the CSCW in Oslo, Ellen Yap at the School for International Studies at Simon Fraser University, and the Moynihan Center at Syracuse University. Financial support was provided by the Norwegian Research Council, the Centre for the Study of Civil War at PRIO, Syracuse University, and the Simons International Endowment at Simon Fraser University.

I end by stating the obvious. This book would not exist if it were not for the dedication and perseverance of its contributors. They not only complied – many times – with my requests for changes and revisions, they also helped a recovering "Euroholic" rediscover his roots in what we used to call security studies. When I left the field 20 years ago, the central actors were superpowers with their ICBMs; today, they are more likely to be imploding states and rebel groups. It is my modest hope this book tells us something new about the latter.

JTC
Vancouver

PART I

Civil war – mobilizing across borders

1 | *Transnational dynamics of civil war**

JEFFREY T. CHECKEL

Civil war has become the dominant mode of organized violence in the post-Cold War international system. Depending upon the counting rule employed, such wars have afflicted from a third to a half of all nations. This internal warfare is not just extremely common, it is persistent, with 20 percent of nations experiencing at least ten years of civil war since 1960. During the mid 1990s – to take just one example – nearly a third of the countries in sub-Saharan Africa had active civil wars or conflicts (Blattman and Miguel 2010, 3–4).

Equally important, this form of 'internal warfare' is rarely internal, with 55 percent of all rebel groups active since 1945 having transnational linkages (Salehyan 2009, 5). Indeed, civil wars nearly always create opportunities and incentives for outside actors to intervene; these actors may be other states, rebel groups, transnational civil society, or the international community, and this intervention may be malign (fanning the war) or benign (transnational NGOs targeting the use of child soldiers). Moreover, such wars are often fueled by cross-border flows of goods, including material (weapons), money (diaspora financing) and human (new recruits for rebel groups). Finally, civil wars can spur social mobilization across borders – by strengthening senses of community among ethnic co-brethren, say.

So, the transnational clearly matters, with scholars documenting a strong correlation between various transnational factors and actors and changes in civil war dynamics. In this important sense, such wars are no different. Across a variety of subfields and research programs in comparative politics and international relations (IR), it has become a

* For helpful comments and discussions, I thank the project participants, the students of my May 2011 Ph.D. seminar, "Qualitative Methods and the Study of Civil War," and, especially, Andy Bennett, Lars-Erik Cederman, Matt Evangelista, Marty Finnemore, Scott Gates, Stephan Hamberg, Andy Mack, Martin Austvoll Nome, Martha Snodgrass, Elisabeth Wood, and two anonymous reviewers for Cambridge University Press.

truism to argue that the external and the internal, the global and the local, the state and non-state actors are inextricably linked. The theoretical challenge – for scholars in general and students of civil war in particular – is to explain the interactions across these various levels.

This introduction and the essays that follow take up this challenge, exploring the relation of the transnational to the local in the context of civil war. How do we conceptualize this transnational dimension? In material or social terms? How does it affect civil war dynamics? By bringing new material resources into play? By affecting cost/benefit calculations? By promoting learning among actors? Under what conditions do transnational factors increase or decrease levels of civil violence? What is the nature of the causal connection between the transnational and the local? Put differently, what is the causal mechanism at work?

We argue that to address these issues requires three moves. Theoretically, the finding of transnationalism's importance in civil war needs to be linked to existing literatures in other subfields that have extensively conceptualized and empirically documented such non-state dynamics; key here is work on transnational politics in IR theory and sociology. Analytically, one needs a more robust understanding of causality, where the goal is the measurement of causal mechanisms and not simply establishing causal effects. Methodologically, the central challenge is practical – to measure mechanisms in action.[1]

The volume thus addresses gaps and promotes learning across three literatures. For students of civil war, we supplement political economy models and correlational analysis with process-based evidence on its social and transnational dimensions. We thus provide new insights to enduring questions related to civil conflict – agency and motives, group mobilization, and international intervention, to name just a few. For those studying transnationalism, we build upon but go beyond a focus on the benevolent side of world politics by exploring and theorizing transnational violence – that is, cross-border activities with malevolent intent and consequences. For scholars interested in process, we provide detailed evidence for the advantages – and disadvantages – of a move to mechanism-based theorizing.

The remainder of this introductory essay is organized as follows. I begin with a brief review of work on transnationalized civil war, arguing that a diffusion metaphor is often invoked to link the external

---

[1] More formally, we measure their observable implications; see below.

and internal. To operationalize it, I draw upon – in the second section – theories of transnational politics. Work by international relations specialists and sociologists offers a rich menu of mechanisms – framing, learning, brokerage, persuasion – to explain *how* transnationalism matters in civil war. The third section connects the theory to data by focusing on method; special attention is paid to process tracing, as this is particularly well suited to measuring causal mechanisms. In the final section, I conclude and preview the volume's structure.

Civil war and the transnational

Over the past decade, new research on civil war has put its study squarely in the academic mainstream. At first quantitative in nature, it has been complemented in recent years by a growing qualitative literature on civil conflict. My purpose here is not a wide-ranging review of this rich literature – for this, see Tarrow 2007, and Blattman and Miguel 2010; rather, the concern is how this work conceptualizes and measures transnationalism (see also Wood, this volume).

Early efforts emphasized aggregate measures (Fearon and Laitin 2003), thus overlooking the sub-national, international, or transnational dimensions of civil war. There was an inclination "to treat civil wars as purely domestic phenomena" and a consequent neglect of "transborder linkages and processes" (Cederman, Girardin, and Gleditsch 2009, 404). More generally, the analytic starting point was individual states treated as independent entities – a so-called closed polity approach (Gleditsch 2007). Cognizant of this limitation, several scholars spearheaded a two-pronged move to develop more disaggregated databases. Some have disaggregated geographically and spatially, using so-called geo-referenced conflict data (Buhaug and Gates 2002; Buhaug and Rød 2006).

More important for my purposes, others have disaggregated by moving away from state-level, aggregate proxies – for example, by coding the attributes of non-state conflict actors (Cunningham, Gleditsch, and Salehyan 2006). This has allowed researchers to document the impact of new actors and interactions across state boundaries in a wide array of cases. Work of this sort is important, not only advancing the civil-war research program, but also – by adopting an open polity perspective – aligning itself with the bulk of

IR scholarship. It has allowed scholars to offer a more nuanced picture of civil conflict, including its transnational dimensions.

As one important example, consider Salehyan's book-length study on what he calls transnational insurgencies (Salehyan 2009). In it, he utilizes rich and disaggregated data embedded in a rigorous research design to document that external sanctuaries have played a central role in more than half of armed insurgencies since 1945 (see also Malet 2010). Salehyan also explains exactly how international borders shape the behavior of rebel groups involved in such conflicts. Simply put, insurgencies seeking to challenge a state often have the option of mobilizing abroad – and especially in neighboring states – where they are safely out of reach of domestic foes. The book is anything but a closed polity approach; rather, it demonstrates the analytic power to be gained when civil wars are viewed in their broader international and transnational contexts (see also Kalyvas and Balcells 2010).

Theory and analytics

Scholarship on the transnational dimensions of civil conflict has illuminated the broad trends at work, and has done so in a methodologically self-conscious way that enhances the reliability of the findings. This is no small feat, especially when one remembers that the data come from violent and inaccessible parts of the world, from failed or failing states. Moreover, there has been a concern to integrate the data with theoretical arguments of increasing sophistication – for example, Salehyan's theory of transnational rebellion that draws upon work on political opportunity structures and conflict bargaining (Salehyan 2009, ch. 1). This is a welcome and progressive move (Checkel 2010).

At the same time, such theorizing is typically not linked to the now voluminous literature on transnationalism in world politics (Risse 2002). This seems odd – for a more systematic connection to this research would alert scholars to alternative theoretical starting points for understanding the cross-border dynamics of civil conflict (see also Tarrow 2007, 588–590).

The work of Kristian Gleditsch and his collaborators is typical in this regard. More than any others, they have documented the role of various transnational factors in civil war (Gleditsch and Salehyan 2006; Gleditsch 2007). It is somewhat puzzling, however, that these effects are interpreted primarily through the lens of rational choice, where transnationalism influences the dynamics of civil war by altering material incentives and shifting cost/benefit calculations (Gleditsch and Salehyan 2006, 341; Gleditsch 2007, 294–299; see also Gates 2002; Fortna 2004, 487–490; Kalyvas 2006, 2008; Humphreys and Weinstein 2007; Blattman 2007, 7–13; Toft 2007, 102–107). Part of the justification for this focus is that non-material factors such as norms, ideas, and learning are difficult to measure (Salehyan 2009, 39)[2] – an assertion that is hard to understand in light of advances in empirical constructivist research over the past 15 years (Adler 2002).

The literature on transnational politics is much more agnostic on social theory, with some preferring rational choice (Cooley and Ron 2002), some social constructivism (Price 1998), while still others combine the two (Risse, Ropp, and Sikkink 1999a). If the goal is to understand the full range of dynamics affecting civil war, then we can only gain by adopting a broadened social-theoretic starting point. As Cederman, et al., argue "additional research is needed on the details of the border-transgressing bond, especially as regards the nature of the actor-specific mechanism" (Cederman, Girardin, and Gleditsch 2009, 433). And from a problem-driven perspective, this 'bond' may equally well be captured by rationalist or constructivist perspectives.

Methodological issues

Students of civil war have shown a growing interest in process (Tarrow 2007) – for example, in exploring the linkages from the transnational to a particular civil conflict. Given this shift, it is not surprising that the language of causal mechanisms is now often invoked (Fortna 2004; Gleditsch and Salehyan 2006, 335–336, 360; Salehyan 2008). Yet, it is unclear what is meant by such language. In one recent study where the transnational to civil war nexus is explored, causal mechanisms seem central to the analysis, but are never defined. Instead, it is left to the reader to infer that a mechanism equals a hypothesis, diffusion, spillover effects, or ethnicity (Cederman, Girardin, Gleditsch 2009, 408, 412, 433; see also Gleditsch 2007, 297; and the discussion in Fjelde "Transnational Dimensions," 5). Causal mechanisms can be

---

[2] See also Hanne Fjelde. (undated) "Transnational Dimensions of African Civil Wars and the Triple-R Framework." In Thomas Ohlson (ed.), *From Intra-State War to Durable Peace: Conflict and its Resolution in Africa after the Cold War.* Unpublished Manuscript, Uppsala University, 14–15.

defined as the process by which an effect is produced or a purpose is accomplished (see next section). However, it is not clear this is what the civil war scholars are measuring empirically. Moreover, even in those cases where more effort is devoted to theorizing transnational mechanisms, these then vanish in the empirical testing (Gleditsch and Salehyan 2006, 342, 347–350). There would appear to be a mismatch between the language of causal mechanisms and methodological choice, between conceptualizing cause as a process (→ mechanisms) and measuring it via quantitative techniques (→ covariation).

Even the most sophisticated, mixed method research on transnationalized civil war has problems at this level. Consider again Salehyan's *Rebels without Borders* (2009). Methodologically, the rigor of the book's quantitative first half is not carried over to its case studies, which is unfortunate given the availability of an increasingly sophisticated case-methods literature (Bennett and George 2005; Gerring 2007a, for example). As a result, the case studies – despite the author's claims (Salehyan 2009, 108, 110, 122–123, 164) – fail to provide evidence for the causal mechanisms he posits to explain the correlational findings. For example, bargaining dynamics based on cost/benefit calculations figure prominently in Salehyan's theory; yet, the case study chapters provide no process-level evidence that such dynamics were at work.

Here again, the transnational politics literature offers both conceptual discussions and empirical applications relevant to students of civil war. Conceptually, it has taken seriously the logical implications of open polity models, developing cross-level theoretical frameworks. These move well beyond level-of-analysis approaches (Singer 1961) or arguments about residual variance (Moravcsik 1993), to emphasize cross-level interactions that put the spotlight on process (Keck and Sikkink 1998; Risse, Ropp, and Sikkink 1999a). Such a conceptual move is necessary if one is to explore the role of transnational causal mechanisms.

Empirically, scholars of transnationalism have put a good bit of thought into the methods one needs to measure such dynamics. Moving beyond the measurement of causal effects, they have demonstrated that techniques are available for capturing mechanisms. In particular, they have convincingly shown the utility of a method known as process tracing (Risse-Kappen 1995a; Risse, Ropp, and Sikkink 1999a), which is seen as key for measuring mechanisms (Bennett and George 2005, ch. 10). These empirical, operational applications of the technique should be of great help to students of civil war, who increasingly invoke it while failing to demonstrate how it works in practice (Weinstein 2007, 53–59; see also Kalyvas 2007).

Summary

Scholarly research has documented that transnationalism plays an important role in civil conflict, but the specific causal mechanisms remain poorly understood, for both theoretical and methodological reasons. From a broader perspective, these limitations are understandable and no surprise. The success to date of the civil war research program (Blattman and Miguel 2010) means these studies have reached a new level of sophistication, where open-polity models and transnational dynamics are stressed, and causal mechanisms are invoked. However, it is one thing to speculate about transnational mechanisms; it is quite another properly to theorize and measure them.

Transnational mechanisms of civil war

Progress in addressing these gaps requires a two-fold analytic-theoretical move – to the language and practice of causal mechanisms and to theories of transnationalism. I begin by situating this volume's understanding of causal mechanisms in the (vast) literature on them. Next, I turn to transnationalist scholarship in international relations and sociology. This work suggests specific ways to make operational the diffusion mechanism invoked in much of the civil war literature, a point I demonstrate with examples from the volume's empirical contributions. A third section then turns the tables, suggesting that transnationalists have something to learn as well, in particular, how to theorize transnational violence.

Causal mechanisms – from confusion to emergent consensus

Thinking about mechanisms has a long history in the philosophy of science and in the social sciences. Philosophers – for several hundred years – and social scientists – more recently – have debated the nature and meaning of cause (Kurki 2008 for a state-of-the-art review). Is it best captured by a Humean understanding of constant conjunction and covariation or a realist account of cause as process? Among sociologists and inspired by the work of Robert Merton and his colleagues at Columbia University, mechanisms were the subject of intensive inquiry in the early years after World War II (Hedström and Swedberg 1998, 1–2). Thus, in the distant and not-so-distant past, the interest in mechanisms was there.

Such interest has blossomed among political scientists over the past decade, due both to a growing dissatisfaction with structural theories (Hall 2003, 375–388) and the rise of a new generation of scholars (see also Bennett, this volume). Rationalists now do mechanisms (Elster 1998), constructivists see them as a core component of their social theory (Wendt 1999), quantitative researchers increasingly invoke them (Gleditsch and Salehyan 2006, 341–344), and – among qualitative methodologists – new research on case studies gives mechanisms a pride of place (Bennett and George 2005; Gerring 2007a).

One not surprising result of all this attention is that different authors define a causal mechanism in different ways, a fact now widely noted and bemoaned (Mahoney 2001; Gerring 2007b; Falleti and Lynch 2009). At an intuitive level, it is easy to define a mechanism – it connects things and captures process. However, the devil, as always, is in the detail. Are mechanisms easy or hard (i.e., unobservable) to see? Must the use of mechanisms be premised on an ontological stance of methodological individualism?

Building upon recent discussions in the literature, I define a causal mechanism as "the pathway or process by which an effect is produced or a purpose is accomplished" (Gerring 2007b, 178; see also Caporaso 2009). Mechanisms are thus "relational and processual concepts … not reducible to an intervening variable" (Falleti and Lynch 2009, 1149); they are "the operative or motive part, process or factor in a concrete system that produces a result" (Wight 2006, 34). These minimalist definitions capture other extant usages of the term (Gerring 2007b; see also Gerring and Barresi 2003).

Moving from conceptualization to a more operational level, there is also a growing consensus on measurement. Philosophers of social science – and especially scientific realists – view causal mechanisms as ultimately unobservable ontological entities that exist in the world, not in our heads; they are thus more than mere "analytical constructs that facilitate prediction" (Wight 2006, 31–32, quote at 31). If mechanisms are real but unobservable entities, the implications for measurement are clear: we measure not hypothesized mechanisms, but their observable implications.

Given the invocation of scientific realism in the last paragraph, I should highlight one area where considerable confusion remains: the philosophical foundation of empirical, mechanism-based social science. As a number of sharp-thinking analysts have noted, there is a tension between the growing use of mechanism-based thinking in American political science and this same community's continuing adherence to a philosophical position – positivism – at odds with a turn to mechanisms (McKeown 1999, 163–164; Johnson 2006; Wight 2006, 31–32; Gerring 2007b, 164). For sure, such philosophical disputes, by their very nature, will not be resolved any time soon (if ever).

In this volume, our response to such confusion and disputes is two-fold. First and pragmatically, we just get on with it, doing methodo-logically self-conscious mechanism-based social science. Implicitly, all contributors adopt a variant of scientific realism. With its emphasis on measuring causation via mechanisms and a practical stance of "epistemological opportunism" (Wight 2002, 36), it well suits our purposes. The latter point is important, as methods flow from epistemology. This opportunism thus legitimates and indeed mandates a plurality of methods when it comes to the measurement of mecha-nisms. Contributors to this volume thus measure mechanisms in a variety of ways, from case studies and process tracing to agent-based modeling.

Second and conceptually, we step back and use our results to assess the fit between research practices and their philosophical foundations (Bennett, this volume). Is scientific realism really such a good basis for what we claim to be doing, especially given the strong critiques recently leveled against it (Chernoff 2002)? Would a form of pragmatism or analytic eclecticism be better (Sil and Katzenstein 2010a, 2010b)? Whatever the philosophical foundation, can we articulate clear and agreed community standards for what counts as good mechanism-based social science?

Transnational politics and civil war

Students of transnational politics – mainly in political science and sociology – have been thinking about international-domestic connec-tions for quite some time. Over nearly four decades, this work has gone through three distinct phases. The earliest research simply challenged realist assumptions about states as the key actors in international politics, getting transnationalism on the scholarly agenda (Keohane and Nye 1972). A second generation, appearing in the 1990s, marked a significant analytical shift – exploring when and under what conditions transnationalism mattered (Risse-Kappen 1995a; Evangelista 1999; Risse, Ropp, and Sikkink 1999a).

More recently, a third set of scholars has disaggregated key assumptions about transnational actors and domestic politics. They have begun to look inside entities such as NGOs, asking what motivates them to act (Schmitz 2004) and why they mobilize around some issues but not others (Carpenter 2007). If earlier research stressed ideational and normative motivations, this new work sees transnational actors as highly strategic and calculating as well (Cooley and Ron 2002; della Porta and Tarrow 2004; Bob 2005). On domestic politics, newer work theorizes it in greater detail and does so more systematically, thus avoiding the ad-hocism that often prevailed in earlier research (Orenstein and Schmitz 2006; Schmitz 2006).

These multiple disaggregation moves have led to a greater interest in the different kinds of causal mechanisms connecting transnational actors and factors and domestic change (Price 1998; Tarrow 2001; Tarrow and della Porta 2004; James and Sharma 2006; Checkel 2007; see also Symposium 2006). Indeed, we now have a growing roster of transnational causal mechanisms, including emulation, persuasion, flows of resources (ideational or material), framing, and power transitions – to name just a few.

Students of civil war can benefit in four specific ways from this IR/sociology work on transnational causal mechanisms. First, it highlights that mechanisms can have varying social-theoretic bases. Some are captured by rational choice – power transitions; others by constructivism – persuasion; and yet still others by both social theories – learning in its simple and complex variants. This social-theoretic pluralism would align civil-war studies with the philosophy of science literature, where it is argued that accounts employing causal mechanisms are in principle "quite compatible with different social theories of action" (Mayntz 2004, 248; see also Mahoney 2001, 581).

Second, this roster of causal mechanisms offers opportunities for better specification of the diffusion metaphor invoked in the civil-war literature. To begin, what exactly is transnational diffusion? Research on the topic defines it as the spread of policies, institutions, or beliefs across borders (Simmons, Dobbin, and Garrett 2006, 787–790).[3] On its own, however, the term obscures more than it reveals, a point now well appreciated in both the transnationalist and policy diffusion literatures (Symposium 2006). Instead, the cutting edge is to unpack diffusion and explore the underlying causal mechanisms – coercion? learning? emulation? – driving it (see also Tarrow 2010). Indeed, it is precisely the latter that are hinted at but not theorized or tested in recent work exploring the transnational dimensions of civil war (Cederman, Girardin, Gleditsch 2009, *passim*).

Third, the mechanisms cited above have undergone extensive empirical testing (Risse-Kappen 1995a; Keck and Sikkink 1998; Price 1998; Risse, Ropp, and Sikkink 1999a; Risse 2000; Lynch 2002; Checkel 2003, 2007; della Porta and Tarrow 2004; Schmitz 2006; see also Levy, Young, and Zuern 1995; Johnston 2001, 2008; Gheciu 2005; Lewis 2005). For example, scholars have now applied a number of techniques for measuring these mechanisms – panel interviews, surveys, text analysis, process tracing – while maintaining a healthy appreciation of their limits (Gheciu 2005; Johnston 2008). And, again, this research is neutral in social-theoretic terms. Some use these methods to document rationalist cost/benefit causal mechanisms (Schimmelfennig 2005), while others use them to measure non-instrumental constructivist learning (Checkel 2001).

Theorizing non-instrumental mechanisms may be especially helpful as scholars of civil war continue their explorations of transnationalism's effects. To date, they have neglected the role of "noninstrumental factors, such as norms and emotions" (Kalyvas 2006, 13; see also Blattman and Miguel 2010, 18), or – specifically on rebel groups – have been "silent on the internal psychology of the recruit," thus making it difficult to uncover "the root causes of ... indoctrination" (Blattman 2007, 25–26, 27; see also Annan, et al. 2009; and Wood 2008, 2009). Those root causes – to take just one example – may be partly captured by the non-instrumental socialization mechanisms (role playing, persuasion) emphasized by the transnationalists (Checkel 2007).

Fourth, the work by transnationalists provides students of civil war the raw material for developing better mechanism-based theories that are bounded, contingent, but still 'small g' generalizable (George

---

[3] Wood, this volume, provides an excellent analysis of the broader diffusion literature and its utility to students of civil war.

1993; Hall 2003; Gerring 2007b). After some false starts – in particular, vague invocations of middle-range frameworks – scholars are thinking hard about how to produce rigorous mechanism-based theory (Elster 1998; Gates 2008; Lichbach 2008) and exploring its requirements in terms of research design (Johnston 2005; Wood 2008, 556). Recently – for example - they have proposed so-called typological theory, where combinations of mechanisms interact in shaping outcomes for specified populations (Bennett, this volume; see also Bennett and George 2005, ch. 11).

If the foregoing suggests an "in principle" contribution from the IR/sociology transnationalists, several examples from the chapters that follow indicate its practical utility. In her study of the Chechen civil wars, Kristin Bakke theorizes and traces the diffusion mechanisms through which transnational insurgents affect domestic challengers to the state. Via mediated or relational diffusion, these insurgents engendered learning and emulation among key Chechen rebel groups, in turn (re-)shaping domestic processes of mobilization (Bakke, this volume; see also Adamson, this volume, for a related argument as applied to diasporas). Hans Peter Schmitz takes a hard case for external influences – the Lord's Resistance Army (LRA) in the Ugandan civil conflict – and demonstrates that even here transnational emulation and social adaptation played roles in shaping its behavior and evolution (Schmitz, this volume).[4]

Turning to a very different type of transnational influence, Stephan Hamberg asks whether transnational advocacy networks have had any real influence on rebel groups' use of child soldiers. Examining the case of the Sudan People's Liberation Army (SPLA), who in the early 2000s demobilized several thousand child soldiers, he argues that social shaming – the most common mechanism of transnational activism – failed to induce a change in rebel group behavior. Rather, child soldiers were demobilized – including by the SPLA – only when the international community granted material concessions or at least promised them to rebel groups (Hamberg, this volume).

A final example returns to the diffusion of civil conflict, but employs computer techniques instead of empirical case studies to capture the causal mechanisms at work. In their chapter, Martin Nome and Nils

---

[4] It is a hard case because the LRA's long-time leader, Joseph Kony, has always sought to isolate it from external influences.

Weidmann utilize agent-based modeling to analyze the diffusion of social identities as a key process underlying the spread of civil conflicts. They disaggregate – and thus better specify – diffusion as occurring through two possible causal mechanisms: social adaptation in a transnational context, and transnational norm entrepreneurship. Their simulations indicate that norm entrepreneurship is the more robust mechanism of diffusion, which is an important confirmation of a finding in the qualitative, IR/sociology literature.

These examples provoke two final – cautionary – remarks. First, we well appreciate there is an issue of aggregation here. That is, while cataloguing various transnational causal mechanisms is a useful starting point, more is needed. After all, the broader international relations literature is by now replete with such (non-cumulative) lists. In fact, it is possible to construct an orderly taxonomy of theories on the causal mechanisms of civil conflict – one that provides a comprehensive and useful checklist so scholars can ensure they are not leaving out important mechanisms in their explanations. This is a task Andrew Bennett takes up in his chapter (Bennett, this volume).

Second, we recognize that the IR/sociology work on causal mechanisms is not the definitive last word. One should maintain a healthy skepticism for how well mechanisms theorized by scholars whose prime interest is peaceful change travel to situations where violence and institutional collapse are the norm. More positively, we can use this translation exercise to push research on transnationalism in new directions, as suggested below (see also Wood, this volume).

Theorizing transnationalized violence

The issue is how to theorize transnationalized violence. And here, the IR/sociology transnationalists – to turn the tables – have much to learn from work on conflict processes. They have focused on peaceful and non-violent change in world politics (the spread of human-rights norms, socialization by international institutions), thus failing to appreciate that their theories may mis-specify social dynamics in settings marked by violent civil conflict.

Consider work on small group dynamics, which clearly play a role in civil war – say, in the transborder recruitment of rebel group members. Students of transnationalism have analyzed them through the prism of socialization, or the process of inducting actors into the norms and rules of a given community (Risse, Ropp, and Sikkink 1999a). To do this, they have drawn upon a particular strand of socialization literature, one where stable institutions are at work and power and coercion are back-grounded (Checkel 2007).

Yet, this process of induction could surely work in more coercive ways. For example, research on professional militaries and urban gangs explores hazing, physical coercion, and even rape as causal mechanisms leading to socialization. Such mechanisms might be highly relevant in civil war settings, as Harpviken and Lischer argue in their chapter on refugee return (Harpviken and Lischer, this volume; see also Wood 2009, 2010; Cohen 2010). The point is not to reject previous work by transnationalists, but to expand their roster of causal mechanisms, thus capturing the full array of social dynamics at work in the contemporary transnationalized world – both its good and evil sides (Checkel 2011).

Summary

This volume brings together students of conflict processes, IR theorists, comparativists, and methodologists to explore the evident fact that civil wars are rarely contained within the borders of one country; they have transnational dimensions that need to be captured. We ask two questions. (1) What are the transnational mechanisms that influence group mobilization during civil war? Under what conditions do they enable organized violence? (2) What are the causal mechanisms at work when transnational actors intervene to end violence in civil conflict?

These questions intentionally capture two key aspects of transnational influence on civil war. The first, a bottom-up perspective, explores how actors in civil conflict may use or be affected by broader transnational processes. The second is a top-down view, asking how transnational actors may intervene to re-shape domestic conflict dynamics. The difference between the two is subtle, but important and essentially concerns the locus of agency. We do not *a priori* give analytic priority to one or the other.

Providing operational, empirically grounded answers to these questions requires the following steps. First, we think in terms of transnational causal mechanisms, which are defined – adapting Gerring (2007b) – as the transnational pathway or process by which an effect is produced or a purpose is accomplished. We theorize and test a number of causal mechanisms relevant to transnationalized civil conflict.

Second and regarding methods, we argue that there is no one technique that is best for measuring mechanisms. Contributors thus utilize a broad range, from the purely qualitative, to cutting-edge methods such as agent-based modeling. The mix varies, depending upon the specific question asked and a contributor's methodological proclivities.

Third, we critically evaluate our contributions. In part, this is done in a standard way, as individual authors consider alternatives and challenges to their arguments and evidence (see Hamberg, this volume, for an excellent use of this strategy). However, we also step back and – in two concluding essays – conduct net assessments. Conceptually, can our findings be used to clarify the outlines of a cumulative civil-war research program centered on mechanisms (Bennett, this volume)? Theoretically, in what specific ways do we advance the research program on civil war and its transnational dimensions (Wood, this volume)?

Causal mechanisms in action – the challenge of measuring process

This section connects the analytics and theory to data by focusing on method. The discussion proceeds in three stages, beginning with a brief review of the best work exploring the methods-mechanisms nexus. Next, I describe and assess the technique known as process tracing, which seems particularly useful for measuring causal mechanisms. Finally, I address feasibility. Can mechanism-based social science – with its inherent requirement for significant data – be conducted in situations where violence and institutional collapse are the norm?

State of the art

While progress is evident in methods work on mechanisms, there is still a clear need to bring the discussion down to a more operational level – how one actually uses mechanisms in empirical social science. Important efforts by four sets of scholars – Bennett and George, Gerring, McAdam-Tarrow-Tilly, and Wood – are indicative of the challenges that lie ahead. If by methodology, one means how we come to know, then the common denominator for these authors is that we come to know about mechanisms by studying processes, dynamics, and narratives.

In their wide-ranging overview of the case-study approach, Bennett and George devote an entire chapter to process tracing (Bennett and

George 2005, ch. 10). This method "attempts to identify the intervening causal process – the causal chain and causal mechanism – between an independent variable (or variables) and the outcome of the dependent variable" (Bennett and George 2005, 206). The chapter is exemplary in noting process tracing's compatibility with both rationalist and constructivist thinking, in highlighting its different varieties, and in giving several methodological tips to the novice.

However, this same novice will be frustrated at a practical level, as basic questions sure to be on the lips of any first-time process-tracer remain unanswered. How does one know when to stop with the process tracing? When is there enough evidence to document the workings of a particular causal mechanism – that is, what are the data requirements (see also Gerring 2007a, 181)? What counts as good process tracing? What are the community standards (see also Bennett and Checkel forthcoming)?

More recently and from a methodologist's perspective, Gerring (2007a) has produced what critics are rightly calling the state of the art on the case study approach. Like Bennett and George, he devotes an entire chapter to process tracing. Yet, in an otherwise superbly crafted book, this chapter is short and lacking in practical guidance on how to execute the technique (see also Symposium 2007b, 5, 14). Indeed, Gerring (and co-author Craig Thomas) despair of offering systematic advice on process tracing, as it is as much "detective work" and "journalism" as a rigorous social science method (Gerring 2007a, 178).

In light of the foregoing, the very title of McAdam, Tarrow, and Tilly's essay – "Methods for Measuring Mechanisms of Contention" – would seem promising (McAdam, Tarrow, and Tilly 2008). Indeed, they start by criticizing Bennett and George (2005) for failing "to tell us how to describe – let alone measure – the causal mechanism or mechanisms at the heart of the processes that interest them" (McAdam, Tarrow, and Tilly 2008, 2–3).

In contrast to others, McAdam and co-authors get down to the brass tacks of how to measure mechanisms, offering two direct measures (events data, ethnography) and two indirect ones (comparative cross-national and intra-national data). This is excellent and very much what work on causal mechanisms requires. However, by drawing illustrations only from the contentious politics research program, the utility of their analysis is limited. In addition, while the empirical examples are interesting, it is difficult to extract a set of best methodological practices from them. Again, the novice – or aspiring Ph.D. student – is left wondering how he/she actually does this mechanism-based research (see also Symposium 2008).

Within the literature on civil war, Elisabeth Wood's social-theoretically plural and carefully documented work on the Salvadoran civil war (Wood 2003) sets the standard for how to capture the presence and role of causal mechanisms. Not only does she theorize a wide range of mechanisms – ranging from (rationalist) calculations of cost/benefit to (sociological-constructivist) morals, emotions, and norms – Wood also provides rich evidence to document and measure them. Her methods are also plural, ranging from ethnography to formal modeling.

Yet this important work could be improved in several ways. At an operational level, it is not entirely clear what procedures Wood followed in reconstructing her group/individual mobilization dynamics. How did she control for the bias generated by her largely micro, individual perspective, where structural factors could be overlooked? How did Wood decide at what level to focus her search for causal mechanisms? How does one decide how close, how micro to go? This problem of so-called infinite regress has been addressed in a general sense (Gerring 2007b, 176), but with little practical advice on dealing with it.

As Wood demonstrates empirically and as others argue from a more methodological perspective (McAdam, Tarrow, and Tilley 2008; Staggenborg 2008, 341), ethnography is important for measuring process and mechanisms. Yet, its use raises two potentially vexing issues. First, how did Wood know when to stop? Arbitrarily after 100 interviews? After 150? While the book provides no clear answer, elsewhere she has argued – quite convincingly – that the ethnographic field work continued until it revealed no new patterns. That is, additional interviews were simply providing further evidence for the operation of her core causal mechanisms (Wood, personal communication, June 2008; see also Gusterson 2008). More formally, one could say that Wood was following a logic of Bayesian inference in deciding when to stop (Bennett 2008).

Second, the epistemological foundation of ethnography – interpretism – sits uneasily with the strong causal emphasis of mechanism-based social science (see also Schatz 2009). How does one square the circle here? Does it matter that Wood, within the covers of one book, utilizes methods – formalization, process tracing, ethnography – from very different epistemological traditions to measure her mechanisms? She provides no clear answer – and is in good company. In his commentary on McAdam, Tarrow, and Tilly's (2008) analysis of causal mechanisms, Lichbach (2008) hints at similar epistemological tensions by invoking the oxymoronic phrase positivist constructivism to describe their contribution. Clearly, this is an area in need of further thought and reflection, one to which we return (Bennett, this volume).

In sum, recent years have seen growing attention to the operational issue of how one measures causal mechanisms. This is a welcome and healthy trend, moving scholars beyond conceptual discussions (what is a mechanism, are they real, etc.). However, in a way quite similar to the quantitative researchers in the civil-war literature, these students of mechanisms are victims of their own success. Their expositions and analysis are generally so clear, it is easy for (even sympathetic) critics to see the remaining gaps and challenges.

Capturing mechanisms – process tracing

Recall our baseline definition of a causal mechanism: "the pathway or process by which an effect is produced or a purpose is accomplished" (Gerring 2007b, 178). Given this definition and the foregoing discussion, a number of methods seem relevant for documenting mechanisms. These include ethnography, interview techniques, process tracing, and even formal models; in addition, agent-based modeling is a promising technique for exploring the logic and hypothesized scope conditions of mechanisms (Nome and Weidmann, this volume; see also Cederman 2001; Weidmann 2007). Finally, statistical methods play a more indirect, but still important role: establishing that there is a relation in the first place that requires explanation.

Full detail on these techniques can be found in the chapters that follow, as authors operationalize them in specific empirical contexts. Here, I concentrate on practice, that is, how we have sought to craft and implement mechanism-based empirical studies. After a few points on design, I advance several evaluative criteria for accounts that employ process tracing.

On design, a good mechanism-based explanation builds on four components (Earl 2008, 356–357). As a pre-condition – step no. 1 – one needs to be able to distinguish the elements from the mechanism(s) in the explanation, so we can study the mechanism. What is X and Y and the mechanism that links them? Then – step no. 2 – we need to show that relations among the elements were changed. More important – step no. 3 – we need to show that the hypothesized mechanism was responsible for altering that relationship and that other, alternative mechanisms were not (see also the discussion of equifinality below). So, for example, if diffusion (X) leads to conflict (Y), we may hypothesize that learning was the mechanism explaining that relation. Even more important, we then – step no. 4 – need to ask in a very empirically grounded way "what are the observable implications of learning?"

Bakke's study of transnational diffusion and the Chechen civil wars is an exemplary illustration of this design in practice. She operationalizes such diffusion as – in part – mechanisms of learning and emulation; develops operational indicators for them; and thinks temporally. For the latter, it is crucial to ask whether domestic learning occurred *after* intervention by transnational insurgents. Bakke also explores whether alternative – domestic, in her case – mechanisms might have produced the same outcome (Bakke, this volume).

Turning now specifically to process tracing, I argue it is possible to articulate a three-part standard for what counts as a good application of it (see also Symposium 2007b, 5; Bennett and Elman 2007, 183; Bennett and Checkel forthcoming; Bennett, this volume). Meta-theoretically, it will be grounded in a philosophical base that is ontologically consistent with mechanism-based understandings of social reality and methodologically plural, such as that provided by scientific realism (Wight 2006, ch. 1), analytic eclecticism (Katzenstein and Sil 2008; Sil and Katzenstein 2010b) or pragmatism (Johnson 2006). Contextually, it will utilize this pluralism both to reconstruct carefully causal processes and not to lose sight of broader structural-discursive context. Methodologically, it will take equifinality seriously, which means to consider the alternative causal pathways through which the outcome of interest might have occurred.

With these three signposts in hand, good process tracing needs then to address specific operational issues regarding theory, data, and method (see also Checkel 1997, 2001, 2003, 2007, 2008a). Theoretically, the study of causal mechanisms raises an infinite regress or stopping point issue. When does the process tracing on mechanisms stop? How micro should we go? In my own work on socialization, I took one mechanism – socialization – and broke it into three sub-mechanisms: strategic calculation, role playing, and persuasion. These were then subjected to process tracing (Checkel 2007). Why stop at this point, though? Persuasion, for example, could be further broken down into its own sub-mechanisms, most likely various types of cognitive processes.

Luckily, an answer to this "how micro" question is straightforward and dictated by the state of disciplinary knowledge. In my case, this indicated it was socialization – and not persuasion – that was ripe for disaggregation into smaller component mechanisms. In addition and at a more practical level, how micro one goes is also a function of available data. It makes little sense to spend time attempting to process trace what cannot be measured empirically.

A second theoretical issue is causal complexity. Thinking in terms of mechanisms abstracts from and simplifies the real world – less than is often the case, but abstract it still does. Moreover, because of the high data requirements, it is all too easy to conduct process tracing on only one mechanism. Yet, in many cases, the outcome observed is the result of multiple mechanisms interacting over time. There is no easy answer to this dilemma; one cannot conduct process tracing on all possible candidate mechanisms. However, thinking explicitly and early about equifinality, where the outcome of interest may be the result of alternative causal pathways (Bennett and George 2005, 161–162), and using agent-based modeling, which allows for systematic exploration of possible interactions among hypothesized mechanisms (Nome and Weidmann, this volume; Cederman 2003, 146; Hoffmann 2008), can bound the problem.

Regarding data, any empirical research project must be able to answer a basic question: When is there enough data? How do we know when to stop with the data collection? If done systematically, process tracing can help provide an answer, with my work on socialization in European institutions providing a case in point (Checkel 2001, 2003). After two rounds of interviewing, I took a break from data collection. Writing up the results – connecting the data to the causal-process story I was attempting to tell – allowed me to see where my data coverage was still weak. This indicated in a very specific manner the data I would need to collect during future field work. This strategy is consistent with the ethnographic and Bayesian perspectives discussed earlier, which argue that one should stop when new data are simply providing additional evidence for the operation of the hypothesized causal mechanisms.

On method and procedure, good process tracing requires explicit attention to triangulation (more precisely, its limits) and structural context. On the former, there is an assumption that triangulation is a form of methodological nirvana, minimizing threats to causal inference. With triangulation, a researcher cross-checks the causal inferences derived from his/her process tracing by drawing upon distinct data streams (interviews, media reports, documents, say). The belief is that the error term in each stream points in such a way that it cancels those in others. However, what if the errors cumulate, with the result being that the researcher is worse off after triangulating than before (see also Kuehn and Rohlfing 2009)? Indeed, what if there is a "dark side of triangulation" (Symposium 2007a, 10)? Well-executed process tracing thus requires that one think beyond triangulation – for example, by making use of counterfactuals – when seeking to strengthen the validity of causal inferences.

Another 'dark side' to process tracing is how use of the technique can too easily blind a researcher to broader structural context (see also Bennett, this volume). For example, in earlier work, I used a causal-mechanism/process-tracing toolkit to explore the social-psychological and institutional factors that might lead decision-makers to change their minds in light of persuasive appeals (Checkel 2003). Yet, as critics noted, I had overlooked structural context, simply assuming that persuasive arguments were a function of individual-level dynamics alone. It was equally plausible, however, that my persuader's arguments were legitimated by the broader social discourse in which he/she was embedded. In positivist-empiricist terms, I had a potential problem of omitted variable bias, while, for interpretivists, the issue was one of missing the broader forces that enable and make possible human agency (Neumann 2008; Autesserre 2009). In either case, the lesson for the process tracer is clear: his or her design must incorporate explicit checks for this potentially serious problem.

In sum, good process tracing builds in part on fairly standard injunctions and checks that are applicable to an array of qualitative methods. These include attention to design, thinking counterfactually, and being cautious in the application of triangulation. At the same time, it demands adherence to additional best practice standards that address problems related to equifinality and issues of infinite regress. Put differently, process tracing, when correctly executed, is far more than a temporal sequencing of events or "detective work" based on hunches and intuition (Gerring 2007a, 178).

Extensions to violent conflict

Is any of this useful to students of civil war? My examples above often derive from situations where institutions work, social relations are stable, and norms are largely shared; in many cases of civil conflict, none of these conditions hold. Yet, I will argue that a decisive turn to the theory and process-tracing practice of causal mechanisms is an essential next step in the civil-war research program. I substantiate this claim in two steps, addressing both feasibility and necessity.

Regarding feasibility, is a mechanism/process account – with its high demands in terms of data, time, and proximity to the subject matter – realistic in a conflict situation? In fact, a growing array of primary and secondary source material indicates the data problem is not as severe as some might expect. Researchers can now draw upon a growing civil war memoir literature (of former child soldiers – Beah 2007a, 2007b) and carefully designed surveys of ex-combatants (Blattman 2007; Annan et al. 2009). In addition, more and more scholars are addressing the proximity challenge by going directly to the source, conducting extensive interviews with ex-combatants as a way of measuring causal mechanisms (Wood 2003; Checkel 2008b; Autesserre 2009; Cohen 2010; see also McAdam, Tarrow, and Tilly 2008, 10–11).

A nagging question remains, though. While there may be more data available on processes and mechanisms, even in conflict situations, is it reliable? In such settings, individuals have multiple reasons to lie or to otherwise dissimulate. Two techniques, however, allow one to bound this problem. First, just as in non-conflict situations, one triangulates (cautiously – see above) across multiple data streams. On the particular issue of interviewees and their possible dissimulation, one looks for changes and discrepancies in accounts as a function of different audiences addressed. Second, the silences, gestures, jokes, and apparent lies of interviewees should be recognized as valuable data in their own right, helping researchers better appreciate how the current social-political landscape shapes what people are willing to say (Fujii 2010; see also Wood 2003, 33–40).

Of course, in conflict/post-conflict situations, it is not just individuals who may have incentives to lie. Organizations as well may intentionally distort historical events in a manner designed to meet current (political) needs, or simply lack the resources to get the story right. However, here too, good research practices suggest ways to deal with such realities. In her work on the Peruvian civil war (1980–2000), Leiby sought to document the frequency of wartime sexual violence, and the Peruvian Truth and Reconciliation Commission (TRC) was a key data source in this regard. Finding serious gaps and omissions in its work, she worked systematically to correct them by consulting other published documents, as well as primary sources – recoding a random sample of 2,000 of the 17,000 witness files compiled by the TRC. The end result was a much richer account of the nature and frequency of sexual violence in wartime Peru (Leiby 2009a; see also Leiby 2009b).

This discussion of feasibility begs a different and prior question. Do we even need to bother with adding mechanisms and process to our accounts? Here, the consensus answer among all students of civil war – quantitative (Sambanis 2004; Blattman 2007, 24–27; Gates 2008; Blattman and Miguel 2010) and qualitative (Tarrow 2007; Kalyvas 2008; Wood 2008) – is yes. For very understandable reasons, one particular social process of civil war – violence – has received significant attention (Kalyvas 2006). However, as researchers have moved to disaggregate in recent years – creating subnational data sets, exploring transnationalism's role, looking inside rebel groups – new processes have been invoked, including community building and allegiance (Gates 2002, 2011), transnational ethnic kinship (Cederman, Girardin, and Gleditsch 2009), socialization (Cohen 2010), norm-driven behavior (Wood 2008), emotional responses (Wood 2003), framing (Autesserre 2009), and social networks (Tarrow 2007), among others. This fact suggests that not only is research on the processes and mechanisms of civil war feasible, it is also necessary and needed.

Conclusions and preview

This chapter and the chapters that follow argue for improved understanding of civil war and its transnational dimensions by integrating insights, concepts, and methods from heretofore disparate literatures and research communities. Dialogue of this type is no guarantee of theoretical progress or mutual learning; however, its continued absence is a sure-fire way to promote group think, closed citation cartels, and academic hyper-specialization.

If one recent state-of-the-art review of the civil war literature can be read as a plea to reconnect it to central concerns of comparative politics (Tarrow 2007, 589, 596; see also King 2004, 432–433), then our argument is that similar gains are to be had via a reintegration with contemporary international relations theory and methods scholarship. As two of the sharpest (quantitative) scholars of civil war have recently argued, the "empirical salience of ... international issues in driving domestic civil conflicts" will require that future work "draw heavily on the existing international relations literature" (Blattman and Miguel 2010, 30).

Preview

The book has three parts, with this introductory, framework chapter comprising Part I. The six chapters in Part II form the book's core; they utilize process tracing and other techniques to document the causal mechanisms of transnationalized civil conflict. Each chapter follows a similar template, where it: highlights a puzzle linked to the transnational dimensions of civil conflict; advances an argument incorporating one or more of the causal mechanisms articulated in this introduction; addresses questions of methods and data; and – most important – shows these mechanisms in action in one or more cases. This similarity in structure facilitates learning and cumulation, both within the book and among readers.

In Part III, we step back and use our results to address two broader issues. In Chapter 8, Andrew Bennett probes the research frontier regarding causal mechanisms. In particular, he systematizes our findings (Part II) by advancing a taxonomy of theories about mechanisms, followed by a discussion of so-called typological theorizing as a means of addressing combinations of mechanisms. Drawing upon the book's case studies, Bennett argues that explanation via causal mechanisms entails important costs, most notably a substantial loss of parsimony, but that this is the necessary price for improving our understanding of the complexities of civil conflict.

In the book's final chapter, Elisabeth Wood explores how our approach and findings contribute to the theoretical and methodological development of work on civil war and its transnational dimensions. Recent theory on the diffusion of policy serves as her baseline for assessing our contributions to the understanding of transnationalized civil conflict. While Wood finds much to praise, she also critiques our underspecification of the politics at work in any diffusion process, conflict-driven or otherwise. On method, she reinforces the message of both this chapter and Bennett's on the central importance of process tracing as a technique to identify the observable implications of causal mechanisms in conflict situations.

PART II

Transnationalized civil war

2 Copying and learning from outsiders? Assessing diffusion from transnational insurgents in the Chechen wars

KRISTIN M. BAKKE

Ever since September 11, 2001, Russian leaders have eagerly claimed that their struggle against rebel forces in the country's Chechen Republic is part of a global war on terror, linked to international terrorism. Similarly, in Moscow during summer 2005, a young Chechen man explained to me that the second war in Chechnya, which began in 1999, was caused by Moscow and Wahhabis – the name many Chechens use for people with a radical Islamist leaning – and was funded by Arab money.[1] These examples from Russia demonstrate that both state leaders and the man-in-the-street have come to emphasize the transnational influences on a struggle that started out largely as a domestic one. Indeed, in June 2010, the US Department of State (2010) noted that the activities of the Chechen insurgent leader Doku Umarov, "illustrate the global nature of the terrorist problem we fight today." Yet, while policy-makers, public debate, and a growing body of research have begun to call attention to such cross-border dimensions of intrastate struggles, few studies have examined the ways in which transnational insurgents matter, once they have entered a conflict.

The causes or catalysts for intrastate struggles sometimes rest abroad. Scholars have argued, for example, that neighboring states may become sanctuaries for rebel groups (Salehyan and Gleditsch 2006; Salehyan 2007), that nationalist movements may learn or imitate movements elsewhere (Beissinger 2002), and that diaspora communities in either near or far-away countries sometimes fund and support rebellions back home (Adamson 2004; Lyons 2006; Smith and Stares 2007). What this research points to, is that intrastate struggles may not be so *intra*state after all, as domestic challengers to the state are helped or face pressures from abroad. In this chapter, I explore the domestic dynamics of the transnational relations of intrastate conflicts. I aim to explain *how* transnational insurgents influence the domestic challengers to the state.

---

[1] Personal communication, Moscow, June 2005.

Drawing on the literatures on intrastate conflicts, social movements, and transnationalism, I theorize the domestic processes that transnational insurgents are likely to impact and the mechanisms through which they affect these processes.

I begin by briefly describing transnational insurgents. I then situate the study of transnational insurgents in the literature and present a theoretical framework for studying how they influence intrastate struggles. I organize the framework around the domestic insurgents' mobilization processes likely to be affected by transnational insurgents, emphasizing how information and resources may travel through different kinds of diffusion mechanisms. I test the argument through process tracing, in a study of the Chechen civil wars.

Transnational insurgents

Typically, the term "transnational" describes cross-border contacts and interactions that are not controlled by states but rather engage both state and non-state actors (Nye and Keohane 1971, 331). This study focuses on transnational insurgents in intrastate conflicts, by which I refer to armed non-state actors who, for either ideational or material reasons, choose to fight in an intrastate conflict outside their own home country, siding with the challenger to the state (Malet 2007). Transnational insurgents, who are also referred to as foreign fighters, exclude foreign legions and private security firms.

The most extensive data collection effort that traces the whereabouts of transnational insurgents is that of David Malet (2007; 2010; 2011), who shows that of 331 intrastate conflicts between 1816 and 2005, transnational insurgents were present in at least 70. While contemporary policy discussions emphasize so-called Islamist militants who travel from conflict to conflict (see Hegghammer 2010), transnational insurgents can also have ethnic ties or other ideological attachments to the domestic struggle. More than 40 percent of the conflicts featuring transnational insurgents began after the Cold War's demise, in Africa, the post-communist countries, Asia, and the Middle East. Historically, transnational insurgents have also participated – or still participate – in conflicts in the Americas (as in Colombia and Mexico) and Europe (for instance, Greece and Spain). Clearly, understanding the role of transnational insurgents in intrastate conflicts is an important empirical question.

Transnationalism, social movements, and intrastate struggles

The finding that intrastate conflicts are not so intrastate after all fits into a long-standing but recently revived research program on transnational relations (see Checkel, this volume, for details). This literature has primarily focused on peaceful non-state actors, such as multinational corporations, international organizations, epistemic communities, and activist networks' effect on domestic politics (e.g. Nye and Keohane 1971; Haas 1992; Evangelista 1995; Risse-Kappen 1995b; Keck and Sikkink 1998; Checkel 1999; Tarrow 2005). Thus, the conflict literature's discovery that there are *violent* aspects to transnational relations is an important contribution.

The emerging literature on violent transnational relations, as well as the more long-standing literatures on peaceful transnational relations and social movements, has pointed to a number of variables that enable non-state actors, including transnational ones, to access or influence domestic politics. Beginning with the regional context, conflict-ridden neighborhoods may increase a state's chances of experiencing violent conflict (Gleditsch 2002; Salehyan 2007). Features of the state itself matter as well. In particular, so-called failed or weak states may attract actors with not-so-noble intentions (Rotberg 2004; Staniland 2005). Similarly, centralized political systems, where executive power is concentrated, may provide transnational actors with few access points to their target state, while states where power is dispersed may provide more access points for influence (Risse-Kappen 1995b). However, states that block domestic groups from exerting influence may inadvertently force these groups to seek allies outside the state, as such opening the door for transnational actors (Evangelista 1995; Keck and Sikkink 1998; Pickvance 1999). Thus, transnational actors may have a harder *or* easier time gaining access to centralized and state-dominated polities than to states where societal groups flourish.

At the group-level, features of both the transnational and domestic non-state actors can affect whether outsiders enter and influence a domestic struggle. An outside group's access to policy-makers and resources will likely aid its impact (Gamson 1975; McCarthy and Zald 1977; Tarrow 1998). Similarly, ethnic affinity or ideological bonds between foreign and domestic fighters – or the manipulation of such ties – can increase the chances of outsiders getting involved (Saideman 2002). The domestic fighters, for their part, can vary in the willingness and ability to allow transnational actors access. Domestic rebels may be more willing to welcome the resources that outside insurgents bring when they face an unfavorable balance of power vis-à-vis the state.[2] Some domestic resistance movements may also be less able than others to keep foreign fighters out. In movements characterized by factional competition, the actors are not just fighting the state, but also one another, attempting to eliminate rivals (Pearlman 2009; Lawrence 2010; Cunningham et al. 2012). Transnational insurgents can help boost the resources needed to fight this dual struggle that each faction of the domestic movement is waging, and there are multiple entry points, or domestic allies, for the outsiders. Indeed, while a cohesive domestic movement may be willing to let outsiders in, it is also able to say no. A fragmented movement, in contrast, may be less able to control whether outsiders join its ranks. In the only study that systematically has begun to examine both when and how transnational insurgents matter, Staniland and Zukerman argue that both an unfavorable balance of power and a fragmented domestic movement are necessary conditions for the emergence of coalitions between domestic and foreign fighters.[3]

While existing work points to a number of conditions that may enable transnational insurgents to enter domestic struggles, less work has focused on the ways in which these actors influence domestic politics. As Checkel notes in the introduction to this volume, the goal in statistical studies of the transnational aspects of civil war is typically to examine whether – to take one example – location in a conflict-ridden neighborhood leads to violent conflict; however, such correlational analysis masks the mechanisms at work.

Diffusion from transnational to domestic insurgents

My focus in this study is the mechanisms that link the presence of transnational insurgents to violent conflict. Consistent with Staniland and Zukerman,[4] I propose that to understand how these outside actors affect intrastate struggles, one must begin by considering what it is

---

[2] Paul Staniland and Sarah Zukerman. "The Effects of Foreign Fighters on Civil Wars: War-Fighting, Ideas, and Recruitment." Unpublished paper, Department of Political Science and Security Studies Program, MIT. 2007. They argue that foreign fighters may lead to changes in the domestic rebels' ideational motivation, non-fighting capacity, and recruitment.

[3] Ibid.   [4] Ibid.

about the domestic challengers that outsiders can shape. Research on social movements suggests there are three aspects of the domestic movement that may change as a result of interaction with or pressure from an outside group – its goals, its repertoire of forms of (collective) action, and its resources. In military terms, we can think of these as strategy, tactics, and logistics. They are features that matter for the domestic movement's ability to fight the state, either by affecting the movement's legitimacy and support in the eyes of the population in whose name it is fighting, or by affecting its capacity and competence to organize collectively and confront the state. Indeed, they are closely linked to key processes in a movement's mobilization: framing of goals, tactical innovation, and resource mobilization (see also Schmitz, this volume; Adamson, this volume). The transnational actors can affect shifts in these processes through mechanisms such as *mediated* and *relational diffusion*, in turn enabling *learning* and *emulation*.

In studies of contentious politics, the term 'diffusion' is often used to describe how social movements may spread from one locality to another (e.g. Beissinger 2002). However, and as Checkel argues in Chapter 1, it may be useful to think about diffusion as a process consisting of a number of smaller mechanisms. Initially, there is the mechanism that enables the spread of information or resources, which can take place through relational, non-relational, or mediated diffusion (Tarrow 2005, building on Sageman 2004). Relational diffusion is about the transfer of information or resources through personal networks and social bonds. It includes interpersonal interactions. Non-relational diffusion is about the transmissions between people or groups with no direct ties or social bonds, where people in one locale learn from people elsewhere through television, the radio, newspapers, and the internet. Here, I will not emphasize non-relational diffusion, as my starting point is the presence of transnational actors. Finally, mediated diffusion takes place when a third party brings two previously unconnected parties together – or at least brings together information or resources from two previously unconnected parties. Mediated diffusion is also called brokerage, as the third party functions as a broker that brings seller and buyer together. The parties that are brought together can be communities or movements, even individuals, and the broker is typically an individual or group of individuals who may set up institutions. Through either diffusion route – relational or mediated – learning or emulation on the part of the domestic insurgents can be based on ideational or instrumental motives.

Yet transmission of information or resources through these initial diffusion mechanisms does not necessarily mean that they have any effect. The effect would depend on subsequent mechanisms – whether the new ideas resonate with the local population (Keck and Sikkink 1998; Checkel 1999), and whether people actually adopt or adapt to the new ideas or use of new resources (Acharya 2004). If transnational insurgents provoke a change in framing or tactics, one might expect a counter-reaction from the local population, pending on whether the new frame or new tactics match local views on what is acceptable and useful. The counter-reaction can deepen existing cleavages within the domestic movement, even bringing about new divisions. How such counter-reactions occur is a separate research question.[5] The important point here is that the initial diffusion mechanisms can ultimately have either helpful or harmful effects on the domestic movement's mobilization – or no effect at all.

Shifts in framing

The social movement literature has long emphasized framing as a process that affects a movement's ability to mobilize supporters. Framing implies that the actors define what they are fighting for and who they are fighting against, often in binary us-versus-them terms. It includes mechanisms such as the attribution of threat or, in more clinical terms, diagnosis of the ills that need to be cured and prognosis for the solution, including the (re)stating and (re)imagining of a legitimate purpose (Snow and Benford 1992; Benford 1993; McAdam et al. 2001, 48).

Transnational insurgents can contribute to shifts in the domestic movement's framing through both mediated and relational diffusion mechanisms that may engender learning or emulation of new frames. Staniland and Zukerman suggest two routes that correspond to these types of diffusion: in the long-run, transnational insurgents can set up schools or other institutions, such as mosques, that transmit their ideologies to (future) domestic fighters through learning, even

---

[5] Kristin M. Bakke. "Acceptance and Resistance to Foreign Ideas: Transnational Insurgents' Impact on the Chechen Separatists." Unpublished manuscript. Department of Political Science, University College London. 2010.

indoctrination.[6] In the short-term, the domestic fighters' personal contact with the transnational insurgents can cause a more direct shift in goals, especially if the transnational insurgents are successful or possess charismatic leadership, and if the bond that develops is a close one.

In both routes, the mechanism is about diffusion through learning or emulation. The diffusion described in the long-term route is mediated diffusion, or brokerage, where a third party brings together previously unconnected actors (Tarrow 2005, 104). The more direct diffusion described in the short-term route is relational diffusion, where learning or emulation results from interpersonal interaction. Studying recruitment into cults and sects, Stark and Bainbridge note that strong personal bonds mean that, "[r]ather than being drawn to the group because of the appeal of its ideology, people were drawn to the ideology because of their ties to the group" (1980, 1379). Learning or emulation on the part of the (future) domestic insurgents can be either ideationally or instrumentally motivated. They may believe in the new framing, or they may decide to adopt or adapt to this framing if it is effective at garnering support or resources.

While it may be impossible to empirically establish whether cognitive mechanisms such as learning or emulation take place, we can observe the first and last steps of diffusion (but see Nome and Weidmann, this volume). We can observe whether people are connected either directly or indirectly through a third party, and we can observe the consequences of diffusion, namely a shift in framing. Hence, if transnational insurgents affect shifts in a domestic movement's frame, we would see a change in framing taking place *after* the transnational insurgents enter the struggle – timing is key here. If the mechanism is about mediated diffusion and long-term learning or emulation, we would observe the establishment of institutions, schools for example, preceding the shift in framing. While it is more difficult to establish the presence of relational diffusion, accounts of heroic individuals among the transnational insurgents, followed by a shift in the domestic movement's framing, would suggest that such a mechanism is at work. Importantly, we should also consider alternative reasons for a shift in framing, as the change may be homegrown rather than imported.

---

[6] Paul Staniland and Sarah Zukerman. "The Effects of Foreign Fighters on Civil Wars: War-Fighting, Ideas, and Recruitment." Unpublished paper, Department of Political Science and Security Studies Program, MIT. 2007. 7–8.

To the degree that these diffusion mechanisms cause a shift in the domestic movement's framing of the struggle, we should carefully consider the effects on public support. If the new framing resonates with the local population, we may observe that initially hesitant factions of the domestic movement adopt the new framing as a means to ensure public support. Yet the transnational insurgents may fail to strengthen the domestic movement if they foster a new framing of the struggle that fails to resonate with the locals.

Tactical innovation

Just like framing is key to a movement's ability to mobilize supporters and fight the state, so is its repertoire of forms of (collective) action – its repertoire of tactics. Tactical innovation refers to a movement's creation of new tactical forms (McAdam 1983, 736). A long-standing claim in the social movement literature says that movements adopting non-institutionalized or radical forms of contention are more likely to have an impact than movements that operate within the bounds of "normal" politics (Gamson 1975; Piven and Cloward 1979). Yet it is also plausible that movements that adhere to the norms of "normal" politics are the ones most likely to have an impact. A movement's turn to violence, for instance, may backfire if that strategy alienates the very population whose support it needs.

Setting aside the question of whether radical forms of contention help or hurt a movement's ability to fight the state, the question here is how transnational insurgents may affect a domestic movement's tactical innovation. In particular, I want to explore their effect on a movement's use of radical tactics. By radical tactics, I refer to tactics that the international community considers inappropriate wartime conduct, including the intentional killing of civilians, torture, hostage-taking, and extrajudicial executions. Do transnational insurgents encourage tactical innovation among the domestic fighters, towards explicitly targeting non-combatants and resorting to hostage-taking and torture?

Similar diffusion mechanisms as those affecting framing can influence tactical innovation. Mediated diffusion, or brokerage, through institutions or third parties can foster learning or emulation of new ideas about morally accepted or effective and efficient tactics. Relational diffusion through one-on-one interactions with the transnational insurgents, either by fighting side-by-side or in training camps, can engender learning or emulation of new tactics, especially if those tactics have proven successful elsewhere and do not contradict local norms for acceptable behavior. As for observable implications, we would have to carefully examine whether the transnational insurgents do indeed advocate or use radical tactics, as well as whether tactical innovation in the domestic movement, towards more radical tactics, takes place *after* the transnational insurgents enter the struggle, keeping in mind that, alternatively, the sources for innovation may come from within (Giugni 1999).

Again, we should not assume that tactical innovation enhances the domestic movement's ability to fight the state. Tactical innovation can backfire if it fails to resonate with local norms for appropriate behavior or local assessments of useful tactics.

Resource mobilization

Perhaps the most common assumption about the traits of a resistance movement that matter for its ability to fight the state is the movement's material resources – its ability to mobilize resources and use these resources to mobilize people (McCarthy and Zald 1977). Resources include fighters, weapons, communication, know-how, and finance. In the literature on revolutions, scholars have long pointed to the importance of overcoming the collective action problem (Popkin 1988; Lichbach 1994). It is reasonable to expect more resource-rich movements to be better able to distribute selective incentives that can lure participants to engage in collective action, even risk their lives, than resource-poor movements that can offer few, if any, rewards. Besides helping prevent free-riding, resources, especially coercive resources such as fighters and weapons (and knowing how to use those weapons skillfully), are critical in and of themselves: the more coercive resources the movement possesses, the better able it is to fight the state.

To the degree that transnational insurgents join forces with the domestic fighters, they may bring fighters and weapons – or funds to buy those – that increase the coercive strength of the domestic movement. That is, they may directly transmit resources to the domestic insurgents by bringing competence and capacity. If they do, we should be able to observe an increase in resources following the entry of the transnational insurgents. More indirectly, through mediated diffusion or brokerage, transnational insurgents can link the domestic movement with funding sources elsewhere, as such contributing to the movement's resource mobilization. While it is unlikely that we can observe the movement's cash flow by examining its budget, the evidence for this latter mechanism could be in the form of expert assessments of a movement's funding or statements from the domestic fighters. Again, a consideration of timing would be key to determine whether the link to funding outside the country is established only after the transnational insurgents enter the stage.

Unlike transnational insurgents' effects on goals and tactics, their effect on resources is in the short-run likely to go just one way: the more resources transnational insurgents bring, the better able the domestic challengers are to fight the state. However, if the domestic movement becomes dependent on external sources of funding, the long-run consequences can be dire if the funding sources dry up. Akin to arguments about foreign aid stifling local initiative in developing countries, the long-run consequence of external sources of funding is potentially a vulnerable or dependent domestic movement.

In sum, assessing the role of transnational insurgents requires establishing the following about the domestic movement: Do we observe a change in framing of its goals? Does it adopt new tactics and carry out operations that were previously taboo? Do the local fighters have more resources or carry out operations for which they previously lacked the resources? If we do observe these changes, we can not conclude that they are caused by transnational insurgents until we have traced the changes back to mediated or relational diffusion from these outsiders, as well as considered alternative domestic reasons for change.

Research design

The research task in this study requires a process-tracing approach (Checkel, this volume; George and Bennett 2005; Gerring 2007a). As I am interested in tracing the mechanisms that create variation across three processes of domestic mobilization – framing, tactical innovation, resource mobilization – the case selection must allow for such variation (on the dependent variables). To that end, I examine Chechnya's conflict with the Russian federal government over time, which offers shifts in each mobilization process. The conflict started with the Chechen declaration of independence in 1991, turned into a war in 1994, came to an end with a ceasefire in 1996, again turned violent in 1999, and today has come to an uneasy stalemate, with violence dwindling since 2005.

In terms of framing, the Chechen conflict began as a nationalist struggle much like the rest of the "parade of sovereignties" in Russia in the early 1990s. It remained so throughout the first war, focusing on independence for the Chechen republic. Since the period between the first and second wars, Chechen leaders increasingly made references to the establishment of an Islamic state. In recent years, some Chechen resistance leaders have framed the struggle in terms of nationalism and self-determination, while the movement's dominant branch is fighting an Islamist struggle aimed at creating an Islamic emirate.

As for tactical innovation, one of the infamous characteristics of the second Chechen war was a growing kidnapping-for-ransom industry, which did not to a similar extent characterize the insurgents' tactics in the first war – although both the Chechens and the Russians were known to have carried out kidnappings even in the first war. Another infamous characteristic associated more with the second war than the first was large-scale terrorist attacks outside Chechnya's borders, such as the Dubrovka/Nord-Ost theater siege in Moscow in 2002 and the Beslan school siege in 2004 – although again, attacks had taken place in 1994–1996. Moreover, in 2000 suicide terrorism became a new tool in the Chechen insurgents' repertoire of tactics. These trends suggest that the tactics of the Chechen resistance movement have changed over time, turning more radical in the sense that also civilians have become explicit targets of violence.

In terms of the ability to mobilize resources and muster coercive strength, the Chechen struggle has also changed over time. In the immediate post-Soviet era, the Chechen separatist government inherited weapons from the branch of the Soviet army that had been stationed in Chechnya and received funding primarily from the Chechen community in Russia. In the second war, the Chechens turned to home-made weapons, but they reportedly used them with great skill (Dudayev 2004). Due to the destruction of the first war, the relative popularity of Putin's war on Chechnya within Russia, and the fact that the resistance leaders from 2000 onwards did not officially head their republic (as Putin put Chechnya under central control), the Chechen fighters had fewer domestic resources available than in the first war. Reports indicate, however, that resources from outside increased.

To assess if and how transnational insurgents have affected these mobilization processes, I consult a variety of sources, including personal communication with Chechens living in Moscow; the documentary/ propaganda film *The Life and Times of Khattab*, which contains interviews and footage of the most important transnational insurgent in Chechnya (Waislamah News Network 2002);[7] the Islamist website Kavkaz Center; the separatist website Chechenpress; monitoring of local Chechen papers by the Russian International Institute for Humanities and Political Studies (IGPI); journalistic accounts through the Jamestown Foundation (*Chechnya Weekly, Terrorism Monitor, North Caucasus Analysis, Prism*), which is an independent institute with extensive coverage of the North Caucasus; reports from the Institute of War and Peace Reporting (*Caucasus Reporting Service*); news searches via Lexis-Nexis; and academic and biographical articles and books.

Transnational insurgents in the Chechen wars

While it is impossible to get precise data on the number of transnational insurgents in Chechnya at any given point – and the Russian authorities may have sought to inflate the numbers – it has been suggested that over the course of the two wars, 500–700 transnational insurgents, including members of the diaspora, have fought there (Moore 2007). A total of 500–700 indicates an increase over time, from the 80–90 who were reported to be active in the first war. Some estimate there were 100–200 transnational insurgents present during the second war (B. Williams 2005b), which would suggest that the highest number of transnational insurgents entered in the interwar period and early years of the second war. The first transnational insurgents came to Chechnya in February 1995, just a couple of months into the first war, as followers of the fighter known as Emir Khattab or Ibn Al-Khattab (Gall and de Waal 1998, 308; Tishkov 2004, 172; Gammer 2006, 214–215). Of Saudi Arabian or Jordanian origin, Khattab fought in the civil wars in Afghanistan and Tajikistan before entering Chechnya in 1995, upon the invitation of a member of the Jordanian Chechen diaspora community known as Sheikh Ali

---

[7] It is a 2002 Arabic-language production (with English subtitles) that portrays Khattab as a war hero, giving it a propaganda-feel, using interviews and footage of Khattab. Produced after Khattab's death, the film is a collage of earlier footage. It is presented by Waislamah News Network as Series 1 of Contemporary Heroes of Islam.

Fathi al-Shishani, who had fought against the Soviets in Afghanistan and had moved to Chechnya in 1993 (Moore and Tumelty 2009, 84). According to some accounts, Khattab brought with him a unit of eight Afghan-Arab fighters. In his own words in *The Life and Times of Khattab*, Khattab says he entered Chechnya with 12 "brothers" from Dagestan, then meeting "other groups," although it is not clear who these other groups were. Tumelty (Moore and Tumelty 2009) reports that after Khattab's arrival in Chechnya, he met with Fathi, who had recruited some 90 Arab fighters from Afghanistan, of which 60 joined Khattab. The transnational insurgents active in Chechnya have primarily been from the Middle East, but some have also come from North Africa, Turkey, and possibly Pakistan. The question here is if and how these transnational actors over time have affected the Chechen resistance movement's framing of goals, tactical innovation, and resource mobilization.

Effect on framing

The Chechen insurgency grew out of the Chechen nationalist movement that emerged in the final days of the Soviet Union. In fall 1991, under the leadership of Dzhokhar Dudayev, a Chechen who had served as a Soviet Air Force general, the nationalists overthrew the local communist-led local government and declared the republic independent.

Leading up to and during the first war, the nationalists framed the struggle around an image of an aggressive and exploitative state that consistently had imposed suffering on them (Radnitz 2006). Dudayev proclaimed in a 1991 interview that, "I will restore my people's pride after our enslavement by the Russians" (Sheehy 1991, 26).[8] This sentiment echoed many Chechens' collective memory, which was – and still is – colored by Stalin's deportation of nearly the entire Chechen population from its homeland between 1944 and 1957 (B. Williams 2000; Tishkov 2004, 50–54; Ustinova 2004). To many Chechens, the deportation is part of a repeated history of repression. In 2005, a Chechen man explained to me that the heart of the Chechen question is that with regular intervals, Russia has occupied Chechnya. The tsarist forces did it, then the Bolsheviks, Stalin, and now the current post-Soviet regime.[9] Such views were not uncommon in the early 1990s, and Tishkov (2004, 53)

---

[8] See also "Interview with Jokhar Dudayev by Peter Collins, Voice of America," *Official Kremlin International News Broadcast*, December 11, 1995.

[9] Personal communication, Moscow, June 2005.

argues that Chechens increasingly believed that self-determination was necessary to halt long-time discrimination.

Dudayev was not opposed to Islam, and he was more open to the teaching of Islam than his Soviet predecessors; he even used traditional Sufi Islamic references to mobilize people. The State Islamic Institute in Grozny (the Chechen capital), which received funding both from Dudayev's government and Saudi Arabian and Islamic International foundations, opened in 1991 (Bobrovnikov 2001, 13). This nod to Islam must be seen in light of Dudayev coming to power in the early post-Soviet period, when the Chechens were happy to again freely practice their religion, long oppressed. Yet Dudayev openly favored a secular state (Tishkov 2004, 169). He formed a commission to consider Islamic sharia courts, but the legal system remained secular until after he was killed in 1996 (Muzaev 1997). Indeed, while there were voices calling for an Islamic state in the early 1990s (German 2003, 31; Moore and Tumelty 2009, 83), the Chechens' initial quest for independence had little to do with religion.

This changed when Dudayev was killed by Russian forces in April 1996. His immediate successor, Zelimkhan Yandarbiyev, had ever since the founding of the nationalist movement favored an independent and Islamic Chechen state (Dunlop 1998, 93). In his brief period in power, Yandarbiyev called for the introduction of sharia criminal code (Powell 1996).[10] When asked in an interview whether it would be natural for Chechens to live under sharia law, Yandarbiyev responded that, "We are fighting to protect our independence and to defend the honor and dignity of the free people under the banner of Islam."[11] The struggle was focused on Chechnya, blending nationalism and Islamism:

Our *jihad* is first of all a *jihad* to defend the territory, honor and dignity of the Chechen people. But a *jihad* is not only a war conducted with arms in hand. It is a struggle against everything that contradicts what has been established by the Single God, that is against everything that a Muslim is forbidden by God. In this sense, of course, the *jihad* knows no concrete forms or borders.[12]

---

[10] See also "Guard to be set up in Chechnya to Supervise Implementation of Sharia Law," *BBC Summary of World Broadcasts (ITAR-TASS)*, October 17, 1996.

[11] "Chechen Separatist Leader Yandarbiyev Thinks Peace Process Will Continue," *BBC Summary of World Broadcasts (NTV)*, October 23, 1996.

[12] Quoted in "Interview Granted by Chechen Republic President Zelimkhan Yandarbiyev," *Official Kremlin International News Broadcast (Nezavisimaya Gazeta)*, December 20, 1996.

Among Yandarbiyev's three most serious contenders in the 1997 presidential elections in the republic, all made reference to Islam but to varying degrees (Radnitz 2006). Aslan Maskhadov, the field commander who had negotiated the 1996 peace agreement with Moscow, advocated a secular state, yet viewed Chechnya's Islamic customs favorably.[13] Shamil Basayev, a prominent field commander, called for an uncompromising attitude to Chechen independence and adherence to Islam, but fell short of advocating an Islamic state.[14] The third candidate, Movladi Udugov, who had served in both Dudayev and Yandarbiyev's governments, favored an independent Islamic state. In the elections, Maskhadov emerged as the clear victor, suggesting a popular rejection of the most radical religious agenda.

Over time, the struggle has taken on much more of a religious tone, departing from a Chechen-centered one. This development appears to have taken off in the interwar years, and the second war was, in contrast to the first war, one where Islamist (Salafi) goals played a significant role. President Maskhadov was killed in 2005, and both of his successors, Abdul-Halim Sadulayev, who was killed after only a year in power, and Doku Umarov, have framed the struggle in more Islamist terms. While Sadulayev's framing of the struggle contained elements of both nationalism and Islamism,[15] Umarov's framing is more clearly Islamist. In the fall of 2007, Umarov proclaimed that his struggle was in the name of a unified Caucasus Emirate, not just self-determination for any one ethnic group:

I am announcing to all Muslims that I am at war against the infidels under the banner of Allah. This means that I, Amir of the Caucasian Mujahideen, reject all infidel laws that have been established in this world. I reject all laws and systems that the infidels have established on the land of the Caucasus.

---

[13] "Separatist Leader Maskhadov against Creation of Islamic State," *BBC Summary of World Broadcasts (ITAR-TASS)*, September 17, 1996; "Separatist Commander Maskhadov Interviewed on Talks with Russia, Fundamentalism," *BBC Summary of World Broadcasts (Tyden)*, October 3, 1996.

[14] "Chechen Separatist Chief Admits Arab Involvement in Conflict in North Caucasus," *BBC Summary of World Broadcasts (ITAR-TASS)*, November 4, 1996; "Interview Granted by Shamil Basayev, a Candidate for the Chechen Presidency," *Official Kremlin International News Broadcast*, December 16, 1996.

[15] "Russia's Tactics Make Chechen War Spread across Caucasus – Rebel President," *BBC Monitoring (Chechenpress)*, September 13, 2005. See also the Jamestown Foundation interview published after Sadulayev was killed, published in *Chechnya Weekly*, July 6, 2006.

I reject and outlaw all names that the infidels use to split the Muslims. I outlaw all ethnic, territorial and colonial zones named 'North-Caucasian republics', etc ... We renounce all these names (quoted in Smirnov 2007b).

Indeed, Umarov, who fought in both wars and was a member of Maskhadov's government, has stated that, "Mujahideen in the Caucasus do not fight for democracy, they fight for Sharia" (Smirnov 2007d). From considering himself the president of Chechnya (a position not officially endorsed as the post is held by the pro-Moscow Ramzan Kadyrov), he has moved to consider himself the emir of the North Caucasus Emirate. This framing of the Chechen struggle as a religiously motivated quest aimed at establishing a larger Islamic state differs from the nationalist framing leading up to the first Chechen war.

The question here is whether the change in the Chechen separatist movement's framing can be traced to transnational insurgents. The empirics suggest yes. Transnational insurgents influenced the framing of the movement's goal primarily through Khattab and his initially small group of fighters, who were dedicated to a social and political Islamic order (Wilhelmsen 2004; Gammer 2005; Speckhard and Ahkmedova 2006; Moore and Tumelty 2008, 2009; Sokirianskaia 2010). Indeed, to Khattab, who had fought in both Afghanistan and Tajikistan, the Chechen struggle was yet another piece in a wider Muslim struggle. Timing-wise, while Dudayev also embraced some Islamic teaching and practices, the shift in framing towards a jihadist struggle, particularly visible in field commander Basayev's framing, followed the entry of transnational insurgents with an Islamist agenda. This change happened through both mediated and relational diffusion.

Initially, Sheikh Fathi functioned as a broker who brought Khattab to Chechnya, thus connecting Chechen insurgents with fighters from the Middle East and elsewhere in the region. This is mediated diffusion: a third party established links between previously unconnected parties. Yet the degree to which the Chechen fighters were unconnected to insurgents abroad should not be overstated. Already in 1994, Basayev had taken 30 of his fighters to a military training camp in Afghanistan (B. Williams 2003; Hughes 2007, 101–102). Moreover, in 1992, Basayev had played a critical role assisting the self-determination movement in Abkhazia in its armed struggle against the Georgian state. Thus, even without Fathi, the Chechens had established links to foreign insurgents and insurgencies.

Once in Chechnya, the route through which information was transmitted from Khattab and his followers to the Chechen insurgents was both relational and mediated. Khattab initially set up military training camps in 1995, and in 1996, he established a training center, Kavkaz, consisting of several camps for both military and religious instruction near the village of Serzhen'-Yurt in the mountainous eastern part of the republic (B. Williams 2005a; Moore and Tumelty 2008).[16] *The Life and Times of Khattab* shows footage of Khattab in Chechnya, his voiceover recounting how he entered the republic and started training his "brothers." The camps included training on religion, mine cleaning, land mining, and the use of weapons. The students, mainly young men, were primarily Chechens but also Dagestanis, Arabs, and Muslims from elsewhere in the North Caucasus and Central Asia. According to one account, they were paid to attend (Baiev 2003, 206). The teachers were primarily foreigners speaking Arabic, helped by translators from Dagestan (Sokirianskaia 2010, 212). Hundreds of young people passed through this training center, and many went on to become fighters in the Chechen resistance in the second war (Sokirianskaia 2010, 212; Moore and Tumelty 2009, 85). In terms of mechanisms, these training camps were sites for both relational diffusion – through direct hands-on training by transnational insurgents – and mediated diffusion – to the degree that non-insurgent teachers introduced their students to new ideas.

Khattab's increasingly close relationship to the field commander Basayev, who allegedly in spring 1998 appointed Khattab his foreign security advisor,[17] is also an example of relational diffusion. Indeed, in his online memoir *Book of a Mujahiddeen* [*sic*], written in 2004, Basayev specifically mentions Khattab's lesson on strategies and tactics of war.[18] In 1998, Khattab and Basayev jointly organized the Islamic International Peacekeeping Brigade, which consisted of Chechen and foreign fighters from the Middle East and North Africa (Wilhelmsen

---

[16] Vidino (2005) notes that many reports of training camps come from Russian intelligence sources and Islamist propaganda videos, but Sokirianskaia's (2010) ethnographic study includes interviews with Chechens who passed through these camps, providing confidence in the camps' whereabouts and programs.

[17] Sanobar Shermatova, "'I Feel Secure When I Have Ammunition at Hand'," *Moscow News*, April 16, 1998.

[18] I was made aware of this e-memoir, which I located by searching online, by King (2008, 241). The online location of this publication changes over time. It was last accessed at www.tawhed.net/dl.php?i=0512091i (August 15, 2012).

2004, 34). The two were responsible for the event that triggered the second war with Russia, the attack into neighboring Dagestan in August 1999. Unsanctioned by President Maskhadov, the attack was aimed at creating an Islamic Republic of Chechnya and Dagestan with the help of Dagestani Islamist militants.

While it is true Basayev had led an attack into neighboring Dagestan in June 1995 – taking more than a thousand civilians hostage at a hospital in Budennovsk – that incident was framed as a response to the Russian forces' violent campaign in Chechnya. "Our aim was to reach Moscow ... and our purpose is to stop this war," he argued.[19] It was an attack motivated by revenge and Chechen independence. In contrast, in the 1999 attack into Dagestan, Basayev framed it as a struggle aimed at driving the Russian "infidels" out of the North Caucasus region: "Today there is a great deal of work for brother Muslims from all over the world ... we will fight until the full victory of Islam in the world."[20] These words echoed those of Khattab, who never had seen Chechnya as an isolated struggle. In a 1997 interview, for instance, Khattab said that, "We are preparing ourselves for other *jihad* (holy war) operations in Chechnya or elsewhere."[21] Basayev's shift in framing, towards a larger Islamist struggle, followed Khattab's entry into Chechnya.

Basayev's 1999 attack into Dagestan, which was the manifestation of a shift in framing, was also apparently influenced by the Dagestani Wahhabi preacher Bagaudin Kebedov, who had fled the crackdown on radical Islamists in his own republic and entered Chechnya in December 1997 (Muzaev 1998e; 1999b; 1999d). Prior to the August 1999 invasion, he asked Basayev to assist him in overthrowing Dagestan's pro-Russian rulers and establish an Islamic Republic (Vatchagaev

---

[19] Quoted in "Rebels Execute Russian Captives," *St. Petersburg Times* (Florida), June 16, 1995. See also David Zucchino, "War Stories from Rebel on the Run: Raid Was a Wake-up Call for Russians, Chechen Explain," *The Philadelphia Inquirer*, July 16, 1995.

[20] Quoted in Ruslan Musayev, "Prominent Chechen Warlords Lead Rebels in Fighting Russian Troops," *Associated Press Worldstream*, August 11, 1999; see also "Chechen Says He Leads Revolt in Nearby Area," *New York Times*, August 12, 1999.

[21] Quoted in "Mujahedeen Leader Says Chechnya Still Faces Russian Danger," *Agence France Presse*, May 17, 1997. See also interview in Sanobar Shermatova, "'I Feel Secure When I Have Ammunition at Hand'," *Moscow News*, April 16, 1998.

2007). Yet while it looks like Kebedov may have played a role in influencing Basayev's 1999 Dagestan attack, the timing suggests that Kebedov followed, rather than fostered, a shift in framing. He did not enter Chechnya until late 1997, for the very reason that the increasingly pro-Islamist environment in Chechnya was more suitable for his preachings than the environment in Dagestan.

Diffusion may also have taken place via the more long-term mediated type, in particular, through schools and mosques that introduced young people to new ideas. From 1996–97, Salafi mosques and schools were opened in Grozny and rural regions of the republic, sometimes with financial rewards to the regions that adhered to this new and non-indigenous version of Islam (Speckhard and Ahkmedova 2006, 16). In *The Life and Times of Khattab*, Khattab recounts how these religious institutions had structured programs, with training for memorizing the Koran and courses for giving *dawah* (spreading the message of Islam), organized from basic to advanced levels. The best source of information for whether this kind of diffusion had lasting effects is Ekaterina Sokirianskaia's (2010) extraordinary Ph.D. dissertation on state-building in Chechnya and Ingushetia, based on years of fieldwork. Her assessment is that, while some of the leaders in the insurgent movement may have turned to Islam for instrumental reasons, "for young people who followed these opposition leaders, who went through the training camps of Khattab, Islamism was already in earnest" (2010, 216).

This turn towards Islam at the societal level made it difficult for the government under President Maskhadov not to turn to it as well. While not a proponent of an Islamic state and religious courts, Maskhadov was gradually compelled to establish sharia courts and implement Islamic rules across the republic (Muzaev 1998a; 1998c; 1998d; 1998e; 1999c), and in February 1999 he implemented full sharia law (ibid. 1999a). It is plausible to reason that because Maskhadov's turn towards Islam followed the establishment of Salafi schools and mosques, he may have found that a more religious message was key to keeping the support of his constituents – who may have attended these schools or mosques – and who looked favorably upon the Wahhabis who had come to join the Chechens' struggle (Gammer 2005). In other words, it was an instrumental attempt at co-optation.

Indeed, the motivation for turning towards a more Islamist struggle appears to have been driven both by instrumental and ideational motives. Because there were sometimes financial rewards attached to turning towards the new branch of Islam that the outsiders brought along, including access to financial patronage abroad (e.g. Moore and Tumelty 2008, 419), one cannot claim that diffusion necessarily took place through learning or genuine adoption of these ideas; it may rather have been emulation in response to these rewards. In a 2003 interview, the Chechen commander known as Amir Ramzan, who admitted to receiving financial support from the transnational insurgent Abu Walid al-Ghamdi, said the following when asked if his foreign patrons expected anything in return: "The most important thing for them is that the money is used for the war, for the *jihad*, and that those who receive it are true Muslims."[22] Similarly, Sokirianskaia quotes Yandarbiyev: "Islamic fundamentalism is not dangerous. It is partnership, international relations. You do not consider it a problem if Western investors tour Russia, do you? One cannot divide help into help from Wahhabis and help from others" (quoted in Sokirianskaia 2010, 215). This comparison of Islamic fundamentalism to investors suggests that instrumental motives cannot be ruled out.

While the struggle over time has come to include more references to Islam and establishing an Islamic state, it is not exclusively an Islamist struggle. Even Basayev, who was killed by Russian security forces in summer 2006, stated in a 2005 interview with the Russian journalist Andrei Babitsky, broadcast on ABC Nightline, that religion was not as important as national liberation: "I need guarantees that tomorrow future Chechen generations won't be deported to Siberia, like they were in 1944. That's why we need independence."[23] A few months later, though, in February 2006, a more Islamist frame dominated: "Today, before every Muslim is the duty to take the path of *jihad* and fulfill the command of Allah" (quoted in Jamestown Foundation 2006). Internal communication between Basayev and his soldiers suggest that he, indeed, was motivated by religion. Yet in public statements that could reach a Western audience, he may have been more reluctant to say so (Radnitz 2006, 249), again suggesting that instrumental concerns were key to the framing of the struggle.

Although the framing of the struggle today is more colored by references to an Islamic state, sharia law, and the unity of Muslims in

---

[22] "Next Year the War Will Seize the Entire Caucasus," Kavkaz Center, November 28, 2003. Available from www.kavkazcenter.com/eng/content/2003/11/28/2039.shtml (accessed June 7, 2011).

[23] *ABC News Nightline*, July 28, 2005.

the North Caucasus than in the first war, it also encompasses the rhetoric of self-determination. While the Chechen resistance movement until 2007 had one overarching leader, it is now divided between the nationalist branch, headed by the UK-based Akhmed Zakayev, who served as foreign minister under Maskhadov and is now the self-proclaimed prime minister of the Chechen government in exile, and the Islamist branch under Umarov. So far, this division has primarily played out as a war of words, but Chechnya's trajectory in the interwar period, when the Islamist framing took root, suggests that divisions within the movement can be detrimental. Indeed, the Chechens' second war with the central government in Moscow resulted from Maskhadov's inability to rein in different factions, in particular Basayev and Khattab.

While the empirics suggest that a turn towards a more religious struggle in Chechnya was influenced by transnational insurgents, they also point to a conditioning variable and an alternative explanation: domestic gatekeepers and domestic roots.

First, the Chechen resistance leaders have played a key role in *allowing* foreigners to have an impact (B. Williams 2007; Moore and Tumelty 2008; 2009). Under President Dudayev (1991–1996), who was not a proponent of establishing an Islamic state, the lead foreign fighter in Chechnya, Khattab, was careful not to challenge the goals or strategies of the domestic insurgent movement. Indeed, during the first Chechen war, Khattab was under the command of Chechen field commanders (e.g. Gammer 2006, 215; Moore 2007; Sokirianskaia 2010, 212). In part, the domestic resistance leaders' upper hand vis-à-vis Khattab in the first war is attributed to the war-effort being funded primarily by the Chechen population in Russia and the Chechen diaspora community – and under the control of Dudayev (Wilhelmsen 2004, 41). Under Yandarbiyev's brief reign (1996–1997), Khattab could do more to fulfill his vision of an Islamic state in the North Caucasus as Yandarbiyev already looked more favorably upon the idea of an Islamic state – and was head of a then war-torn, cash-starved republic. While Yandarbiyev's successor, Maskhadov, was a secularist and not initially a proponent of establishing an Islamic state, Khattab's close alliance to Basayev, who increasingly worked in opposition to Maskhadov, ensured that he had access to Chechen insurgents and people.

Thus the influence of transnational insurgents has to a certain extent been controlled by gatekeepers in the Chechen resistance movement.

Once the movement shifted away from the relatively centralized structure of President's Dudayev's National Guard, it became easier for outsiders to have an influence. Indeed, Maskhadov's presidency was plagued by an inability to control the former field commanders, particularly Basayev. By the fall of 1998, Maskhadov's forces were even engaged in combat with some of the former field commanders (Tishkov 2004; Gammer 2006). This kind of environment, paired with the destruction and poverty of the Chechen republic after the first war, provided space for the influence of outside forces.[24] Notably, the Wahhabi preacher Kebedov escaped from crackdowns on Wahhabism in Dagestan to Chechnya precisely in this time period. At the same time, the influence of the transnationals *contributed* to cleavages and clashes among different armed factions – in turn hampering negotiations with Moscow. Aware of the detrimental effects of such infighting, in April 1999, Maskhadov tried, unsuccessfully, to bridge divisions between different factions (Muzaev 1999b; 1999e).

Second, the empirical record suggests there may be an alternative domestic explanation for the shift in framing that has little or nothing to do with transnational insurgents. Prompted about the influence of Arab fighters in a 2006 interview, Umarov, the leader of the Islamist branch, claimed it was exaggerated. Moreover, he pointed out that, "[t]hese Arabs fight everywhere where there is *jihad*, not only in Chechnya, to fulfill their Muslim duty" (quoted in Jamestown Foundation 2006), suggesting that transnational insurgents came to Chechnya because there already was a *jihad* – not the other way around. Indeed, the shift towards a religious struggle may have been part of a purely domestic strategy to unify the different ethnic groups across the North Caucasus in a struggle against the Russian state, drawing on the religion that these groups shared. In earlier wars in the region, Islam had also been the basis for unity among the different ethnic groups (Gammer 2006, 64–66; Smirnov 2007c; 2007d), and Islamic rhetoric has a history in struggles in the region. Writing about the 1990s, the historian Charles King argues:

Web sites such as kavkazcenter.com – a major channel of communication with the rest of the world – consistently appropriated the Islamic lexicon found in [Caucasian rebel leader] Shamil's letters written 150 years earlier.

---

[24] See Paul Staniland and Sarah Zukerman. "The Effects of Foreign Fighters on Civil Wars: War-Fighting, Ideas, and Recruitment." Unpublished paper, Department of Political Science and Security Studies Program, MIT. 2007.

Rather than "Russians," the Web masters spoke of "unbelievers" (*kafirs*). Rather than pro-Russian Chechens, they spoke of "hypocrites" (*munafiqs*). Casualties on the Chechen side were always "martyrs" (*shahids*). There is a world of difference between the Russian Empire's wars in the Caucasus and those of the Russian Federation, but in Chechnya of the early twenty-first century the past still proved a dark template for action (King 2008, 241).

That is, the template for a religious struggle is found both abroad and in Chechnya's own history. Across the North Caucasus, especially in Dagestan, the fall of communism and the centralized Soviet state were associated with a return to Islamic practices from the late nineteenth century, including mass pilgrimages to Mecca and Medina (Bobrovnikov 2001). Thus one could argue that the use of the Islamist framing is a strategic last resort of a weakened resistance movement, hoping to create a larger Caucasian alliance in its fight against the Russian state. The timing of a return to such a template, though, during the interwar period, does suggest that transnational insurgents played a role in its revival.

Effect on tactical innovation

The second Chechen war has become associated with large-scale hostage-takings, suicide terrorism, and kidnappings. While the first war also witnessed attacks directed at civilians, notably the hostage-taking at a hospital in Budennovsk in June 1995 and the Kizlyar-Pervomayskoye hostage crisis in January 1996 (both in Dagestan), the second war has been the scene of the most infamous large-scale terrorist attacks. These include the Dubrovka/Nord-Ost theater siege in Moscow in October 2002, where more than 800 people were held hostage (129 killed, including in the rescue operation), and the Beslan school hostage crisis in September 2004, where more than 1,100 people were held hostage, most of them schoolchildren (a total of 334 killed). Moreover, suicide bombings, which were absent from the first war, began in the summer of 2000 and peaked between 2003 and 2004 (Nivat 2005; Speckhard and Ahkmedova 2006). While the suicide attacks initially targeted only military targets, beginning in 2002, the attacks, several of them featuring women suicide bombers, were also directed at civilians. Suicide attacks have also come to be employed by citizens of other North Caucasus regions, including the bombings of Moscow's metro in March 2010, under the umbrella of Umarov's Islamist struggle. The question for this chapter is whether this tactical innovation – towards more radical forms of action – can be traced to diffusion from transnational insurgents.

The empirics suggest a hesitant yes. Even though suicide attacks did not take place until 2000, Dudayev had apparently seen such tactics as an option since 1994 (Hughes 2007). In terms of large-scale hostage-takings, while there has been an Arab presence in all four major hostage attacks related to the Chechen wars, in each case, those in charge were Chechen field commanders, and the demands raised were specific to the Chechen conflict – an end to the conflict, withdrawal of Russian forces, and independence – and not about a global *jihad* (Moore and Tumelty 2008, 426; Speckhard and Ahkmedova 2006, 10). While the Kremlin played up the Arab presence among the hostage-takers at School No. 1 in Beslan, most of them were Chechen and Ingush, suggesting local motivations (Tuathail 2009). Similarly, the turn to suicide terrorism stems from local grievances, and Chechen resistance leaders have taken responsibility for most of the attacks (Moore and Tumelty 2008, 427). Yet the fact that Arabs were not the dominant actors and the demands were Chechen-centered does not preclude tactics being influenced by transnational insurgents.

Relatively little time passed between the entry of transnational insurgents in Chechnya, with Khattab in February 1995, and the first large-scale hostage event, the Budennovsk hospital siege in June 1995. While Basayev, who orchestrated the attack, early on became a close ally of Khattab, there is too little information about the degree of their contact in the early days of 1995 to assess whether Basayev's choice of tactics was caused by learning or emulation via relational diffusion. Basayev claimed that ten Arabs participated in the attack, which suggests the possibility of relational diffusion, although he also pointed out that he personally supervised the training of these foreigners – not the other way around.[25] He argued that the Budennovsk attack was meant to make Russians feel "the real horror of the war that Moscow had unleashed on his people" (quoted in Quinn-Judge 2004), indicating a homegrown reason for a change in tactics, based on a violence-begets-violence mechanism. Indeed, many members of Basayev's own family, including his wife and two children, had been

[25] "Chechen Separatist Chief Admits Arab Involvement in Conflict in North Caucasus," *BBC Summary of World Broadcasts* (*ITAR-TASS*), November 4, 1996.

killed in a Russian air raid on his hometown just two weeks prior to the attack. Basayev often threatened to again take the struggle to Russian soil and target civilians,[26] but he also claimed that he had not gone to Budennovsk with the intent of taking civilian hostages (Gall and de Waal 1998, 260, 263), and that he did not intend to undertake a similar hostage-taking.[27] Indeed, according to some news reports, the Budennovsk attack was quite spontaneous, almost accidental – allegedly, the rebels were heading for Moscow but had to stop as they ran out of money for bribing the road police. Similarly, the 1996 hostage-takings in Kizlyar and Pervomayskoye, led by Salman Raduyev, appear to have been carried out as a spontaneous second-best alternative after the rebels' attack against a Russian air field in Kizlyar failed (Jamestown Foundation 1996). After the Budennovsk attack, Basayev's deputy, Aslambek Abdulkhadzhiev, emphasized that they never again planned to carry out anything like it, suggesting that such an attack on civilians was, somehow, unacceptable:

Here I must say we do not plan anything like Budennovsk. The Budennovsk tragedy will never be repeated. Moreover, we did not make these plans except as a last resort. Why was the world was silent when Shali was bombed [by the Russians], when some 400 people were killed or wounded? (quoted in Jamestown Foundation 1995)

Abdulkhadzhiev's assessment here is slightly different than later statements posted on the Kavkaz Center website. Consider the following 2009 statement from Umarov, which seems to indicate a degree of acceptance of civilian targets:

(T)his year will be also our offensive year all over the territory of Russia. Why? Because I think that those people who are living today in the territory of Russia, they are also responsible for their soldiers, for their leadership, for those atrocities, for that outrage, that they commit, and for those wars that they wage today against Islam.[28]

---

[26] "Next Time It Could be Moscow, Says Chechen Commando Chief," *Agence France Presse*, June 26, 1995.

[27] Mikhail Markelov, "Shamil Basayev: 'I Am Not Planning Another Budyonnovsk'," *Russian Press Digest* (*Novaya Gazeta*), September 15, 1995.

[28] Emir Dokka Abu Usman: "This Year Will Be Our Offensive Year," Kavkaz Center, May 17, 2009. Available from http://kavkazcenter.com/eng/content/2009/05/17/10700_print.html (accessed August 15, 2012). Umarov had expressed a similar sentiment already in 2005, after his own family was targeted. See "We're Beginning the War on the Territory of Russia," Kavkaz Center,

Thus it looks like radical tactics aimed at civilians have become not just more common over time, but possibly more accepted on the part of the fighters. Indeed, both the Dubrovka/Nord-Ost theater siege and the Beslan school hostage crisis appear to have been more planned as attacks against civilians than the 1995–1996 large-scale attacks.

Such a change in use and acceptance of radical tactics would coincide with the entry of transnational insurgents, but it is important to note that in both quotes above, the actions of the Russians serve as a justification. The second war was characterized by a brutal campaign, including civilian targeting, on the part of the Russian forces (e.g. Politkovskaya 2001, 2003); we thus cannot ignore the possibility that the turn to more radical tactics on the part of the Chechens was a purely domestic response (Speckhard and Ahkmedova 2006). We should also not overlook the possibility that the growing kidnapping-for-ransom industry in Chechnya, beginning in the interwar years, was driven purely by the pursuit of profits by criminals (Murphy 2004, 139; Tishkov 2004, 107–126; Zürcher 2007, 105), rather than the influence of outsiders.

Yet if we accept that transnational insurgents over time contributed to the Chechen insurgents' turn towards increasingly radical tactics, what is the evidence for diffusion mechanisms? The hostage crisis that most prominently featured the influence of radical Islam was the Dubrovka/Nord-Ost theater siege in October 2002, where the hostage-takers ahead of time had made a video where they proclaimed they were seeking martyrdom in the name of Allah. The video, which featured women covered in black veils with Arabic script, aired on Al Jazeera during the attack. Timing-wise, it is plausible that the tactics were a result of learning or emulation via both relational and mediated diffusion from transnational insurgents, as both training camps and Salafi schools had been set up in Chechnya in the mid to late-1990s – although there is little information about the kinds of tactics advocated by the transnational insurgents in these fora. According to one account, Khattab put videos of suicide bombings against Russian military barracks online and trained students in hostage-taking techniques in his camps (Murphy 2004, 33, 39), suggesting these were tactics he

May 9, 2005. Available from www.kavkazcenter.com/eng/content/2005/05/09/ 3778.shtml (accessed August 15, 2012). See also this 2003 interview with another Islamist Chechen commander, Amir Ramzan: "Next Year the War Will Seize the Entire Caucasus," Kavkaz Center, November 28, 2003. Available from www. kavkazcenter.com/eng/content/2003/11/28/2039.shtml (accessed June 7, 2011).

advocated. Similarly, while not independently confirmed, an investigation under President Maskhadov implied that Khattab was behind the kidnapping and killing of six international Red Cross workers in December 1996,[29] again suggesting an acceptance for targeting civilians. Khattab's successor, Abu Walid al-Ghamdi, who had been in Chechnya since the late 1990s but took over Khattab's role when Khattab was killed in the spring of 2002, is reported to have emphasized suicide attacks in Russia over guerilla warfare in Chechnya as an effective tactic (Vidino 2005). In 2003, the second-in-command of the jihad in Chechnya issued a fatwa sanctioning the use of female suicide bombers (Henkin 2006, 198). Moreover, according to Georgian officials, by early 2002 a number of Arab fighters had fled from Afghanistan to the Pankisi gorge in Georgia, located on Chechnya's doorstep, where several hundred Chechen and other insurgents were trained in the use of toxic gases (Vidino 2005; Civil Georgia 2003).[30] By the time of the Dubrovka theater siege in the fall of 2002, then, these reports suggest that the Chechens may have been exposed to and trained by transnational insurgents advocating radical tactics through both relational and mediated diffusions.

Others have suggested that non-relational diffusion also played a role, through news accounts about suicide terrorism in Iraq (Reuter 2004, 6). Indeed, in this respect, Khattab's training camps served as a forum for non-relational diffusion, as the students reported to have seen videos of fighting in Palestine and Kashmir (Sokirianskaia 2010, 213); at least in Palestine, suicide terror had been a tactic since 1994.

As for the domestic insurgents' motivation to adopt or adapt to new tactics, the purpose of the Chechens' video from the Dubrovka theater siege (and a similar video associated with the Beslan school hostage crisis), observers have argued, was to attract funding from external sources in the Middle East (Wilhelmsen 2004, 45; Speckhard and Ahkmedova 2006, 11). Thus, to the degree that diffusion took place, it may have been emulation driven by strategic funding concerns, rather than an internalized learning process.

---

[29] "Warlord Khattab Implicated in Murder of Six Red Cross Workers in 1996," *BBC Summary of World Broadcasts (ITAR-TASS)*, March 27, 2000.

[30] Basayev claimed that the so-called militants in the gorge were actually Chechen refugees. See "Chechen Field Commander Marries Third Wife, Gets Russian POWs as Wedding Gift," *BBC Monitoring Trans Caucasus Unit (Kavkaz Tsentr)*, December 14, 2000.

Just as there is a domestic alternative explanation for shift in framing, there is also a local template for hostage-taking as a tactic. Indeed, hostage-taking has a long tradition in Chechnya, going back to the North Caucasian people's resistance to Russian annexation in the 1700s and 1800s, where both the local population and the Russians resorted to such tactics (King 2008, 53–59). Suicide terrorism, in contrast, does not have a local historical template among the Chechens, despite centuries of conflict with central rulers. Thus in the absence of outside influence, it is unlikely that the Chechens would have turned to such a tactic. Indeed, despite the effect of domestic violence-begets-violence dynamics and the historical template of hostage-taking, the fact that some of the large-scale hostage attacks in the Chechen wars have been aimed at attracting funding from the Middle East suggest that transnational factors have played a role in radicalization of tactics, but perhaps a smaller role than what they are given credit for – especially by the Russian government.

Effect on resource mobilization

Most accounts of transnational insurgents in Chechnya suggest that their key contribution to the domestic resistance movement's resources is not manpower but access to financial resources, primarily in the Middle East, although they have also brought along expertise in communications and use of weapons (Wilhelmsen 2004, 41–46; Vidino 2005; Ware 2005; Hughes 2007; Moore and Tumelty 2008).

Initially, the promise of the transnational insurgents who arrived in February 1995 was their added resources, including both weapons and access to finance, and the know-how and training expertise they brought via relational diffusion in training camps and by fighting side-by-side. In those early days of the war, the Chechen insurgents found themselves overwhelmed against the Russians' airpower. Khattab and his followers were key participants in the Chechens' retaking of Grozny in summer 1996, although the brutal winters in the Caucasus mountains and the lack of knowledge of Russian prevented large numbers of transnational insurgents from joining and contributing to the Chechens' struggle. Indeed, while Basayev admitted to being assisted by Arab fighters in the June 1995 attack on Budennovsk, when asked where he got his weapons, he did not mention foreign sources. Instead, Basayev emphasized that he was buying his weapons from the Russians.[31]

In the interwar years, the ability of the transnational insurgents to bring both competence and capacity increased. *The Life and Times of Khattab* features Khattab saying that after the first war, he was asked by the military and civilian Chechen leadership to help train insurgents, as the Chechens doubted that the Russians would completely withdraw. Khattab and his crew established training camps in Serzhen'-Yurt, contributing to resource mobilization via relational diffusion. Because financial resources in the immediate aftermath of the war were limited, Khattab notes that they initially had to limit the number of people they were training. However, as they made progress, they accepted up to 400 young men per course, not only from Chechnya but also from Ingushetia, Kabardino-Balkaria, Karachay-Cherkessia, Dagestan, Tatarstan, Uzbekistan, and elsewhere. Sokirianskaia's ethnographic study includes interviews with Chechens who attended these camps:

After training in the first camp, the best were selected and transferred to the military camp. Guys from Russia were taught mining, explosives, and the like ... This was real military training, these people knew that there would be another war, they were preparing (quoted in Sokirianskaia 2010, 213).

Besides providing competence through his training camps, Khattab did, per his own account, also provide humanitarian relief to the war-torn population via his camps – which furthered his hero image among some Chechens. He continued to fight alongside the Chechens until he was assassinated in 2002.

The transnational insurgents' contributions to the Chechen insurgents' resource mobilization has also been via mediated diffusion, i.e. their link to funding sources outside Chechnya, especially charities in Saudi Arabia (e.g. Murphy 2004, 140–155; B. Williams 2005a). Throughout the first war, Sheikh Fathi, who recruited Khattab to Chechnya, continued to recruit transnational insurgents and was, reportedly, instrumental in channeling funds from the Middle East to the Chechen insurgents. Khattab himself, attuned to the power of propaganda, released tapes of the Chechens' struggle through a network of mosques, which helped recruitment of foreign fighters to Chechnya (Vidino 2005; Tumelty 2006).

---

[31] "Basayev Takes Firm Stand on Chechnya's Independence," *BBC Summary of World Broadcasts* (*Segodnya*), July 26, 1995.

The Chechens used the same strategy in the second war, releasing tapes from the Dubrovka/Nord-Ost theater siege in 2002 and the Beslan school hostage crisis, portraying their struggle as an Islamist one. These tapes were aimed at attracting funding from the Middle East (Wilhelmsen 2004, 45; Speckhard and Ahkmedova 2006). Without having access to the resistance movement's budgets, it is hard to know where their funding actually comes from, but Andrei Smirnov, a journalist covering the North Caucasus, reports that a Chechen field commander in 2003 admitted to receiving funding from international Muslim foundations (Smirnov 2007d).[32] The Chechen field commander Salman Raduyev stated in 1998 that his group was funded by Islamic parties in the Middle East (Muzaev 1998b). More generally, Khattab was an important broker establishing links between the Chechen insurgent movement and Islamic charities (B. Williams 2007, 162). Similarly, the Dagestani Wahhabi preacher Kebedov, who entered Chechnya in the interwar years, was allegedly funded by charities in Saudi Arabia, Pakistan, and the US (Vatchagaev 2007).

The flow of resources may, in turn, have influenced tactical innovation, especially the large-scale attacks such as the Dubrovka/Nord-Ost and Beslan sieges. There are also accounts suggesting that the shift in framing, towards a more religious message, has been affected by concerns for resources. In other words, the domestic movement's concerns for resources may be a catalyst for shifts in the other two processes of mobilization. That trend has not necessarily been welcomed by the domestic population. The Chechen doctor Khassan Baiev notes in his autobiographical account that: "We welcomed the humanitarian aid we received from Middle Eastern countries, but we did not like it when they told us our Islam was not the true Islam. For 400 years we have fought against people telling us what to do" (2003, 206). Even Umarov has had to balance his message, so that he can gain, or at least keep, support among Chechens who may be motivated by self-determination and also attract funding from prospective funders in the Middle East, especially Turkey, who may be skeptical of his true commitment to an Islamist struggle (Smirnov 2007a).

The flow of resources via transnational insurgents has also influenced the balance of power between domestic and transnational insurgents, which in turn has affected both framing and tactical innovation in a

---

[32] See the interview in "Next Year the War Will Seize the Entire Caucasus," Kavkaz Center, November 28, 2003. Available from www.kavkazcenter.com/eng/content/2003/11/28/2039.shtml (accessed June 7, 2011).

radical direction. In the first war, Dudayev was in control of most funding sources, which came from within Russia. In the interwar years, Maskhadov, more cash-starved in an already war-torn republic, became dependent on warlords with external funding bases, thus giving both the warlords and their foreign funders more power (Wilhelmsen 2004, 40, 46). Indeed, in fall 2007, the resistance leader in neighboring Kabardino-Balkaria, Anzor Astemirov, posited that *he* was the one who had convinced Umarov to completely abandon the idea of a Chechen-centered struggle and declare the Caucasus Emirate. His leverage was Umarov's dependence on non-Chechen fighters (Smirnov 2007c).

This attempt to trace resources suggest that the route through which transnational insurgents influence the domestic insurgent movement may start with the resources they bring to the table (or battlefield). If shifts in framing and tactical innovation follow from a wish to attract resources, the motivation causing shifts in these processes is about strategic emulation rather than genuine learning.

Lessons learnt and further research

While the transnational dimensions of intrastate conflicts have received a great deal of attention among both scholars and policy-makers in the last few years, relatively little research has explored how transnational actors influence such struggles. In this study, I theorize and trace the diffusion mechanisms through which one group of such actors, transnational insurgents, have influenced mobilization in the Chechen separatist struggle against the Russian central government. I argue that through both relational and mediated diffusion, which engender either ideationally or instrumentally motivated learning and emulation, transnational insurgents can affect a domestic movement's framing of goals, tactical innovation, and resource mobilization. While researching mechanisms in a civil war setting can be a challenging task due to data limitations – it is, for instance, difficult to get reliable information about an armed group's training, much less whether the students genuinely learnt something from that training – I have sought to overcome these challenges by highlighting the observable implications of my argument and triangulating data from a variety of sources (see also the discussion in Checkel's introductory chapter).

There are lessons in this study for both scholars and policy-makers. For scholars, the study shows that mechanisms highlighted in relatively peaceful settings by the transnationalism and social movement literatures also apply to more violent realms. For example, just like epistemic communities can influence the framing of a state's foreign policy, transnational insurgents can affect the framing of a domestic movement's goals. Insurgents, too, copy or learn from others. While the emerging scholarship on the transnational relations of civil wars so far has largely assumed that transnational insurgents make such conflicts more likely or more violent, this study draws on the social movement literature to highlight that there are different aspects of a domestic movement's struggle that can be shaped by transnational insurgents – framing of goals, tactical innovation, and resource mobilization. Yet my empirics also point to conditioning variables and alternative explanations, emphasizing the need to carefully consider domestic factors that may either shape or overshadow the role played by transnational insurgents.

For policy-makers, the study suggests that the role of transnational insurgents should not be overstated. Rather than assuming that transnational insurgents influence domestic insurgents and insurgencies, policies ought to be based on a careful examination of if and how these actors influence the different processes in a domestic movement's mobilization effort. Transnational insurgents do not necessarily have unidirectional and identical effects across these processes.

The next step in this research agenda picks up on these varied effects and explores how outsider-induced changes in a domestic movement's mobilization processes are received among the local population.[33] My research so far suggests that it is not a given that transnational insurgents actually strengthen the domestic movement, as the changes they encourage can cause a backlash. While this chapter focuses on how transnational insurgents may influence intrastate struggles by affecting processes internal to the domestic movement, future research should also explore how transnational insurgents, like other activist groups, may shape intrastate conflicts by altering the external political context in which the struggle takes place (see Meyer and Whittier 1994). Indeed, to the degree that concerns about transnational terrorism changes states' policies towards domestic challenges within their borders, these domestic challenges are more indirectly affected by transnational insurgents.

---

[33] Kristin M. Bakke. "Acceptance and Resistance to Foreign Ideas: Transnational Insurgents' Impact on the Chechen Separatists." Unpublished manuscript. Department of Political Science, University College London. 2010.

3 Mechanisms of diaspora mobilization and the transnationalization of civil war *

FIONA B. ADAMSON

Introduction

As Checkel notes in his introduction to this volume, the roles of external and transnational actors are attracting increased attention in studies of civil war. Diasporas are unique in this regard as they consist of populations and actors that are both external and internal. They exist "outside the state ... but inside the people" (Shain and Barth 2003, 451). As such, they epitomize the complexities of disentangling processes and actors in the study of transnationalism and civil war.

The aim of this chapter is to contribute to a broader understanding of the transnational dynamics of civil war through a study of diaspora mobilization and conflict. The chapter does so by briefly pointing to the existing literature, before focusing on several causal mechanisms that can help us to disentangle and disaggregate aspects of diaspora mobilization that may exacerbate violent conflict in the home state. I then employ these mechanisms to examine the case of the conflict between the Kurdistan Workers' Party (PKK) and the Turkish state in the 1980s and 1990s. I conclude by discussing both the contributions and limits of focusing on mechanisms of diaspora mobilization in civil war, placing them within a broader context that includes other factors such as geopolitics and state interests.

Diasporas and violent conflict

In recent years, there has been increased interest in the role that diaspora populations can play in contributing to or exacerbating

* Thanks to Kristin Bakke, Andrew Bennett, Jeffrey Checkel, Matthew Evangelista, Scott Gates, Kristian Harpviken, Sarah Lischer, Elisabeth Wood, and the other project participants for their many helpful comments on the chapter. Elena Fiddian-Qasmiyeh, Maria Koinova, Francesco Ragazzi, and Idean Salehyan also provided a number of useful insights and suggestions on earlier drafts.

violent conflicts.[1] Research on this topic ranges from quantitative studies that operationalize diasporas as independent variables (Collier 2000; Collier and Hoeffler 2004), to collections of individual case studies (Smith and Stares 2007), to broader theoretical and analytic discussions (Anderson 1998; Huntington 1996; Kaldor 1999). A loose collection of studies is emerging that is pushing forward a research agenda on diasporas as potential initiators or exacerbators of violent conflict, as well as mediators of conflict and/or actors in conflict resolution and post-conflict reconstruction (Adamson 2004; 2005; 2006; Brinkerhoff 2006; Koinova 2010; Shain and Aryasinha 2006).

The most cited finding of this research has been that of Collier and Hoeffler (2004), who in a quantitative study analyzing "greed" vs. "grievance," identified diasporas as a significant force in fueling violent conflict. Building on earlier observations (Angoustures and Pascal 1996) regarding the financing of violent conflicts by diaspora groups, Collier and Hoeffler attempted to measure quantitatively the impact of diaspora populations on civil war by correlating the size of a country's diaspora to the incidence of civil war in that country. They suggested that the correlation could be explained by the ability of diasporas to provide financial support to rebel organizations through donations, and argued that this finding lent confirmation to their overall argument that "greed" or political economy factors trumped "grievances" in explaining civil wars.

This quantitative finding that diaspora populations may influence the course of violent conflict appears to be supported anecdotally by numerous other studies. In discussions of how the dynamics of conflicts are changing due to broader patterns of globalization in the international system, Kaldor (1999) notes both the ideational and material impacts of diasporas on conflicts around the world. Support is also provided in a RAND survey of sources of external support in contemporary insurgencies, which noted that one of the major changes in the international security environment post-Cold War was the increased importance of non-state actors in general, and diasporas in particular, as sources of financial and material support for insurgencies and guerrilla movements (Byman et al. 2001, 41). Others have portrayed diaspora

---

[1] There is a broader literature addressing the question of what constitutes a "diaspora" and how to define it (i.e. Adamson and Demetriou 2007, 2012; Brubaker 2005; Cohen 1997; Dufoix 2008; Sheffer 2003). I do not directly address these debates here, although the framework used in this chapter is informed by the literature.

populations as engaged in a form of "civilizational rallying" who come to the aid of their "ethnic kin" in times of violent conflict (Huntington 1996) or foster "long-distance nationalism" that is characterized by "a serious politics that is radically unaccountable" (Anderson 1998, 74).

The implication here is that members of diasporas can involve themselves as supporters of violent conflicts in their home countries, without paying the consequences of living in societies marked by political violence. These observations have recently been extended more broadly to the phenomenon of terrorism – Sageman (2004), for example, claims that 84 percent of those involved in al-Qaeda-inspired terrorism have been recruited in a diasporic context, with the majority of recruitment taking place in Western Europe. In addition, there is a growing body of empirical studies of particular conflicts (Biswas 2004; Danforth 1995; Fair 2005; Gunaratna 2001; Ho 2004; Hockenos 2003; Lyons 2006; Rapoport 2003; Shain 2002; Smith and Stares 2007) that have examined the extent to which members of diaspora groups have been active supporters of political violence.

Yet, although a growing body of literature has established the significance of diaspora populations for understanding the dynamics of violent conflict, there has to date been little attention paid to systematizing the study of such diaspora involvement. The conclusions of Collier's (2000) study, for example, relied on the finding that there is a correlation between US Census data on foreign-born populations and the recurrence of violence in civil wars. While it suggested reasons for this finding it did not attempt to trace the various processes by which a population abroad would impact on a conflict in its "home" country. Similarly, many qualitative studies that have noted the importance of diasporas have been largely descriptive and have not attempted to identify causal mechanisms that could be used to systematically compare diaspora involvement in conflicts across different cases.

Part of the problem in investigating the processes and causal mechanisms by which diasporas come to play a role in conflicts may have to do with how they are conceptualized in much of the literature – as unitary actors treated as "independent variables." Without examining intervening processes of political mobilization, it is difficult to arrive at conclusive statements regarding the role that diasporas play in the international security environment. Indeed, some research (i.e. King and Melvin 2000) convincingly shows that in many cases diaspora mobilization should be treated as a *dependent variable* rather than an *independent variable*, i.e. that diaspora mobilization is a consequence rather than a cause of violent conflict.

A focus on political mobilization points to parallels between the processes of transnational mobilization that are seen in diaspora politics and other instances of transnational politics (Adamson 2002; 2005; 2012). As Checkel notes in his introduction, there is now a well-established literature in international relations, comparative politics and sociology that theorizes transnational processes and movements (Bob 2005; Della Porta and Tarrow 2004; Keck and Sikkink 1998; Khagram, Riker, and Sikkink 2002; Tarrow 2005). Similarly, there is growing literature on civil wars and ethnic conflict that has begun to examine their transnational dimensions (Wood, this volume; see also Gleditsch 2007; Gledistch and Salehyan 2006; Hironaka 2005; Jenne 2007; Salehyan 2009). What is needed is to combine insights from such literatures in ways that can better specify the processes and causal mechanisms by which diaspora politics come to impact on the dynamics of violent conflicts.

Paying close attention to causal mechanisms is important, because one need only examine the wider body of research in diaspora studies to quickly see that the purported effects and outcomes that are attributed to diasporas vary widely. Diasporas, for example, can affect policy-making outcomes in their "host state," particularly in the area of foreign policy-making (Weil 1974; Mathias 1981; Tucker et al. 1990; Uslaner 1991; Huntington 1997; Smith 2001; Saideman 2001). They can enhance economic development or contribute to democratization and the observance of human rights (Koinova 2009; Van Hear 1998; 2002; Shain 1999). Such a wide range of possible impacts would suggest that diasporas in and of themselves do not inherently contribute to any particular outcome – their activities and political impacts vary. This calls into question the utility of conceptualizing diasporas as unitary actors that have fixed effects on outcomes. A more fruitful approach would be to assume that the activities of members of diaspora populations vary, and then to ask under what conditions and for what reasons they are most likely to become participants in civil wars. This involves identifying a set of key causal mechanisms.

Diaspora mobilization in civil wars: identifying causal mechanisms

A focus on causal mechanisms and the use of process tracing in case studies provides an important starting point in helping us to specify exactly when, why, and how diaspora populations may play a causal role in the initiation or perpetuation of civil wars. This involves moving away from the use of primordial and essentialist assumptions that reify "diasporas" as unitary actors, and instead examining the actual processes by, and conditions under which, members of diaspora populations become mobilized as de facto participants in a "long-distance conflict."

Much of the literature on political mobilization, social movements, and contentious politics has focused on processes that occur at the domestic level or within states. Similar mechanisms are found in processes of political mobilization that occur in a transnational setting and that take place across state borders (Della Porta and Tarrow 2004; Keck and Sikkink 1998; Khagram, Riker, and Sikkink 2002; Tarrow 1998; 2005; see also Bakke, this volume). However, as Bennett reminds us, a focus on mechanisms does not mean that we should ignore the broader structural context, such as global inequalities and variations in domestic political opportunity structures (Bennett, this volume). Rather it allows us, within a given set of broader structural conditions, to explicate the specific dynamics and processes that link dispersed populations and that mobilize them to collectively engage in particular sets of actions that affect the course of a violent conflict.

As an initial step, one can separate the study of diaspora involvement in violent conflicts into two stages: the *process* of diaspora mobilization, and the *impact* of diaspora mobilization on the course of a conflict. In the first stage, the mobilized diaspora is treated, loosely, as the dependent variable. In other words, the phenomenon to be explained is how and why transnationally dispersed populations come to be mobilized to be engaged in a violent conflict thousands of miles away. In the second stage, the mobilized diaspora becomes the independent variable. The focus is on how mobilized diaspora populations then come to impact on the onset, duration and intensity of a violent conflict. By separating diaspora involvement in violent conflict into its constituent parts, we gain greater analytical leverage and can begin the process of exploring variations in each of the mechanisms in greater detail.

In the following sections, I identify five causal mechanisms that provide a starting point for understanding how and when diaspora populations become actors in civil wars. Like Checkel and Gerring, I define a causal mechanism as "a pathway or process by which an effect is produced or a purpose is accomplished" (Checkel, this volume). In actuality, of course, there are numerous and multiple mechanisms that could play a role in diaspora mobilization and the transnationalization of conflict; many have been identified and elaborated upon by scholars working on transnationalism and/or contentious politics (McAdam, Tarrow, and Tilly 2001; Tarrow 2005). Other factors, such as the origins and process of migration, state repression, and human rights abuses in the country of origin, and the emergence of political opposition in both the home state and the diaspora, are important for understanding diaspora involvement in violent conflict, but will not be the primary focus of this chapter.

The five causal mechanisms examined here are divided into two subsets. The first set – *transnational brokerage, strategic framing*, and *ethnic or sectarian outbidding* – are related to diaspora mobilization. The second – *resource mobilization* and *lobbying and persuasion* – relate to the impact of the mobilized diaspora on the conflict. It may be tempting to treat the two elements of mobilization and impact as two stages in a sequence (first the diaspora is mobilized, and then the mobilized diaspora impacts on the conflict), however, in reality the two processes may overlap, reinforce each other, or create feedback loops in ways that do not lend themselves to a strictly sequential mapping or analysis.

The process of diaspora mobilization

It is common in quantitative approaches to civil war and ethnic conflict to reify a particular collective actor – such as an ethnic group or organization – and to treat the group as "acting" in a conflict. However, beginning with the assumption of a pre-existing collective actor begs the prior question of how that collectivity itself becomes constituted and comes to be viewed as an "actor" and why that collective actor comes to have an "interest" in a conflict that is occurring primarily in a different geographical locale. In other words, it is necessary to look at questions concerning the formation of collective agency, group identity, and collective interests/preferences as part and parcel of our understanding of conflict processes. A mechanism-based approach can help us shed light on the micro-dynamics of this process.

Transnational brokerage

Social network theorists have identified "brokers" as particularly powerful actors in their ability to link together disparate networks.

When two networks are separated by a "structural hole" a broker can gain power by filling the gap and bringing together two unlinked networks (Burt 2005; Goddard 2007; Padgett and Ansell 1993). A focus on the mechanism of transnational brokerage helps explain how networks defined by diasporic ties become connected with "conflict networks" that are actively engaged in political violence. A necessary yet insufficient condition of diaspora involvement in conflict is linking of diasporic networks in one or more so-called "host states" with those networks that perpetuate or sustain conflict in the "home state."

A broker plays a role in connecting a group or network symbolically but also materially to a conflict. Here one can compare with the literature in social movements that examines how transnational brokerage brings about a "scale shift" in incidents of transnational contention (McAdam and Tarrow 2005; Tarrow 1998; 2005). To apply this to civil wars, it is necessary to understand how transnational brokers emerge and connect diasporic networks in different states and to conflict networks in the so-called "home state." This is a prior step to understanding how ideas, material resources, expertise, recruits, or other elements are transferred back and forth between the diaspora and the conflict zone.

Strategic framing

The concept of "strategic framing" has been largely developed in and drawn from the literature on social movements (Benford and Snow 2000). However, it is also found separately in work on policy frames (Rein and Schoen 1996), as well as being increasingly employed as a useful analytical tool by scholars of international relations (Bob 2005; Busby 2007; Khagram, Riker, and Sikkink 2002; Payne 2001); it also plays a central role in the chapters by Bakke and Schmitz in this volume. Frames have been defined as "schemata of interpretation" that are "intended to mobilize potential adherents and constituents, to garner bystander support, and to demobilize antagonists" (Benford and Snow 2000, 614; Goffman 1974, 21, as cited in Benford and Snow 2000) or as persuasive devices used to "fix meanings, organize experience, alert others that their interests and possibly their identities are at stake, and propose solutions to ongoing problems" (Barnett 1999, 25, as cited in Payne 2001, 39). Social movement approaches conceptualize framing as "the conscious strategic efforts by groups of people to fashion shared understandings of the world and of themselves that legitimate and motivate collective action," and have identified the linking of different frames, or "frame alignment" as an important way to explain the emergence and growth of social movements (McAdam, McCarthy, and Zald 1996, 6 as cited in Busby 2007, 251).

The process of diaspora mobilization is dependent on the ability of actors to devise and articulate frames that resonate with members of diaspora groups in ways that successfully align the perceptions, values, or interests of diaspora members with those of civil war actors or conflict entrepreneurs. Deploying notions of national belonging and duty or "kinship" could be one possible framing strategy, but there are certainly other powerful frames that could be deployed to mobilize members of a diaspora. For example, some studies have noted that diaspora entrepreneurs can successfully deploy frames emphasizing guilt or obligation in order to tie members of diasporas to their country of origin, such as the obligation to send remittances to family members.[2] A focus on strategic framing processes emphasizes that involvement by individuals in so-called "homeland politics" or a conflict thousands of miles away is a puzzle to be explained rather than a situation to be expected.

Ethnic or sectarian outbidding

Ethnic outbidding broadly refers to the politicization of ethnic differences by elites or political parties (Rabushka and Shepsle 1972; Horowitz 1985). In dynamics of ethnic outbidding, parties or elites attempt to outdo each other, leading to a cycle of polarization that fuels extremism (Brubaker 1996; Gagnon 1994; Chandra 2005). Outbidding can involve the use of violence, both as a means of demonstrating strength and resolve, and as a way of marginalizing more moderate alternative groups. The taking of extreme positions can be seen as a means of increasing one's bargaining leverage (Jenne 2007). The aim of the process of outbidding, including the use of repression and violence, is to draw a firm distinction between what

---

[2] Laura Hammond. "Obliged to Give: Remittances and the Maintenance of Transnational Networks Between Somalis 'At Home' and Abroad." Unpublished Manuscript. 2007.

Kydd and Walter (2006) have referred to as "zealots" vs. "sellouts." In other words, the taking of extreme positions – either rhetorically or through the selective employment of violence – can, under certain conditions, mobilize public support, thus leading to increased radicalization. It is this strategic deployment of both language and action to simultaneously increase power and legitimacy (thus creating a feedback loop in the form of additional support – material as well as social) that makes this mechanism interesting.

Diaspora organizations can operate in a manner similar to ethnically defined political parties (sometimes they are directly affiliated with home-state political parties). Indeed, they may have increased incentives to do so to retain support. Because the "diaspora" as a construct is defined according to an ethnic or national category (or, at the minimum, a connection to a real or imagined homeland), this may create incentives for diaspora organizations to attempt to outbid each other in their articulation of a national or ethnic identity as a means of increasing their power and standing in the diaspora. When organizations are competing for diaspora support, incentives may exist for ethnic outbidding. This is arguably even more likely to occur if there is instability, political uncertainty or conflict in the so-called home state. After all, in some respects the "diaspora" ceases to exist if a distinct identity is not mobilized and fostered, as arguably occurred with the "Irish diaspora" in the US following the 1998 Good Friday Agreement (Cochrane 2012).

The impacts of mobilization on violent conflict

Once a process of mobilization takes place, how does a transnationally mobilized population impact on violent conflict? Two additional mechanisms – resource mobilization and lobbying-persuasion – help to explain the direct and indirect impacts a mobilized diaspora can have on a conflict. These mechanisms are drawn directly from the literatures on social movements and transnational advocacy networks, and are common to both non-violent and violent forms of mobilization (McCarthy and Zald 1977; Pichardo 1988).

Resource mobilization

Diaspora mobilization emerges as a strategy in civil war when members of diaspora populations have access to needed resources.

Political entrepreneurs can engage in resource mobilization activities and then channel them into the support of conflict-related activities. Resources can include capital and financial resources, but also human resources – technical expertise, or even recruits. Identifying the mechanism of resource mobilization provides a means for examining the processes and pathways by which diaspora organizations manage to mobilize resources and channel them both to diasporic activities and directly to the zones of conflict.[3]

Lobbying and persuasion

Lobbying and persuasion are additional mechanisms by which actors in the diaspora can impact the course of violent conflict. There are numerous studies of persuasion or argumentation in the field of international relations (Checkel 2007; Johnston 2008; Price 1998; Risse 2000). One of the most applicable models to diaspora involvement in civil wars is that of the "boomerang pattern" (Keck and Sikkink 1998, 12–13). In this model of transnational lobbying, NGOs in a state where political mobilization is difficult will network with NGOs outside it. In turn, these external NGOs place pressure on their own governments and on international organizations, which then place pressure on the original state. This is a useful model for understanding how actors in a civil war situation can turn to diasporic elites to lobby internationally on their behalf (see also Hamberg, this volume).

Diaspora mobilization in the Kurdish conflict in Turkey (1980–2000)

Having identified a set of causal mechanisms, I now turn to their application in a case study of the Kurdish conflict in Turkey, which has been notable for its high level of diaspora involvement. The civil war between the Kurdistan Workers' Party (PKK) and the Turkish state has claimed approximately 40,000 lives since 1984, has resulted in thousands of villages being destroyed, and has produced an estimated 3 million refugees/displaced people. It is a conflict for which there is extensive data, including a number of academic reports, as well as

---

[3] For a similar understanding of the role played by resource mobilization in other instances of transnationalized civil war, see Bakke and Schmitz, both this volume.

studies of the dynamics of Turkish and Kurdish transnational politics (e.g. Barkey and Fuller 1998; Lyon and Ucarer 2001; Østergaard-Nielsen 2001; 2003; Romano 2006; Wahlback 1999; Watts 2004; White 2001).

By utilizing these existing studies, and supplementing them with primary research such as the use of press reports, government documents, and ethnographic research, it is possible to engage in a process-tracing exercise that sheds light on both the mechanisms of diaspora mobilization and the impacts of this mobilization on the conflict. This case study does not present a full overview of the conflict, its various stages, iterations and complexities, and relation to other developments in Europe and Turkey. Rather, my aim is to show how the identified causal mechanisms shed important light on the transnational dimensions of the Kurdish conflict in Turkey during the period of 1980–2000.

The historical roots of the contemporary conflict can be traced to the founding of the Turkish Republic with the Lausanne Treaty of 1923. As part of Turkish nation-building, expressions of Kurdish or other minority identifications were severely repressed by the state and viewed as threatening to Turkish national unity. An ideology of secular Turkish nationalism, derived from the principles of Kemalism put forth by Turkey's founder, Kemal Atatürk, came to dominate the political discourse in Turkey. In this context, there were several regional Kurdish rebellions and uprisings within Turkey in the 1920s and 1930s, and low levels of political activity around the Kurdish issue in Eastern Turkey in the 1960s, but the most significant event was the founding of the PKK by Abdullah Öcalan in 1978.[4]

The PKK began to agitate among Kurdish areas of southeastern Turkey in the late 1970s. During these years, as Turkey descended into a state of internal anarchy characterized by violent clashes between the extreme left and right, the PKK began to attack targets and established a presence in Kurdish areas of the country. The 1960s and 1970s had seen a significant migration from Turkey to Western Europe, especially Germany. This was a response to the labor shortage in Germany following World War II. Between 1961 and 1974, the number of Turkish workers in Germany grew from 2,400 to 617,500

---

[4] For general background on the Kurdish conflict in Turkey, see McDowall 1996, 395–458; Barkey and Fuller 1998; Gunter 1990; Izady 1992, 67–72, 215–218; Entessar 1992, 81–111.

(Akgündüz 1993, 161); by 1974, their number was greater than that of any other nationality. The number of Turkish citizens in Germany continued to grow even after recruitment stopped in the 1970s, due to a combination of family reunification policies and political asylum, eventually reaching approximately 2 million.

In 1980, Turkey experienced a military coup and the PKK, along with other left-wing organizations as well as trade unions, was severely repressed, with the government banning a number of political parties and arresting political activists. In 1982, the new Turkish constitution strictly prohibited the use of the Kurdish language, Kurdish publications, and the establishment of Kurdish political parties or other manifestations of Kurdish identity. Following the 1980 military coup and the severe repression that followed, the PKK regrouped in Syria and Lebanon and formed an armed organization that mounted attacks in southeastern Turkey beginning in 1984.

One of the key features of the Kurdish conflict in Turkey has been its transnational dimensions and the active role that Kurdish populations in Europe have played in it. This role has not remained static, but instead has evolved over time. A full study of the transnational dimensions of the Kurdish conflict would have to account for the fluctuations that occurred as populations from Turkey became more established in Europe; as external events (such as the arrest of the PKK leader Abdullah Öcalan in 1999) shifted the dynamics of the conflict; and as the relationship between Turkey and Europe has evolved in the light of European Union (EU) negotiations. It would also need to take note of the changing political situation in Turkey with the introduction of constitutional reforms due to the EU harmonization process, the easing of restrictions on the Kurdish population, and the emergence since 2001 of the Islamic Justice and Development (AK) party as a major political force. Nevertheless, it is possible to trace the basic contours of diaspora involvement in the conflict by employing the five mechanisms discussed above.

Transnational brokerage: linking Europe with the conflict in southeastern Turkey

To understand the transnational dimensions of the civil war, it is important to understand how populations in Europe became linked with the conflict in Turkey. A key factor in this respect was the emergence of a group of "transnational brokers" who managed to connect migrant populations in Germany and elsewhere with conflict networks and actors in southeastern Turkey. These brokers were largely members of the National Liberation Front of Kurdistan (ERNK), which was the political wing of the PKK, and which embedded itself in populations in Europe and undertook mobilization activities in support of the war in Turkey. A key development in this respect was the exodus of a group of Kurdish intellectuals, activists, and militants to Europe from Turkey following the 1980 military coup; this group interacted with already-settled populations from Turkey in Europe. Some of these activists began to organize a Kurdish nationalist move-ment in Western Europe and establish European branches of the ERNK in a number of European states.

The vast majority of Kurdish cultural associations, information centers, and publications during the 1980s and much of the 1990s were associated with or controlled by European branches of the PKK through the ERNK or its affiliates. Throughout the mid 1980s to early 1990s, the political wing of the PKK operated legally in most of Europe, with its above-ground cultural, social, and political organizations existing side-by-side with a parallel covert and tightly organized underground structure (Stein 1994, 86). The European Central Committee of the ERNK had headquarters in Cologne and Brussels with national organi-zations in Germany, Belgium, France, Holland, England, Switzerland, Italy, and the Scandinavian countries (Stein 1994, 91; Barkey and Fuller 1998, 38; Helfer 1988, 20).

Throughout the 1980s and 1990s, the PKK pursued a dual strategy. It used political violence against the Turkish state (and segments of the Kurdish population) by perpetuating an armed conflict in southeastern Turkey, in which institutional voids in Lebanon and Syria and, following the Gulf War, Northern Iraq, were used as bases to train militants and plan incursions into southeastern Turkey. At the same time, it engaged in political activities in Europe as a means of mobili-zing populations that could provide resources and political support for the conflict. Most of the Kurdish leadership in Germany during this period was already connected in some way to the Kurdish student activist networks that had arisen in Turkey in the 1970s. There was thus an established link between Kurdish activists in Germany and the PKK leadership that operated out of Syria and southeastern Turkey (Barkey and Fuller 1998, 32). Members of this group of exiles in

Europe maintained contacts with networks of PKK members who had fled to Syria and Lebanon, and who had begun to take up arms against the Turkish state from across the border. Exiles in Germany and other countries in Europe managed to build a pan-European counterpart to the PKK's political wing, the ERNK, and successfully created a transnational structure that was organized as a network of local cells that spanned the continent and beyond (Bundesamt fuer Verfassungsschutz 1996, 7). This Kurdish movement "became an almost invisible network spread across the globe" (Bruinessen 1998, 48).

Thus, the political organization of the Kurdish diaspora was undertaken by political entrepreneurs who were well connected with the PKK structures in Syria and southeastern Turkey – often the same individuals were moving back and forth between Europe and Damascus. This provided a transnational brokerage mechanism for directly connecting diaspora populations in Europe with the PKK conflict networks in Syria and southeastern Turkey. Although numerous social, familial, political, and official ties connected Kurdish populations in Europe with Turkey, the process of political mobilization around the conflict cannot be understood without an account of the ERNK/PKK's transnational activities. As an organization, it successfully managed to cultivate transnational brokers who linked populations and resources in Europe to the armed insurgency in southeastern Turkey and surrounding regions.

Strategic framing: constructing a politicized Kurdish identity in Europe

The political activities undertaken by the transnationally connected Kurdish activists in Europe involved mobilizing migrant populations from Turkey as Kurds. To understand how this occurred, one has to examine the use of strategic framing in the construction of a politicized Kurdish identity amongst populations in Europe. In his provocatively titled article, "How Turks Became Kurds, Not Germans," sociologist Claus Leggewie made the claim that "there have always been Kurds among the Turkish 'guest workers' and refugees, but most of them did not discover their 'Kurdishness' until they came to Europe" (Leggewie 1996, 79). Similarly, Bruinessen argues, "among the Turkish 'Gastarbeiter' who had migrated to Western Europe since the late 1950s, there were many who 'discovered,' in the course of the past few decades, that they were not Turks but Kurds" (Bruinessen 1998, 44–45).

Many who grew to identify themselves as Kurds in Europe may have migrated to Germany or other countries as self-identified Turks, grew up speaking Turkish, not Kurdish, or had parents who came to Germany as labor migrants in the 1960s and viewed themselves as secular and Kemalist Turks. This replicates some aspects of the situation in Turkey, where "assimilated Kurds" often readily identify themselves as Turkish, and even highly politicized Kurds may speak Turkish, rather than Kurdish. In both Turkey and within the immigrant community in Western Europe, there have also always been Kurdish-speakers and self-identified Kurds, but very few members of this category drew upon their Kurdishness as a basis for political activism during the 1960s or early 1970s.

The *politicization* of a Kurdish identity and the development of a Kurdish nationalist movement within the "Turkish" immigrant community in Germany occurred largely during the 1980s and the 1990s. This was due to the efforts of the transnational brokers who emigrated from Turkey to Germany and other European countries following the 1980 military coup. When Kurdish political entrepreneurs arrived in Germany and other European states in the late 1970s and early 1980s, they had access to immigrant populations that provided a large pool of potentially active Kurds. Early migration patterns from Turkey to Germany produced networks that were disproportionately drawn from the ethnically Kurdish regions of Turkey, due to the low levels of economic development in southeastern Anatolia. By the mid 1970s and the ending of the official recruitment of workers, there were significant portions of the "Turkish Gastarbeiter" population in Germany that originated from ethnically Kurdish regions, yet most of this population did not identify with a Kurdish political identity or project. Bruinessen writes: "Until the late 1970s, relatively few migrant workers emphasized their Kurdish identity. Most of the workers, especially those of rural origins, were reluctant to become involved with politics. Moreover, their European surroundings defined them as Turks, and this remained in most contexts the relevant identity" (Bruinessen 1998, 45).

When activists from the PKK arrived in Western Europe in the 1980s, they went about explicitly constructing and politicizing a distinct Kurdish national identity. Through processes of strategic framing, they were able to create and deploy a new form of nationalism that appealed to a population that felt doubly marginalized by the Turkish state and its official national narrative, as well as by European states. This was particularly strong in Germany, in which second-and even third-generation migrants were viewed as "foreigners" (*Auslaender*) who were denied German citizenship, and often remained socially and economically marginalized. At the same time, official agreements between Germany and Turkey meant that this population was still living in the grip of the Turkish state within Germany – whether via schooling provided by Turkish teachers, religious life dominated by *imams* from the Turkish Presidency of Religious Affairs (*Diyanet*), or Turkish officialdom in everyday life in Germany, such as in the registration of births.

This encouragement of diaspora members to discover their Kurdish identity and to construct Kurdishness as a form of resistance to state hegemony in both Europe and Turkey had a certain appeal, especially amongst segments of the second-generation Turkish immigrant population. A variety of frames and techniques were used to mobilize a Kurdish national movement in Europe. First and foremost was the attempt to elevate Kurdish language and culture to a status on par with its Turkish counterparts. This was symbolically important as an act of protest because of the restrictions on Kurdish linguistic and cultural expression in Turkey at the time, but also because of the continuing involvement of the Turkish state with "its" diaspora in Germany. Absent *jus soli*/place-of-birth citizenship criteria in Germany, births to Turkish citizens had to be registered with Turkish authorities – meaning that any restrictions on giving Kurdish names to infants in Turkey were replicated for Turkish citizens in Germany.

The promotion of Kurdish cultural activities, such as Kurdish-specific festivals and ceremonies became another form of symbolic protest. Most important amongst these was the celebration of the festival "Newroz" (New Year) which during this period was banned in Turkey. Similarly, the publication of Kurdish-language books, poetry, and newspapers, as well as the promotion of Kurdish music and the establishment of a Kurdish-language satellite television that could compete with Turkish stations were cultural activities that could be freely pursued in Europe, but were also deeply political acts owing to their illegality in Turkey (Hassanpour 1998). This promotion of Kurdish culture, language, and customs became a political act in itself – a form of resistance that carved out a publicly available alternative identity category for members of the diaspora that posed a challenge to the hegemonic categories of both "German" and "Turkish."

The promotion of a Kurdish national identity, combined with the radical politics of the PKK and its Marxist ideology that endorsed armed struggle, fostered a culture of resistance in Europe that equated Kurdish nationalism with resistance to Turkish and German nationalism, American hegemony, capitalism, and traditional authority structures (feudal and tribal systems). This frame of resistance to existing power structures resonated with a large number of young Turks/Kurds in Europe and, while it was not the only set of frames available, it was particularly successful in appealing to a segment of the population that was predisposed to identify culturally as Kurdish.

Kurdish political entrepreneurs in the 1990s were thus able to formulate political categories and ideologies that presented individuals with identity options that countered both German and Turkish national identities. They constructed categories of belonging that resonated with the lived experiences of many young members of the Turkish-Kurdish community in Europe, and used this as a means for expanding their base of political support. As Eccarius-Kelly (1999, 16–17) noted:

Once the PKK succeeded in establishing an emotional link with such a subculture group [of German Kurds] it [was] easier to mold members into PKK structures ... In exchange for membership and activism within the PKK structures, young Kurds are offered a Kurdish dream world complete with myth of origin, sense of ethnic harmony, social status and respect.

The conflict itself helped to foster and reify a Kurdish identity – thus creating a feedback loop between mobilization in the diaspora, conflict activities in southeastern Turkey, and further mobilization. The fact that Germany vocally denounced the PKK only added to the attraction it had for many who joined "the movement to become part of an 'elite organization' with an almost mythic fame for its defiance of the German state" (Eccarius-Kelly 1999, 24).

Ethnic outbidding: the PKK and its alternatives

The PKK was not the only Kurdish group active in Europe in the 1990s and it also faced stiff competition from a range of non-Kurdish entities including Turkish nationalist, Turkish leftist, and religious organizations. A number of Kurdish organizations with links to Kurdish Social Democrat movements in Turkey – who eschewed political violence – also existed in Germany; they operated largely under the guise of the umbrella organization KOMKAR, which viewed itself as working simultaneously for the rights of Kurdish immigrants within Germany and for an improvement of the political situation of Kurds within Turkey. In addition, there were some smaller Kurdish organizations operating in Germany at the time. Generally, however, the PKK was successful in acquiring a relative monopoly over the segment of the "Turkish" immigrant community that came to identify as "Kurdish." This was accomplished through a combination of successful mobilization and propaganda, the creation or co-optation of an extensive organizational structure, as well as coercion.

The relationship between the PKK and other Kurdish groups in the 1990s can be viewed as a case of the PKK winning a competition of "ethnic outbidding" within Kurdish diaspora communities in Europe. Under conditions of intense suppression of Kurdish identity in Turkey and discrimination in Germany and Europe, the PKK was able to devise a strategy that equated "Kurdish" with resistance, and not assimilation. Thus, other groups were constructed as less "Kurdish" to the extent that they were constructed as promoting integration into German society or collaboration with the Turkish state. By taking an extreme position, that included the use of contentious politics, resistance, and violence, the PKK established itself as the acknowledged representative of the Kurdish cause in Europe. It was thus able to gain hegemony over Kurdish politics in the diaspora, despite the fact that many individual diasporans may have disagreed with its tactics and many of its actions.

The PKK did not hesitate to use violence to suppress its rivals within Europe. But while coercion did play some role in the PKK's monopolization of the Kurdish movement, the high levels of support that it had within Kurdish communities in Europe was also attributable to its recognition as the only organization that could viably challenge the interests of Turkish state elites. Some estimates put political support for the PKK as high as 90 percent among those who identified as Kurds in Europe in the 1990s, with at least 10,000 active members in the party or related organizations and 50,000 active mobilized sympathizers in Germany (Bundesamt fuer Verfassungsschutz 1996, 8; Barkey and Fuller 1998, 32).

Thus, the PKK, as the most radicalized of the Kurdish organizations operating in Europe in the 1990s, was viewed by many as the "legitimate representative" of the Kurdish cause – the organization that was willing to mobilize and use violence to press for Kurdish rights and autonomy. The context here is important and a key to why this strategy worked. A "radical" message or strategy will not be necessarily a winning strategy in terms of mobilization success, but can be if an audience is persuaded that it is the most legitimate strategy in a particular context.

In this case, a context of restricted membership in European societies, severe repression in Turkey, and the perception that European foreign policy enabled Turkish repression all worked to make the radical strategy of the PKK appear to offer a more effective pathway of resistance than the more incrementalist approaches of the non-violent Kurdish parties. At the same time, the PKK was skilled at altering its frames over time to respond to changes in the context, as well as co-opting the successful frames of other groups. For example, one sees a shift over time from a more radical Marxist-Leninist message in the 1980s and early 1990s to the emergence of a more human rights and political and cultural autonomy frame in the mid to late 1990s – the PKK effectively co-opted the successful elements of other organizations' agendas into its own.

Resource mobilization: the diaspora as a source of material support

Kurdish nationalist political entrepreneurs were able to draw upon the politicized transnational networks that they activated in Europe as a source of material support that the PKK used to build up its organizational structures within Europe and, in the 1990s, to fund the armed conflict in southeastern Turkey. Much of the financial support for the PKK was raised in Europe. The PKK harnessed material resources from the Kurdish diaspora by collecting voluntary donations and "taxes" of up to 20 percent of individual salaries and business profits (Marcus 1993). The relationship between political mobilization, resource mobilization, and impact on violent conflict is not necessarily sequential – contributing to a cause can have a binding and mobilizing effect on individuals, and the creation of a strong identity movement can have an independent legitimizing effect on a conflict. Nevertheless, the mobilization of material resources from the diaspora population is one of the most direct impacts of the diaspora on the conflict.

Some sense of the scale of resource mobilization undertaken by the PKK can be gleaned from official sources and police and intelligence reports. The German government estimated that the PKK collected between Deutsche Mark (DM) 30 and 50 million annually via donations and racketeering from the Kurdish community in Germany in the 1990s – over DM 1.5 million annually in the city of Berlin alone.[5] Rates of "donations" or "taxes" were set according to one's financial means and status, with the unemployed and asylum seekers expected to pay DM 30–50 per month; gainfully employed members of the community DM 100–300 per month, and rates of up to DM 3,000 a month for successful business owners.[6] In the early days of the conflict, money collected in Europe was reportedly transferred first to a PKK office in Sweden, where it was consolidated from networks across Europe and transferred directly to Abdullah Öcalan at his headquarters in Damascus.

In the wake of Öcalan's arrest in 1999, individual couriers reportedly transported revenues directly from Germany to southeastern Turkey.[7] The official ban of the PKK in Germany in 1993 apparently led to an increase rather than decrease in the revenues that it collected in Germany (Gunaratna 2001, 13–14). In addition to collecting money from immigrant communities in Germany, the PKK also actively collected revenues in a number of other European countries. One Turkish source cited a British intelligence report that the PKK collected £2.5 million in 1993 from immigrants and businesses in England (Turkish Democracy Foundation 1997, 47).

Individual supporters of the PKK regularly provided voluntary donations to the organization in amounts ranging from several thousand to over DM 10,000. Many of the large donations came from well-established first-generation immigrants who managed to save a substantial amount over the course of their stay in Germany, and wished to exercise influence in the local Kurdish community by making generous donations to Kurdish organizations (Imset 1992). Many economic migrants during the first wave of migration from Turkey in the 1960s and 1970s came from rural and economically depressed regions of southeastern Turkey. Despite what were comparatively poor living conditions in Germany, most first-generation

---

[5] Sources include Bundesamt für Verfassungsschutz 1996, 6; Landesamt für Verfassungsschutz Berlin 1994; *Der Spiegel*, February 22, 1999, 35.

[6] "Hilflos vor dem Terror," *Der Spiegel*, March 25, 1996, 35–38, cited in Eccarius-Kelly 1999, 22.

[7] Imset 1992, 156; *Der Spiegel*, February 22, 1999, 25.

migrants were members of German unions and earned middle-class wages, which enabled them to save enough to start their own businesses or purchase land in Turkey. This meant that many in the first generation were actually able to save substantial amounts of money that could later be drawn upon for the funding of cultural and political projects. Organized political fundraising activities sponsored by the PKK were known to raise very large sums of money – one source claims that the PKK was able to raise DM 100 each from 120,000 participants in a fundraising event in the Netherlands in 1998 (White 2001, 193).

In addition to voluntary contributions that were harnessed from immigrant communities in Europe, an important source of revenue for the PKK was extortion and protection money. This included protection money collected from Kurdish and Turkish businesses in Germany and other European countries, and forced donations from individuals. According to one source, 69 out of every 100 incidents of extortion that occurred in Germany in 1994 were somehow connected with the PKK.[8] The German government established a number of special commissions in various cities throughout Germany to examine the problem of extortion and racketeering, in particular by the PKK.[9] In the Netherlands, a prime source of revenue was apparently extortion money obtained from Kurdish-owned pizza parlors.[10]

Another source of revenue was the corruption of the asylum process. A Swiss source argued that the PKK was collecting 20–60 percent of the state support provided to Kurdish refugees who were waiting for their asylum hearing, which resulted in annual revenues of millions of Swiss Francs transferred from Basel, to Paris, and eventually to PKK headquarters in Damascus (Helfer 1988, 48). Kurdish organizations in a number of European countries, including Germany and the UK, were responsible for certifying political asylum seekers as genuine. Both the Turkish and German governments argued that the PKK, in addition to receiving donations or other forms of payment from refugees and asylum seekers, was also involved in controlling the market for forged visas and passports, as well as human smuggling operations (Turkish

---

[8] Statement by Rolph Tophoven, Director of the Terrorism Research Forum in Germany, cited in Turkish Democracy Foundation 1997, 48.

[9] Bundesamt für Verfassungsschutz 1996, 6.

[10] Helle Bering, "Europe's Kurdish Headache," *Washington Times*, February 24, 1999.

Democracy Foundation 1997, 48). The system was also reportedly used as a means of sending PKK organizers from Turkey to Western Europe and in engaging in human smuggling as a source of additional revenue (Helfer 1988, 47; Dalman and Tabak 1995). The PKK, according to some accounts, benefited directly from the asylum regime in three respects: first, it charged refugees or others up to $3,000 to be smuggled into Europe; second, it used this inflow of new refugees as a means of bolstering the legitimacy of its claims regarding the extent of human rights abuses in Turkey; and third, it mobilized and recruited these refugees into European branches of the PKK, thus expanding its organizational structure and strength within the continent (Eccarius-Kelly 1999, 22).

Money raised by the PKK in Europe from donations and various underground activities was, according to reports, used to purchase arms originating from Germany, Iran, and Iraq (Imset 1991, 160). In addition to purchasing arms and funding the PKK's extensive organizational structure, the Kurdish diaspora in Western Europe was also a source of PKK recruits for the conflict in the southeast. Figures on the number of recruits that originated from Europe are difficult to verify, but estimates put the number at 4,000 to 5,000. These recruits often became militants after a period of training in Lebanon, and others worked as "organizers, diplomats, technicians of various sorts" (Bruinessen 1998, 45). Thus, the PKK, despite having a political support base consisting of populations that were socially marginalized in both Turkey and Western Europe, was successful in exploiting the resources available in the diaspora as a means of funding the armed conflict in southeastern Turkey.

Lobbying and persuasion: getting the Kurdish issue onto the European political agenda

Perhaps as important as mobilizing political and material support in the Kurdish diaspora in Europe, was the strategy of mobilizing political support for the Kurdish cause in European capitals. This, in a sense, was a version of the Keck and Sikkink "boomerang pattern" in which blocked opportunities in one state (Turkey) created incentives to harness the political clout of powerful actors in other states in a form of "leverage politics." Through a combination of agenda-setting, framing, lobbying, and coalition-building, Kurdish political entrepreneurs were largely successful in raising public awareness of the Kurdish issue in Europe, making the human rights practices of Turkey more generally, and the Kurdish issue in particular, one of the central focuses of discussions surrounding Turkey's accession to the EU. Turkish state policy towards the Kurds, and their military response to the PKK, came under greater public scrutiny. The Kurdish cause gained a degree of legitimacy in the broader public, and the Turkish state came under public and diplomatic pressure.

A European-wide network of Kurdish information centers, for example, provided points of contact for the press and politicians in Germany and other states, disseminating alternative sources of information on the situation in Kurdistan. PKK information centers in Germany issued press releases, maintained partnerships with German press outlets, and organized debates with German politicians. Activities designed to raise public awareness of the Kurdish conflict ranged from forms of contentious politics such as mass demonstrations and festivals, the taking over of buildings or other confrontational strategies such as self-immolation, and hunger strikes. On a mundane level, posters, placards, and graffiti were used as a means of ensuring that the Kurdish conflict in Turkey became partially embedded within the fabric of everyday life in Germany and other European states.

In addition to these "confrontational" strategies, Kurdish political entrepreneurs also worked through institutional channels within Europe (Østergaard-Nielsen 2001). This included meeting with German politicians, civil society groups, organizing educational events, and pressing for Kurdish language classes in schools. The recognition of identity claims by German authorities through such symbolic acts as the sponsorship of cultural festivals or Kurdish language classes served to legitimize the existence of a distinctive Kurdish identity – thus strengthening the nationalist cause. This in turn provided the basis for Kurdish political entrepreneurs to draw on human rights discourses in order to make claims concerning the relationship between a Kurdish political identity and Turkish state practices – and, by extension, the nature of German foreign policy toward Turkey.

In addition to working through institutional channels, Kurdish groups networked with leftist organizations in Germany and other European states to organize events, including fact-finding missions to southeastern Turkey, which were sometimes joined by German politicians. German pro-Kurdish solidarity groups traveled to Turkey and staged protests in the southeast on behalf of Kurdish villagers.[11] Kurdish political entrepreneurs in Germany also cultivated a sustained relationship with political parties – for example, a number of Kurdish politicians at the local level in Berlin were members of the Green Party (Sayan and Lötzer 1998, 25).

One of the strategies used by Kurdish nationalist political entrepreneurs was the establishment of an embryonic government-in-exile. A Kurdistan parliament-in-exile was established in late 1994, and has met intermittently in cities throughout Europe since that time. In 1999, it regrouped as the Kurdish National Congress (KNC). Largely dominated by the PKK, and its political wing, the ERNK, its members were elected from transnational constituencies and its activities include holding press conferences, publishing literature on the Kurdish issue, and dispatching delegations to third-party states, and to international organizations, such as the United Nations, European Parliament, and the Council of Europe. In 1995, the European Parliament recognized the PKK as a Kurdish liberation organization, arguing that it was "what the FLN was for the Algerians and the ANC for South Africans" (Watts 2004, 24). During the mid 1990s, its meetings attracted representatives from various human rights groups, NGOs, and political parties. Members of the KNC established ties with national parliaments in England, Poland, Italy, and Spain (Watts 2004, 25).

Kurdish political entrepreneurs drew on human rights norms and discourses as a way of framing demands and articulating grievances within Europe. By drawing on such discourses, they were able to patch together transnational coalitions of support that brought together civil society groups, non-governmental organizations, and actors within various European governments. The networks of human rights organizations and other organizations that make up a "transnational advocacy network" on behalf of Kurdish human rights took on a greater significance from 1999 onwards.

During this period, several major events occurred, including the arrest of the PKK leader Abdullah Öcalan in Kenya following his expulsion from Syria due to Turkish military pressure, his attempt to obtain political asylum within Europe, and the opening of EU accession talks with Turkey, that raised international awareness of the

---

[11] Reuters News Agency, "Turkey Holds Eleven Germans after Pro-Kurdish Protest," April 17, 1995.

Kurdish issue and significantly altered the incentives and constraints faced by Kurdish political entrepreneurs in Europe. These events dramatically shifted the dynamics of the Kurdish conflict and ushered in a new era defined by a weakened PKK who called for a ceasefire in the conflict, but also by a wave of reforms and liberalization that accompanied the process of EU membership negotiations; the latter, in turn, led to the removal of many of the restrictions on Kurdish language and identity in Turkey.

The domestic landscape in Turkey changed further in 2001, when the Islamic Justice and Development (AK) party came to power. Despite reforms, the PKK abandoned its ceasefire in 2004. The conflict has continued to persist in recent years, but in a radically changed context in which significant legal reforms have provided many of the cultural, linguistic, and political rights to Kurds that had originally been demanded by the PKK.

Conclusions

A growing body of research has shown that diaspora populations often play a role in promoting or exacerbating violent conflict. However, it has lacked detailed examination of the causal mechanisms at work in the transnationalization of civil wars through processes of diaspora mobilization. Rather than assuming diaspora support for conflict as natural, or treating diasporas as unitary actors that have independent effects on conflicts, this chapter has instead identified a number of causal mechanisms that can be used to more closely and systematically examine cases of diaspora mobilization in particular conflicts.

I have focused on a subset of five causal mechanisms and suggested how they operated in the Kurdish-Turkish case. It is certainly possible to identify many other relevant mechanisms and to engage in a greater level of micro-analysis of each of them, as Bennett argues in his contribution to this volume. However, my aim has been more modest: To suggest the utility of a mechanism-based approach for understanding the relationship between diaspora mobilization and violent conflict.

At the same time, it is important to acknowledge the limits of focusing on the role of diaspora politics in violent conflicts. While such an emphasis can illuminate some of the underlying dynamics, it does not necessarily shed light on outcomes. Mobilization, fundraising, and lobbying may occur in a conflict, but such activities may not necessarily be the only factors contributing to a particular conflict outcome. The case of Kurdish nationalism and the PKK, for example, can be contrasted with that of Kosovar nationalism and the Kosovo Liberation Army. Both involved very similar causal mechanisms and processes of diaspora political mobilization in Europe – including resource mobilization and lobbying – but resulted in very different outcomes in the same year: a NATO military intervention in Kosovo on the one hand, and the arrest of the leader of the PKK on the other. The explanation for these different outcomes rests not in the processes of diaspora mobilization, but in geopolitics: Turkey is a member of NATO and thus any military intervention by the US or Europe would have been unthinkable.

4 | Refugee militancy in exile and upon return in Afghanistan and Rwanda*

KRISTIAN BERG HARPVIKEN AND SARAH
KENYON LISCHER

Introduction

Over the past 25 years, it has been increasingly acknowledged that refugees have some degree of political agency in exile and that this agency has strong transnational dimensions. A main form of cross-border mobilization includes organized violence within displaced populations with the aim of gaining political influence in the country of origin. Popularly referred to as "refugee warriors," the phenomenon has been thoroughly analyzed (Lischer 2003; 2005; Stedman and Tanner 2003; Terry 2002; Zolberg, Suhrke, and Aguayo 1986; 1989). In the original definition, refugee warrior communities possess "a political leadership structure and armed sections engaged in warfare for a political objective, be it to recapture the homeland, change the regime, or secure a separate state" (Zolberg, Suhrke, and Aguayo 1989). Less attention has been devoted to the question of what happens to militant refugees when they return (Harpviken 2009; 2010). What are the mechanisms by which returning refugees continue to engage in organized violence? To what extent can post-return militancy be explained by processes that started in exile (or even prior to exile)?

Refugee militarization is generally part of a larger transnational complex in which hosts and exiles have a history of interaction. Militarized refugee groups have the advantage of being able to shift between the territories of a contender and host governments that are either sympathetic to the rebels or unable to control their activities

* Research for this chapter was funded by the Research Council of Norway (grant no. 185958). We are grateful for comments on earlier versions from Fiona Adamson, Kristin Bakke, Jeff Checkel and Mark Naftalin, as well as constructive feedback from members of the 'Working Group on Transnational and International Dimensions of Civil War,' Centre for the Study of Civil War, Peace Research Institute Oslo.

(Salehyan and Gleditsch 2006). Transnational ties serve to channel flows of personnel, arms, money, or knowledge, perhaps also fostering political and diplomatic support. Particularly when rooted in common networks that pre-date the period of exile, there is considerable potential for the growth of transnational organization.

In addition to exile-based interactions, transnational factors also play a role in the reverse situation, when militarized exiles return home. We argue that three primary mechanisms explain whether refugees militarized in exile engage in violence upon return: (1) socialization; (2) resource distribution; (3) security entrapment. With socialization, we focus on transformative learning that fosters militant attitudes, often occurring in exile, but, when effective, with long-term consequences. By resource distribution, we refer specifically to the militant group's ability to selectively distribute various types of resources – money, positions, land, business opportunities – to attract and sustain membership. Security entrapment describes a dynamic where a returning militant group and its members perceive that the only way to withstand an existential threat is to use force. These key mechanisms may interact sequentially, as when recruits that were initially attracted by the group's resources over time are effectively socialized to share the group's militant worldviews. The mechanisms may also operate concurrently, such as when resource distribution and security entrapment reinforce the leaders' commitment to militarization.

The United Nations High Commissioner for Refugees (UNHCR) estimates that nearly 25 million refugees returned to their countries of origin between 1990 and 2010 (UNHCR 2010a, 10). A proportion of those returnees have been involved in political violence while in exile, and some may do so upon return. Despite that, the potential for militant return has received little attention, in part, as Richard Black points out, because it lies "outside the core mandate of the key policy organization involved with refugees – UNHCR – and after the period in which the distinctiveness of the 'refugee experience' might be expected to be most visible" (2006, 24). The neglect is similar across a number of relevant analytical literatures. A case in point is international security studies, despite a concern with the military role of refugees (Loescher 1992; Weiner 1992; 1996). The peacebuilding literature most commonly sees return as an indicator of a successful peace process, although at least one perceptive observer has questioned this assumed relationship (Adelman 2002). Studies of disarmament, demobilization, and reintegration (DDR), a subfield at the interface of security and peacebuilding, are similarly mute on what happens when militarized refugees return to their homeland.

In the following section, we explain our mechanism-based approach and elaborate on the three main mechanisms at play. Following Checkel, we adopt Gerring's definition of a mechanism as "the pathway or process by which an effect is produced or an outcome is accomplished" (Gerring 2007b, 178). Hence, we establish a framework that can elucidate the processes and interactions involved in returnee violence. We then apply this framework to the cases of refugee mobilization and return in Afghanistan and Rwanda, both of which have had large scale militarization of refugees. For each case, we then refine the analysis of the mechanisms through an iterative process, going back and forth between the framework and the empirics. In both Afghanistan and Rwanda, we find that the socialization and resource distribution mechanisms are most useful for understanding returnee-related violence, but with security entrapment playing a key role in instances where there is a delayed remobilization following an initially peaceful return. We take a historical perspective to uncover continuities (and ruptures) in the way the mechanisms at hand play out in exile and upon return, seeking to define their sequential interaction over time. We conclude with further implications for the study of transnational mechanisms in the context of refugee and returnee militarization.

Mechanisms of returnee violence

Socialization

Returnees who have undergone systematic socialization that breeds radical or militant attitudes are more likely to engage in organized violence for political purposes, particularly if the socialization has fostered a vision of returning home as a means for rectifying past injustices and building a new polity. Socialization involves transformative learning, in the form of acquiring new skills, and also new ways of thinking about the world. Socialization is often understood as the outcome of interaction between individuals (what Bakke in her chapter refers to as relational diffusion; see also Checkel, this volume); yet institutions – schools and educational centers, organizations with a major component of on-the-job training (i.e. armies), or cohesive solidarity groups – are a prerequisite to bring about societal transformation. We assume, in line with Checkel (2001), that people in novel or uncertain environments, such as refugee camps, are most likely to be susceptible to socialization.

Our main focus is on political and ideological socialization, although we recognize that convictions may be solidified by developing supporting skills. In military socialization, the acquisition of new skills and the transformation of consciousness intertwine, as learning to fight and kill is inextricably linked to changing perceptions of self, as well as to justifications for exerting violence. Elisabeth Jean Wood offers a valuable analysis of the transformation of social networks during war, which includes her conception of military socialization (Wood 2008). She explains that military recruits "have to be socialized in the use of violence for group, not private, purposes." She continues by noting that "[t]raining and socialization to the armed group take place both formally, through the immersion experience of 'boot camp'... and informally, through initiation rituals and hazing" (Wood 2008, 546). Dara Kay Cohen, in her work on sexual violence during war, draws on Bard O'Neill (O'Neill 2001) explaining that "socialization may be achieved through the mutual hatred of an enemy group, as a result of guiding ideology in which all the group members believe, or ... a set of group benefits that may be experienced from a group activity" (Cohen 2010, 24). While socialization can be conceived of in both rationalist and constructivist terms (Checkel 2005), we contend that effective socialization may breed militant commitment even among recruits who initially joined for solely instrumental reasons (Wood 2010).

Socialization is reinforced by engaging in violence, as when fighters from the refugee setting circulate back and forth across the border. The likelihood of post-return violence will depend on whether militant socialization continues, takes on new forms, or comes to a halt, as a consequence of return. At its most effective, however, socialization may foster attitudes that will persist over time, even in the absence of organizational regularity or other forms of maintenance. For our purposes, where the main interest is in post-return militancy, we expect exile socialization to be essential.

The combination of formal and informal socialization is likely to be particularly robust, and – particularly relevant for our purposes – can bring about attitudinal change that survives the dissolution of the fighting entity, rendering a latent militant potential that can be reactivated in the face of major upheavals. More broadly, the likelihood of violence increases when a large number of refugees sharing a radical vision return together, as often occurs following major political and military changes at home. Thus, in many conflict settlements, rapid and voluntary return may carry with it the prospects for destabilization.

The observable implications of socialization include changes in institutions and in discourse (both public and private). Seeing them as the main harbingers of new worldviews, we want to capture both the transformation of existing, and the formation of new, institutions. Data on institutional innovation can be solicited from the broader case literature (on the conflict and its specific groups), with the caveat that the socialization efforts that take the form of direct interaction or that are of a more informal character are often harder to document. Furthermore, institutional capacity does not necessarily bring about attitudinal change, and we therefore need to capture transformations of the discourses on goals and motivations, as well as tactical choices and justifications. The changes in the discourse can be documented through interviews with group members or knowledgeable observers. For institutional change, we will still examine what happens in exile, both because institutions are often exile-specific (even though schools and education centers are sometimes repatriated wholesale), and because effective socialization outlives its institutions (and a return to country of origin).

Resource distribution

In addition to socialization, an important mechanism related to returnee violence is the ability to distribute valuable resources, both during and after exile. In situations of civil war, political and military organizations cannot succeed without ensuring individual contributions to the cause. The driving engine of the resource distribution mechanism is the ability to offer penalties and rewards that target the individual, often referred to as selective incentives (Olson 1965). Resource mobilization theorists (McAdam, Tarrow, and Tilly 1996; Tilly 1978) view robust access to resources as key to the success of opposition movements of any sort (see also Bakke, this volume). In the first instance, and in its concern to create incentives for individual behavior, the mechanism operates with an assumption of – possibly bounded – rationality (Checkel 2005). Yet, at a deeper level, individual commitment hinges on the ability of the organization to either build upon, or gradually foster, a coherent network and a deeper sense of shared purpose (Gates 2002). The sequence is one where the resource distribution and socialization mechanisms combine, as members are either coerced or paid to join, but where systematic socialization later fosters loyalty and shared purpose.

In many refugee crises, large-scale returns take place as a response to peace agreements or regime changes. Refugees may return when they are attracted by either the prospect of controlling opportunities for, or receiving the benefits of, patronage. The type and value of a resource varies with context and can include: positions in government and the military; claim to land and property; business advantages (such as mineral concessions or a share in state-run enterprises); and control over aid. The potential for offering selective incentives to followers increases if the exile group has a stake in the new power structure. Since the most attractive opportunities will fill quickly, a sense of urgency may develop among returnees. Thus, there is an inherent risk that those returning will use violence, or at least threaten to use it, to maximize control over resources. It is important to note that this mechanism applies primarily to those returnees who are already enrolled in political-military entities, and have previous experience of political violence.

What are the implications that one can observe when the resource distribution mechanism is operating? We can observe the group's discourse on resources, what it does to gain control over them, and whether resource distribution is converted into armed capacity. The discourse over resources can be explicit, focusing on unfair distribution or on the prospective rewards when gaining power; or it can be more implicit, as when the setting up of a shadow government signals the promise of future control over resources. Expert opinions and interviews with members are the prime sources. Establishing the resources made available to the group is not necessarily any easier, as both suppliers and receivers have an interest in restricting information. Again, the reporting by experts and interviews with key informants are the best sources. Ultimately, however, our core interest is in whether the distribution of resources affects the commitment of individuals and the group's capacity for violent action. Observable implications here are whether increased commitment – in particular to militant or violent action – is linked to favorable access to various types of resources or whether failure to comply with a group's expectations results in resources being withheld. Assessing whether the access to resources, and the ability to distribute them selectively, affects individual commitment and group capacity requires deep familiarity with the trajectory of both the group and the conflict context.

Security entrapment

When the political settlement that initiates a return process does not include a trustworthy and enforceable role for the group and its members, it is highly likely that return will be followed by continued violent engagement. Potential resolutions include internationally brokered power-sharing deals (with or without international peacekeepers), domestically negotiated agreements, and decisive military victories by one party. The literature on civil war finds that a weakly enforced external compromise increases the likelihood of violence (Walter 2003). In that situation, returnees will fear for their safety, especially if they return as minorities to a majority-held area. A military victory, on the other hand, can either guarantee or erode protection for the returnees, depending on which group emerges victorious.

To the extent that a post-return security dilemma reproduces security threats that were associated with earlier flight, this further heightens the likelihood of post-return violent engagement. In some instances, perceptions of insecurity may develop over time during the reintegration phase, leading to violence. For example, if a peace agreement starts to unravel, previously militarized returnee groups may react to the security vacuum by taking up arms. This may be important, not only for those who are core members of the movement taking part in an "armed return," but also as a mechanism for remobilizing former loyalists who have left the movement (who may or may not be earlier returnees from a militarized exile). Security entrapment may also bring the principled bystanders (those who held back on joining) on board, as the alternative is insecurity or even death.

What are the observable implications of security entrapment? The starting point is the very nature of the security architecture, which in most, but not all, cases of refugee return comes in the form of a peace settlement. Is there a formula for power-sharing that accommodates the fundamental security concerns of all major parties, and is there a credible external guarantor? The analyses by party representatives and seasoned observers, both at the moment of transformation and in retrospect, are interesting here. Second, and even more important, there is the tracing of the main parties through the process of political transition to detect the emergence of constellations in which the parties with their members and larger constituencies will feel entrapped. The sources are similar to the ones tapped to document the security architecture, perhaps with more emphasis on insiders' perspectives; however, the empirical challenges may be greater now, both because the processes may unfold within very short time periods and because secondary sources may be in short supply. Finally, there are important exacerbating factors that feed into the entrapment mechanism. Most important, historic experiences of entrapment (prior to flight; in exile) and their embodiment in narratives that may be activated by leaders intent on mobilization can greatly stimulate the sense of entrapment, and therefore the will to fight. Likewise, the reactions to dramatic events, such as the death of a key politician (even if by natural causes), are worth scrutinizing, as the ensuing analysis and reactions (or absence thereof) are firm indicators of whether there is an evolving sense of entrapment.

The security entrapment mechanism often interacts with other mechanisms. It connects with the socialization mechanism in that people who have been trained to hate and trained to fight are more likely to react violently if entrapped. In relation to resource distribution, it can be seen as a functional equivalent to it (i.e. even if the organization cannot give you money, it can give you security, which is the key thing when threatened). And obviously, a group's access to resources has diminished (and will diminish further) in situations of security entrapment.

Refugee militancy and violent returns in Afghanistan

While Afghanistan has become the model case of refugee militarization, there has been virtually no analysis of what happened to the militarized refugees upon return (but see Harpviken 2009; 2010). The militarization of large parts of the refugee population in Pakistan, and its importance for the evolution of the conflict, has been thoroughly demonstrated, not the least in the pioneering work of Zolberg, Suhrke, and Aguayo (1986; 1989). In this case study, we will focus on the mechanisms by which some returnees came to engage in violence upon return, while others did not.[1]

Afghanistan has been characterized by armed conflict since the late 1970s, accompanied by the largest refugee movements in recent times, with an estimated peak at over 6 million refugees in Iran and Pakistan by 1990 (UNHCR 2001). Identifying the mechanisms at work, our point of departure will be the militarization of refugees in Pakistan, from 1978 to 1992, followed by an examination of refugee return in the transition from the People's Democratic Party of Afghanistan to the so-called Mujahedin government (a resistance coalition) in 1992, and the Taliban challenge to the internationally supported Karzai government in the aftermath of the 2001 US-led intervention. We will see that socialization is important to exile-based militancy, but with varying impact upon return, depending on whether the resource distribution and security entrapment mechanisms are at work, and that understanding the interaction between mechanisms is critical.

The emergence of a state-in-exile (1978–1992)

What would become the core of the Pakistan-based resistance of the 1980s originated in the ideological socialization of Islamist study circles at Kabul University in the 1960s and early 1970s. Politically radical, with ties to the international Muslim Brotherhood, this was a small group with little resonance in the larger Afghan population. After the kingdom was converted into a republic through the 1973 coup, a group of some 1,000 Afghan Islamists were welcomed by Pakistan, which saw them as a potential asset against a troublesome neighbor (Roy 1986, 74–79). At the turn of the decade, this small group of Pakistan-based radicals would become the pool from which the host country's intelligence service selected the leaders of the refugee-based insurgency and its state-in-exile (Rubin 1991). In April 1978, the Soviet-oriented People's Democratic Party of Afghanistan (PDPA) took

---

[1] This case study is based on an examination of the relevant secondary literature (including academic, journalistic, and biographic accounts), as well as 20 interviews with key informants (conducted by Harpviken in 2008 and 2009), and 110 interviews with Afghans who have been engaged with a variety of political-military organizations (conducted by a group of Afghan surveyors in 2009). The study also builds on previous work by Harpviken on political mobilization in Afghanistan (Harpviken 2009).

power in a coup, with a forceful reform agenda that immediately sparked local uprisings. When the Soviet Union intervened in December 1979, Afghanistan became a hotspot of the Cold War, and within two years, the refugee population was an estimated 3 million.

Resource distribution

For the Afghan refugees in Pakistan, we see the resource distribution mechanism at work in its crudest form. The early resistance had largely been led by local notables, often instrumental in facilitating flight for their followers, intent on continuing warfare from the relative safety of exile (Harpviken 2009, 55; Suhrke and Klink 1987). In exile, the embryonic political structure among Afghan refugees transformed quickly. The host government effectively decided on a set of seven groups that would represent the Afghan resistance. Each group was led by one of the long-standing exiles. Intent on supporting the Afghan resistance, but concerned about being drawn into the war, Pakistan sought to maximize influence over all sorts of international assistance, ranging from military supplies to humanitarian aid (Fielden 1998; Schöch 2008).

A particularly effective measure was to link refugee aid and politics. Refugee status was made conditional on membership in one of the political parties, with the net result that the absolute bulk of refugees became party members (Amstutz 1986, 229). The majority of the refugees were settled in camps, often under the control of a specific party. The parties had considerable influence over the distribution of aid in the camps (Centlivres and Centlivres-Demont 1988). Traditional notables were often marginalized, as a younger generation with a different skill set – and a different political orientation – took over. The control that parties gained over the distribution of all sorts of refugee assistance was key to the political enrolment of refugees, but also key to keeping a tab on refugees over time.

Male refugees, in return, were expected to be at the service of the party. A common pattern was that fighters would spend up to six months at a military base in Afghanistan, then come back to Pakistan for a similar period, stock up on supplies, perhaps get refresher training, rest and spend time with family. Truly mobile military groups were rare, so most would be fighting in their area of origin (Roy 1986, 176–183). Despite the ties to local residents, however, there were clear limits to the involvement of military groups in the day-to-day life of the society (Dorronsoro 2005, 212). This led to a relative seclusion; the checks and balances of civil society lost out to the influence of the political parties, which played a central role in most areas of life.[2]

Socialization

The political parties also emphasized socialization. While the pioneer migrants were largely socialized prior to migration, the bulk of the post-1978 refugees were – often reluctantly – brought into the orbit of the political parties through resource distribution, with socialization following suit. Socialization in this context would imply education (both conventional and religious schooling), military training, and lastly, combat socialization. The key, in relation to the prospects for post-return violence, is that sustained education efforts in exile – reinforced during combat tours across the border – fostered a radical and militant vision. Post-return violence, then, is the delayed effect of socialization that has produced robust convictions. The refugee context for Afghans in Pakistan was well suited for effective socialization. The refugees faced great uncertainty. They lived in urban centers or in densely populated camps (often in remote areas), with the latter being most dependent on the parties.

Conventional schooling was considered important by the Afghan parties, particularly by the Islamist ones. In his doctoral thesis, Farhad Rastegar (1991) offers a unique understanding of Afghan refugees in Pakistan. Rastegar contrasts Hezb-e Islami with Jamiat-e Islami, the two main Islamist parties. While Jamiat advocated a bottom-up political transformation as the ultimate outcome of individual change, Hezb pursued a top-down strategy whereby institutional change will force social and individual change. To bring about the change of the polity, however, requires capacity that can only be built in the schools, in the form of a critical mass committed to revolutionary violence (Rastegar 1991, 119–127). Schools, says Rastegar (1991, 261), "provide movements with both a socially desired service outlet, and an easily reproducible mobilizational structure." As we shall see, upon their 1992 return, both Jamiat and Hezb, with their weight on exile socialization, proved capable of engaging in sustained large-scale fighting.

---

[2] In the aftermath of the 1987 Geneva Accords between Pakistan and the Soviet Union, the resistance parties issued threats against what they saw as an act of treason, seeing return as contrary to the holy war against infidels in which they were engaged (Rizvi 1990).

Other groups, particularly those of a more fundamentalist political-Islamic orientation, emphasized religious schools. This was particularly the case for the Harakat-e Inqelab, led by Mohammad Nabi. The party was rooted in the informal networks of Sunni Islamic scholars, in which particular personalities with their own madrasas and entourage were the building blocks (Borchgrevink 2010). The rapidly expanding madrasa sector in Pakistan, catering both to Afghan refugees and Pakistani nationals, contributed significantly to a hardening of political sentiments. But the role of the madrasas, as is often alleged, was not to build military competence – that was taken care of elsewhere – but rather to foster a new political consciousness (Zahab and Roy 2004). In that sense, the madrasas played a role similar to that of ordinary schools (Fair 2009). Both schools and madrasas, particularly when run by a political group, not only fostered militant worldviews, but also served as effective conduits for recruits to the military branch of the organization, where they would also develop their skills as fighters.

While many of the parties had some capacity to train their own personnel, the bulk of the military training was arranged by Pakistan's security apparatus. Mohammad Yousaf headed the Afghan Bureau of Pakistan's Inter-Services Intelligence (ISI) from 1983 to 1987, and has described the training:

At the end of 1983 we were operating two camps in Pakistan, each with a capacity of 200 trainees. By mid-1984 we were putting over 1000 a month through the system, and by 1987 we had seven camps operating simultaneously. (Yousaf and Adkin 1992, 117)

The overwhelming majority of the trainees had a refugee connection in that their families resided in Pakistan.

The close interaction between political consciousness raising and military training – even if it was kept physically separate – is interesting. In Olivier Roy's words, "politicization has arisen through militarization and not as a result of implanting political parties or ideological discourse" (Roy 1989, 45). Military socialization – at exile training centers and in combat – became the fundamental carrier for ideological reorientation. It is not so much an overarching ideological project that necessitates militancy as it is a military engagement that brings with it attitudinal political change. With militancy having become as much the end, as a means to an end, it becomes difficult to foster reorientation and compromise. Militant attitudes alone – fostered through the various forms of schooling – are one thing; however, when that is followed by practical military training – and an ability to practice the newly gained skills – militancy becomes particularly robust.

Regime change and civil war (1992–2001)

When, in April 1992, the remains of the PDPA regime collapsed, massive repatriation followed swiftly. The seven exile parties negotiated a deal, and their leaders moved to Kabul in the company of their armed entourages, each taking control in various parts of the city. Government ministries were quickly converted into the armed fortifications of the party who had the interim minister. The outgoing regime had split into factions that merged with various resistance fronts. A particular case was Rashid Dostum's Junbesh-e Milli, a militia whose changing of sides was pivotal to the government collapse. Within a few weeks, Kabul was thrown into massive violence, first with Sayyaf's Ittehad forces shelling Shia majority areas in West Kabul (Harpviken 1996, 113). Not long after, Hezb-e Islami, whose leader was given the prime ministership in the treaty, started rocket attacks across Kabul (Rasanayagam 2003, 142–143). Over the next years, Kabul became a battleground in which the former resistance parties fought each other with great intensity and with massive civilian costs. The main parties to the armed politics playing out in Kabul were the two Islamist groups built up in Pakistani exile, plus Hezb-e Wahdat (an alliance of Shia parties with offices in Iran) and Dostum's militia-based group. That other exile groups did not display an appetite for engaging in the fighting makes comparison interesting.

Socialization

When peace broke down in 1992, to what extent did the socialization of exile manifest itself in sustained violent engagement? One of the main contenders, Dostum's Junbesh-e Milli, was not bred in exile. The other groups were not exclusively exile-based, and they had all incorporated elements from the army of the previous regime. Nonetheless, the one group that proved to be the least reconciliatory, and that has to take a major part of the blame for the spiraling violence in Kabul from 1992 – Hekmatyar's Hezb – was also the group that had the most systematic approach to militant socialization. While the disconnect between the Hezb and existent social structures helps explain its failure to mobilize broadly (Harpviken 1997), the same seclusion also permitted effective socialization around radical political visions. There were local groups that peeled off, and there was the inclusion of army elements, but the Hezb leadership managed to sustain its capacity throughout a fight that most Afghans saw as totally illegitimate (Roy 1995, 63–75).

Resource distribution

The resource distribution that works so well to instill and maintain organizational loyalty in exile is hardly reproducible upon return, when the sources of support are changing, the expectations of armed groups and their constituents are altered, and the conditions by which a group monitors members and fosters dependence are less favorable. The 1992 transition did not abide by the logic of a peace treaty. Rather, gaining control over territory (and elements of the fragmenting state apparatus) became decisive for what political claims any group could expect to successfully make. Rapid mobilization – and therefore rapid return – was critical. Fieldwork findings from 1992 to 1994 (Harpviken 1996) are reconfirmed by the interviews conducted for this project in 2010. For those who have served the party in, or from, exile there is an instinctive expectation of a fair share in the spoils of peace, with real prospects of getting access to good positions with the new administration. This is reflected in the peak of returns just after the regime change: 1,274,000 returnees were registered by UNHCR in 1992, less than 300,000 the following year (UNHCR 2003).

Over time, the willingness to take risks for the party diminishes if resource distribution fails. Hezb-e Islami, arguably the party with the strongest party loyalty, did lose some of its commanders as international funding dried up after 1992 (Giustozzi 2009, 70–71). Yet, the ability to maintain its military engagement despite a severing of resource distribution capabilities indicates that strong socialization can in large measure render resource distribution unimportant (Humphreys and Weinstein 2006). In contrast, those groups who had a poor socialization record and lacked access and ability to distribute resources quickly fragmented (Giustozzi 2009, 71–73; Rubin 2002, 256–264).

Security entrapment

The early returners expected to be part of an orderly transition to a new regime, not to a new round of civil war. The fighting, particularly as it played out in the capital, created a situation where one's security depended entirely on protection from one of the armed groups. The forces of the various parties carved out their own territories, in large measure associated with a particular ethnicity: Jamiat being dominantly Tajik, Hezb-e Islami mainly Pashtun, Jumbesh heavily Uzbek and Hezb-e Wahdat almost exclusively Hazara. The escalating insecurity spiral in Kabul from April 1992 onwards placed anyone at risk, and those who had an affiliation with any political group – indeed the case for almost all returnees – found themselves compelled to seek protection there (Harpviken 1996, 116–119). Such protection, naturally, would come at the price of not only loyalty, but also tangible contribution to the armed struggle. An alternative was to escape; perhaps as many as 1.5 million people did. These were mostly those who resided in Kabul under the old regime, and who therefore lacked the connections that were necessary to solicit the protection of the new rulers.

Meanwhile, a great deal of those who had fought from exile in Pakistan during the 1980s had disassociated themselves from the national power struggle. For them, the holy war – the jihad – was won (Roy 1995, 68–72). This was the common pattern both among the so-called traditionalists and the fundamentalists. These were groups that had largely lost out in the transition from the PDPA, even though they were maintaining some posts in the government structure. They also stood at the sidelines when the battles for Kabul played out. Why? While these groups were centrally placed in the madrasa sector in exile, their religious education was more traditional, less ideologized, and, at least in part, disconnected from military struggle. The fundamentalist groups had never gained the same degree of control over resource distribution in exile as had the Islamists. One could still have expected that their claim to possible influence would stimulate military action in the context of return, but while the leaders did return to Kabul with their trusted armed men, they never threw themselves into the new civil war. Ultimately, these were groups whose roots were in the rural areas; as a result, the consistent, enduring, security entrapment that ignited military action within other groups rarely occurred.

The coming to power of the Taliban, through a massive armed campaign from 1994 to 1996, will not be analyzed in any detail here. Yet, it is worth noting that the Taliban in large measure incorporated the constituency of the parties that held a more traditionalist or fundamentalist orientation – the very parties who had not taken part in the fight over Kabul post-1992. Undoubtedly, a religiously founded political vision brought about by socialization in exile was instrumental to the Taliban mobilization, yet its ability to sustain itself was contingent on resource distribution, with Pakistan being a willing supplier and enabler. Mobilizing as much within the refugee population as within Afghanistan itself, the Pakistani dual role of refugee host and source of support was key to Taliban expansion.

International intervention and armed remobilization (2001–)

The armed resurgence of the Taliban, following its ousting by the US-led intervention from 2001, took two or three years to gain momentum. In an intervention in which the ground forces were exclusively Afghan (with a few international advisors and special agents), the remobilization of fighters in exile played a prominent role (Rashid 2008). Examples of this are Abdul Haq, a legendary resistance commander who was captured and killed by the Taliban in the Jalalabad area, and Hamid Karzai, the president-to-be who went across to Kandahar with his own men and a US support team (Barfield 2010, 288–290; Schroen 2005, 273–278). Also, the so-called Northern Alliance, and the strongest party within it – Jamiat-e Islami which by 2001 maintained control over perhaps 10 percent of the territory (and the country's UN seat) – drew heavily upon exiles. While it is clear that the refugee return component of the events in 2001 and beyond was significant, the focus here shall be on the Taliban resurgence that followed what at first appeared to be a decisive and widely popular intervention.

The literature on the Taliban resurgence (Giustozzi 2007; Rashid 2008) discusses the importance of Pakistani support – including access to sanctuary – but does not explore its transnational dimensions (but see Franco 2009; Stenersen 2009). Yet, there is little doubt that the post-2001 Taliban mobilization was firmly related to the migration and refugeehood that had characterized the past 20 years, and that recruitment among recent returnees, as well as among exile Afghans in Pakistan, was essential to the organization. Patterns of movement across the border, however, had become increasingly complex. What is often referred to as the neo-Taliban was neither a purely refugee-based insurgency nor a purely returnee-based one, but it was certainly one that drew on refugees and returnees alike, and not least on decades of intensive mobility that had fostered dense networks of interaction across the border.

Socialization

What was the role of socialization in the resurgence? Most importantly, the combination of exile political training with battlefield socialization did breed a sense of common purpose. In the immediate aftermath of September 11, 2001, the sense of common purpose was severely weakened, as a large share of former Taliban sought distance from an ideologized religio-political platform – rooted in Wahabist Islamic thinking – that many felt was foreign. The Taliban leadership responded to this by modifying their political message, in Thomas Barfield's words, portraying "themselves less as Muslim zealots and more as God-fearing nationalists seeking to expel infidel foreigners from the country" (Barfield 2010, 327). This resonated better with the dominant mode of thinking in the refugee environments in Pakistan and in most madrasas on both sides of the border.

Triggered by an international military campaign that focused on the "war-on-terror" – at times with severe consequences for civilians, while everyday security under the new government was declining severely – the Taliban's message resonated fairly well with ingrained attitudes. The pool of recruits that would over time swell the ranks of the new Taliban was easy to miss in 2002 and 2003, since they were either getting on with their ordinary lives in Afghan society, or spent most of their time in the refugee environments across the border; however, they had both the right ideological outlook and the necessary military practice. Once the sentiment within the mainly rural Pashtun population in Afghanistan's south and east started to turn against the Karzai government and the international forces, the Taliban tapped into an attitudinal base that gave it strong momentum.

Resource distribution

Resource distribution was not a key element of Taliban remobilization. Historically, the control over resources had been important to draw Afghan refugees to the various political parties, and the Taliban built on this. The resource distribution that the Taliban represented was limited to basic security and Islamic justice, and, at the personal level, recognition and positions of power. The Taliban was never a welfare organization; its vision of the state's responsibilities was very narrow. Neither, despite the common reference to non-ideological, easy to convert, "ten-dollar-a-day" Taliban (e.g. Miliband 2009), was it an army of guns for hire. Most important, though, was the relative promise that stemmed from the fact that great expectations of aid and economic development in the wake of the US-led intervention were not met. The impression early after 2001 was that the Pashtun south received far less than its fair share of international assistance (International Crisis Group 2003). With deteriorating security, neither the government apparatus nor the internationals managed to change that impression, even though there was significant economic growth in more shady trades, drugs included. So, while the Taliban did not find themselves in a position where they could use resource control to attract followers, this was not as significant an impediment as it could have been, given that the government and its supporters failed to offer an alternative.

Security entrapment

The key to Taliban resurgence is security entrapment. The intervention was, in the early period, widely popular among Afghans, including a large share of those who had sided with the Taliban. Facing a combination of supreme air power and Afghan ground forces, the Taliban regime collapsed, and within a couple of months, the war was effectively over. As the main leadership fled, often to Pakistan, the rank and file Taliban's fighters effectively demobilized, over-whelmingly with the intention not to re-engage in war (van Bijlert 2009; Strick, van Linschoten, and Kuehn 2011). Over the next couple of years, however, an increasing number of former Taliban supporters reconsidered their retirement ambitions, joined by a new younger generation (Nixon 2011).

We are focusing here on the insurgency in the south of the country, where it started first. The international forces – a continuation of the intervention, Operation Enduring Freedom – were not set up to offer security for citizens. Rather, they were focused on tracking down al-Qaeda and high level Taliban, with a net effect that was negative. Both non-aligned citizens and demobilized Taliban fighters had to bear the cost of collateral damage to life and property. The UN-mandated International Security Assistance Force (ISAF) at first had a remit limited to the capital Kabul, but expanded to the south in mid 2006. By then, the resurgence had already gained significant speed, and rather than attempting to change the dynamics, the ISAF forces adopted an offensive anti-Taliban strategy that came with significant costs in terms of insecurity and damage.

Also the government, whose structure was in large measure built on people whom the Taliban had driven from power in the 1990s, constituted a threat rather than a source of protection. While there were virtually no ordinary armed forces, there were groups under the command of local officials and other strongmen, engaged in a variety of pursuits from local power struggles to subcontracting for international forces, but again with a net negative effect on local citizens' security (Gopal 2010; Moghaddam et al. 2008). Once insecurity triggered armed protest, and neither the international forces nor the government proved capable of reacting effectively, a spiraling insecurity dynamic unfolded in which the armed responses by various actors were mutually reinforcing. Distancing oneself from the conflict became more difficult by the day, and for many, there was no alternative to joining the Taliban.

What are the overarching patterns in the Afghan case? For the Afghan refugees in Pakistan in the 1980s, a rich resource supply from states and aid agencies was placed at the disposal of political parties handpicked by the host state. These parties used the resources effectively to draw refugees into their institutions of socialization. The parties ran effective socialization programs in exile, combined with battle socialization in extended periods of cross-border mobilization. With the transition in 1992, the promise of government positions and other privileges was immediately important, but as fighting broke out, was replaced by a genuine sense of security entrapment, in which nobody but militant groups could offer critical security to their potential followers. Similarly, for the Taliban remobilization post-2001, entrapment seems to have been the dominant mechanism at play.

Refugee return and political violence in Rwanda

The Rwandan conflict represents the most complex and violent instance of refugee return in Africa since 1990. Political violence involving refugee populations has influenced Rwandan politics since at least the mid twentieth century. During the period of Belgian colonialism, the minority Tutsi enjoyed favored status relative to the Hutu. This power balance reversed in the late 1950s when the Belgians withdrew support for the Tutsi king. Following independence in 1961, at least 200,000 Tutsi civilians fled to Uganda, Tanzania, and Zaire.

Thirty years later, a Tutsi-led exile army invaded Rwanda from its base in Uganda with the goal of toppling the oppressive Hutu government. The Rwandan Patriotic Army (RPA) was led by refugees (or their descendants) who had fled decades earlier. In the context of civil war and political upheaval, extremist Hutu militants, soldiers, and ordinary citizens killed up to 800,000 Tutsi and moderate Hutu in the spring of 1994. As the RPA approached the capital city, the government army and extremist militias fled to eastern Zaire, along with over a million Hutu civilians. Tens of thousands of Hutu militants infiltrated the refugee camps, intimidated refugees, stole food aid, and launched cross-border attacks against Rwanda. In 1996, the Rwandan Patriotic Front (RPF) government responded by attacking Zaire and forcing hundreds of thousands of refugees back over the border to Rwanda. The government, dominated by the Tutsi returnees from Uganda, prevented the previously militarized Hutu returnees from regaining political power.

The mechanisms of socialization and resource distribution, within the context of security entrapment, help explain that violence. To trace the mechanisms at work requires examining Rwandan politics during the 30-year exile of Tutsi refugees in Uganda, the civil war and genocide of 1990–1994, and the reintegration period from 1994–2010. The relevant mechanisms began germinating decades before the genocide and have continued to shape politics in the years following. By examining those time frames, the remainder of this case study isolates the relevant mechanisms.[3]

Tutsi refugees in Uganda, 1959–1990

Socialization

As discussed earlier in the chapter, socialization involves learning new skills and ideas which can be transmitted through formal institutions or informal networks. The socialization mechanism is not inherently militaristic. Such influences can either encourage or discourage violence,

---

[3] The following study is based on field research conducted in Rwanda in April – May 2009. About two dozen interviews with Rwandan and international staff of local NGOs, religious organizations, community reconciliation and reintegration programs, United Nations and other international organizations, US government agencies, and returned refugees were conducted. It also draws upon secondary sources, interviews with scholars with extensive field research experience, and resettled refugees in the US. Due to the severe restrictions on freedom of speech in Rwanda, most informants agreed to speak only under strict conditions of confidentiality.

depending on the social environment. The power of socialization may be particularly strong among refugee populations, considering the inhabitants' limited sources of information, geographical isolation and anxiety. In her discussion of socialization in pre-genocide Rwanda, Lee Ann Fujii cites a Rwandan whose own understanding of what affects people's behavior "assumes that people are influenced by those around them and thus will inevitably take on the beliefs and attitudes of others. According to this logic, the social environment is powerfully transformative" (2009, 101). This is especially likely in a context of insecurity and resource scarcity.

Observable implications of socialization in exile include the transformation of refugee-based institutions from peaceful to explicitly militaristic. The successful RPF invasion had its roots in years of organized exile activity, which included ties with Rwandans in distant countries. As discussed earlier in the chapter, such conditions increase receptivity to militant socialization. The experience of persecution both in Rwanda and in Uganda encouraged many refugees to join Tutsi refugee organizations, such as the Rwandan Refugees Welfare Association and, later, the Rwandan Alliance for National Unity (RANU). These groups created community and socialized members in a way that facilitated a transition from peaceful community building to support for militarized return. For example, during the mid 1980s, RANU sent refugees from Kenya to Uganda for military training (Kuperman 2004, 66). Leaders also benefited from the ability to distribute resources received from the diaspora. These resources provided material encouragement once the militarized socialization programs took root. Prunier reports that the nascent RPF army received financial support, and even recruits, from the Tutsi diaspora (Prunier 1998, 124, 131–132). Thus, the decades of socialization facilitated the leaders' later efforts to form an exile army.

Security entrapment

Socialization was not the only contribution to militarization, however. Security entrapment and resource distribution mechanisms interacted with socialization in exile. As the Ugandan exile persisted, local resentment intensified due to a perception of preferential treatment by the government and the United Nations. In response, the Ugandan government attempted to confine the refugees to camps, leading to an isolated and impoverished existence (Mamdani 2001, 164–165). Mamdani explains that "a refugee self-consciousness developed first and foremost in response to anti-refugee prejudice promoted by the state and shared by many in the society at large" (Mamdani 2001, 165). In the late 1960s Ugandan President Milton Obote cracked down on Tutsi economic activity (van der Meeren 1996, 261). Idi Amin then took power in the 1970s and recruited a few Tutsi refugees to fight with him, although eventually the relationship soured. Obote regained power in 1979 and increased violent scapegoating of the refugees to the extent that Mamdani labels it a "pogrom" (Mamdani 2001, 168).

That oppression increased refugees' fears for their survival and led the Tutsi to support Yoweri Museveni's rebel forces, which were victorious in 1986. By that time, around 3,000 of Museveni's 14,000 rebels were Rwandan Tutsi exiles (Kuperman 2004, 66). During their time with the Ugandan rebels, the exiles that later formed the RPF were socialized under tight military discipline and learned basic guerrilla warfare skills. Mamdani observes that: "The electric example of a home-grown guerrilla movement that had defeated an internationally recognized government without substantial external support was not lost on RPF leaders" (Mamdani 2001, 173). By the late 1980s the refugees' situation in Uganda became increasingly untenable, however, as Museveni realized that the Tutsi constituted a political liability. Following anti-refugee violence, "the guerrillas harvested youthful recruits from the victimized population" (Mamdani 2001, 170). In December 1987, the Rwandan refugee organization altered its focus to emphasize the goal of return to Rwanda, by force if necessary, and renamed itself the Rwandan Patriotic Front (Lemarchand 2001, 12). Prunier points out an observable implication of the socialization spurred by this security entrapment: "the result of these changes occurring at the top was that many people lower down decided to turn to the RPF and its radical project of reconquest" (Prunier 1998, 127).

Resource distribution

As discussed earlier, the ability to provide resources (or withhold them) offers significant leverage to military groups in exile. Upon return, those groups who maintain that capability will be more likely to mobilize militarily. While in exile, Rwandan refugees had four main resource streams – the Ugandan government, international organizations, diaspora funding, and their own income-generating activities such as farming. Humanitarian assistance provided one important source of resources, even including UNHCR scholarships for youth. Such aid, however, created resentment from the local Ugandan population and stoked violence against the refugees (Mamdani 2001: 165). The Rwandan Tutsi exile organizations in Uganda gained recruits whenever the resources provided by the Ugandan government and international organizations decreased and the relative importance of diaspora funding increased.

Political and economic oppression by the Ugandan government solidified the militant resolve of the RPF and its search for additional resources. As the Uganda-based exiles coalesced, the "new militants from the exiled left-wing intellectuals in Europe and North America" increased their support (Prunier 1998, 128). RPF adherents viewed the diaspora-funded organization as a better resource relative to the other dwindling options. Kuperman (2004, 67) reports that the RPF received up to $1 million per year from the diaspora. In addition, the RPF could promise its members future opportunities for land and employment if they toppled the Rwandan government. As Mamdani (2001, 167) observes, "the question of entitlement becomes acute at times of political crisis." In the context of uncertainty about the future in Uganda, the socialization and resource distribution mechanisms complemented each other to ensure the success of the RPF invasion and its consolidation of power. RPF socialization strengthened cohesion and the promise of resources increased that solidarity upon return.

As the various push and pull factors fell into place, the RPF army crossed the border into northern Rwanda in October 1990. After initial setbacks, the invaders made significant progress, though at a high cost to civilian life – both Hutu and Tutsi (often killed in retaliatory attacks by local forces). The RPF secured territory fairly easily, but it failed to establish political dominance. As the rebels advanced, the terrified population fled wholesale, leaving the RPF in control of abandoned towns, villages, and farms. Military socialization in exile was not sufficient to enable the RPF to build a government in the conquered territory.

Civil war and genocide, 1990–1994

Security entrapment

As the RPF gained a military advantage, the international community pressured all the combatants to negotiate. This pressure reflected Western norms favoring power-sharing and ethnic diversity, as well as a reluctance to commit military resources to the region. Western states and the United Nations cajoled the parties to sign the Arusha Peace Agreement in Arusha, Tanzania. The Agreement did not reflect the preferences of either the Tutsi rebels or the government of President Habyarimana, and left both in a situation of insecurity. The RPF agreed to withdraw its forces to specified points and the government promised to embark on democratization, including the integration of the Tutsi forces into the army and government (Arusha Peace Agreement 1993). The RPF had lost its stronghold in Uganda and, thus, its fall-back option. The weak United Nations commitment exacerbated the security entrapment since the agreement was not enforceable. The fears of the Tutsi were magnified by their historical experience of insecurity in Uganda. The leaders could call upon the narrative of past oppression to mobilize followers.

The uncertainty about the future peaked after the president's plane was mysteriously shot down in April 1994. At this point, the Hutu extremists unleashed the genocide and the RPF took up arms. Surprisingly, the Rwandan government put up little resistance to the Tutsi rebels, seeming to focus its energy on committing genocide rather than defeating the well-organized and armed RPF. As the RPF advanced, fleeing Hutu militants herded nearly 2 million Hutu civilians to neighboring states. Over one million Hutu huddled in IDP camps. The rebels captured the capital, Kigali, in July 1994 (Lischer 2005, 41–54; Prunier 1998).

Socialization

In tracing the story of the civil war and genocide, one sees that the socialization process that unfolded in exile continued to affect returnee violence upon return. During the actual combat and mass killing, there was not much opportunity for organized socialization, such as the diaspora had experienced. Rwanda was in a state of uncertainty and chaos, with more than 20 percent of the population displaced. Rather, the period from 1990 to 1994 highlights the results of the transformative learning that occurred in exile. As the war progressed, the Tutsi rebel army, led by Paul Kagame, demonstrated the value of the exile experience in terms of military cohesion and capability. It appears that Kagame also used this time to plan a strategy for implementing his vision once in power. An essential component of this vision included the reintegration of returned refugees as significant political actors (Kinzer 2008).

Transnational interactions among mechanisms

The Hutu refugees in Zaire also attempted to transform their institutions to promote militarized return. The militants' goal was to return in military victory to Rwanda and complete the genocide against the Tutsi. To that end, the militant leaders transferred the government structure from Rwanda and established a government in exile. The interaction of the socialization, resource distribution, and security entrapment mechanisms reinforced the power of the quasi-government. The use of propaganda transformed refugee world views by describing the genocide in terms of a civil war. Leaders supplemented this propaganda with manipulation of humanitarian aid resources to benefit supporters. Refugees were torn between the security entrapment created by militant coercion in the camps and the security fears of what awaited them in Rwanda. However, pressure such as forced recruitment and extortion reduced the utility of other socialization programs (Boutroue 1998).

The transnational nature of this conflict became more pronounced as the Hutu militants increased cross-border attacks. In 1996, the RPF perceived a significant existential threat from the hostile Hutu state-in-exile in Zaire. In alliance with Zairian insurgents, the RPF invaded Zaire and forcibly repatriated hundreds of thousands of refugees back to Rwanda (UNHCR 2010b). In the coercive repatriation of the Hutu refugees, one sees the unusual phenomenon of a cross-border conflict between two state-in-exile refugee groups. Andrea Purdeková explains: "Rwanda represents a unique case study not only due to the scale and complexity of movement in a relatively brief period, but also because the victors of the war were themselves returning exiles" (2008, 5). Mamdani concurs that "what has come to be known as the RPF invasion of Rwanda also needs to be understood as an armed repatriation of Banyarwanda refugees from Uganda to Rwanda" (Mamdani 2001, 160). The return of militarized Tutsi refugees in Rwanda demonstrates the significance of socialization and resource distribution, within a context of insecurity. The RPF, as a mobilized diaspora in Uganda, developed the political, military, and social organization that underpinned its successful invasion. Upon their return, the coercive Hutu militants lost their ability to control the refugee population, solidifying the power of the RPF.

Reintegration and consolidation of power, 1994–2010

Socialization

Upon taking power, the RPF government clearly realized the impact of socialization in exile, likely due to its own experience in Uganda. A report on post-genocide violence commissioned by the Rwandan government proposed a wide-ranging socialization campaign to reduce what it described as "wickedness." Recommendations included:

The education and the sensitization of people through all agents and organs of socialization such as solidarity camps (ingando) ... sketches and plays, movies, profane songs, religious songs, media, local and national festivals, civil society (religious confessions, local and international NGO's, various associations including those of national unity and reconciliation), operational political parties on the ground, public administration, public and private firms and education system (secondary schools, higher institutes and universities). (Republic of Rwanda. National Unity and Reconciliation Commission [NURC] 2008, 114)

An observable implication of the socialization mechanism includes public and private discourse which reflects changed world views. In Rwanda, group labels radically changed to reflect the government's attempt at transformative learning in the realm of ethnic identity (typified by the quote above). Following the genocide: "The state language in Rwanda ... divide[d] the population into five categories: returnees, refugees, victims, survivors, and perpetrators" (Mamdani 2001, 266). Within the unspoken designation of Hutu and Tutsi, the categories played a significant role in the political landscape. For example, the term "survivor" described a Tutsi civilian who lived in Rwanda during the genocide. Mamdani comments that no Hutu are labeled survivors since "the assumption is that every Hutu who opposed the genocide was killed ... The dilemma is that to be a Hutu in contemporary Rwanda is to be presumed *a perpetrator*" (Mamdani 2001, 267; italics in original). Subcategories among the Hutu also often referenced a person's judicial status. The term "perpetrator" (or, more colloquially, "génocidaire") referred to those convicted (or even suspected) of participation in the genocide.[4] Surprisingly, the

---

[4] As pointed out by Lee Ann Fujii, those labels were not necessarily accurate since some people were imprisoned on false charges and many génocidaires had never been imprisoned (personal communication, 2010).

categories of "refugee" and "returnee" held less resonance for Rwandan citizens than might be supposed, considering the extensive usage of the terms in secondary literature. Perhaps that was because such a large percentage of the population had an experience of exile.[5]

More formal discourse included laws against so-called "divisionist" speech, which limited public discussions of ethnicity, and constrained private communications as well.[6] These laws provided for severe penalties of up to 25 years in prison for offenses ranging from murder to "threatening, intimidating, degrading through diffamatory [*sic*] speeches, documents or actions which aim at propounding wickedness or inciting hatred" to "marginalizing, laughing at one's misfortune, defaming, mocking, boasting." Remarkably, children under 12 years old could be convicted of the crime of genocide ideology and taken to a "rehabilitation centre" for up to one year (Republic of Rwanda 2008).

Those many cleavages and unspoken divisions were products of and affected the process of socialization. This is apparent in the extent to which these guidelines were followed in public and private conversations. The observable implications of this discourse are of a socialization that relies on coercion in an attempt to change popular conceptions of ethnicity. It is difficult, however, to ascertain the extent of such transformations (see also Bakke, this volume); in a context of insecurity, this is made more difficult since informants do not speak freely. Outwardly, the socialization has succeeded in transforming discourse. It will take a longer time to see if such measures can create transformative learning among a reluctant, suspicious population.

The new institutions which developed reflect the operation of the socialization mechanism. The centerpiece of the anti-genocide ideology campaign was the government's rigorous program of returnee socialization called ingando which aimed to deprogram the Hutu extremist socialization that occurred in exile. These non-voluntary re-education camps included "sensitization training" covering "Rwandan history, civic education, national unity and reconciliation, gacaca, micro-financing and public health (particularly HIV/AIDS)" (Waldorf 2009, 11). Purdeková describes these camps as "a space of tightly upheld military-like discipline and instruction rather than debate" (2008, 18).

---

[5] Interviews, Rwanda, April – May 2009.
[6] These restrictions on free speech meant that most of my informants agreed to speak only on condition of confidentiality.

Repatriating ex-combatants spent two months in a separate ingando camp upon their return to Rwanda. According to MONUC, the UN peacekeeping force in the Democratic Republic of Congo (DRC, formerly Zaire), the program effectively prevented violence after return.[7] In addition to former soldiers and militants, the ingando program expanded to target prisoners in transition between partial and full release, as well as civilians such as teachers, civil servants, and post-secondary students.

In judging the success of the socialization, one can observe outcomes such as the level of violence and nature of public discourse. The ultimate goal of the ingando program, to change the thinking of the participants, is not easily observable. Interviews with ingando participants and with experienced observers also provide insight into the process (Thomson 2011). In the short term, violence involving repatriates is low, although a multitude of factors (including coercion) can contribute to that.

Resource distribution

In some instances, resource distribution works through providing patronage jobs, yet in others it operates by cutting off resources selectively. Excluding or withholding resources can influence the potential for remilitarization. An indicator of this mechanism at work is the selective distribution of resources to potential enemies in exchange for pacification (if not loyalty).

The Rwandan government, through the disarmament, demobilization, and reintegration (DDR) program, was the primary provider of resources to former combatants. After completing the ingando training, the ex-combatants received basic needs kits. Some received further funding, depending on their rank and affiliation (Waldorf 2009, 10–11). Using reintegration packages and other demobilization resources, partly funded by the World Bank, the government fostered dependency and encouraged compliance from the ex-combatants. Mgbako comments that "the government is offering a chance at reintegration and economic aid to all rebels, fearing that if it does not assist these rebels in peaceful resettlement they will revitalize the insurgency" (2005, 210).

The second main resource needed by returnees in Rwanda was land. Rwanda is the most densely populated country in Africa and the vast

---

[7] Interviews, UN officials, Kigali, Rwanda, April 2009.

majority of people rely on subsistence farming. Land issues were immensely complicated by the numerous migration flows in and out of Rwanda since independence. In terms of resource distribution, the government took control of this valuable resource, in part due to weak private property laws.

Following the 1990–1994 civil war and genocide, Rwandan Tutsi who had lived in exile for up to 30 years claimed the right to the lands they abandoned, even though they were now occupied. Minear and Kent explain that:

the old caseload refugees posed a very complex problem . . . these returnees after so many years in exile had high expectations. Those among the 600,000 who lacked housing, employment, and land – or whose homes and lands had been occupied in the interim – represented a potentially explosive political and emotional issue. (1998, 64)

As discussed above, the ability to distribute resources increases the power of a militarized group. The RPF needed to follow through on its promises to retain the loyalty of its followers. The Arusha Peace Agreement of 1993 outlined a power-sharing deal that attempted to defuse that thorny issue. The Accords mandated the following:

All refugees shall therefore have the right to repossess their property on return. The two parties recommend, however, that in order to promote social harmony and national reconciliation, refugees who left the country more than 10 years ago should not reclaim their properties, which might have been occupied by other people. The Government shall compensate them by putting land at their disposal and shall help them to resettle. (Arusha Peace Agreement 1993, Chapter I, 1.1.4)

In the context of extreme land scarcity, massive migration flows, and a weak transitional government, the vision of the Agreement was not implemented.

The shortage of land and perceived injustice of the resource distribution continued to threaten political stability in Rwanda in the years following the genocide. One can observe the changes wrought by the preferential distribution of resources in the wide-scale bulldozing of slums in Kigali and relocation of mostly Hutu residents to distant, inhospitable areas. The cleared areas are then awarded to government supporters for so-called economic development projects. An Anglican priest, and genocide survivor, remarked caustically that soon the entire map of Kigali would read "no poor people allowed."[8] UNHCR warned that "the threat to stability of the reintegration process is real by creating categories within the returnee community (between those having received a house and those who haven't)" (UNHCR 2002, viii). A 2007 Norwegian Refugee Council report worried that the complicated relationship between ethnicity and land issues is "disregarded and even suppressed by the government" (Bruce 2007). To the extent that the resource distribution patterns reinforce cleavages among competing groups, former militants might be induced to take up arms to rectify perceived injustices.

In Rwanda, socialization was the foremost mechanism influencing returnee violence, but the role of resource distribution was essential in enabling leaders to capitalize on the socialization process. As the Tutsi refugees reached consensus on the need for military return, the RPF leaders were able to provide material benefits (in particular the promise of future benefits) as incentives to their followers. When they invaded Rwanda, the returnees were able to take over the land of the Hutu civilians displaced by the fighting. As part of the 1993 Arusha Peace Agreement, the RPF negotiated for restitution of property or government compensation for the Tutsi refugees who had been displaced to Uganda. Thus the returnees were able to mitigate fears of security entrapment by remaining within the group formed during the socialization process in exile.

Concluding remarks

This chapter examined a form of conflictual transnationalism: the potential for violent engagement upon return from militarized exile contexts to the country of origin. Our approach privileges the role of mechanisms in understanding returnee violence. The socialization, resource distribution, and security entrapment mechanisms help elucidate the conditions under which previously militarized refugees engage in violence upon return in both Afghanistan and Rwanda. At the empirical level, our findings highlight the advantages of a mechanism approach, particularly when dealing with complex levels of variation and interaction within and between cases.

We conceive of socialization as transformative learning and are particularly interested in socialization that encourages militant attitudes.

---

[8] Interview with the author, Kigali, Rwanda, May 7, 2009.

This occurs most readily in the seclusion and uncertainty experienced by many refugee populations. Such socialization can lead to violence upon return to the home country. Our second mechanism focuses on the way in which the distribution of resources – widely defined to include anything from emergency aid, to jobs and property – stimulates recruitment and allegiance, building interdependence between refugees and the leaders of militant groups. The final mechanism discussed is security entrapment, which plays out when return exacerbates external threats to individuals with the militant group being the only possible guarantor. Security entrapment can also create incentives for militarized return when refugees perceive threats while in exile.

It is unlikely that we will find trajectories of refugee and return militancy where only one of the mechanisms is operating. There is a logical sequence in which socialization takes place mainly prior to flight and in exile, resource distribution happens in exile and (in part) upon return, whereas security entrapment happens mainly after return. But the mechanisms can also interact jointly, as when Afghan refugees in Pakistan in the 1980s were enrolled in socialization campaigns as a reflection of controlled resource distribution, or when Rwandan Hutus in Zaire were affected by all three mechanisms (nearly) simultaneously. In both our cases, militarization hinged on a combination of socialization and resource distribution; security entrapment, while often important, clearly played a secondary role.

In exploring the mechanisms by which mobilized refugees contribute to violence upon return, the chapter contributes to larger debates in at least two substantive bodies of literature: (forced) migration as well as civil war and transnationalism. To the former, we contribute an in-depth framework for exploring political violence involving militant refugees upon their return. This is an extension of the emerging realization that refugees have agency – and that such agency can sometimes have a "dark side." To the debate on civil war and transnationalism, our findings highlight the dynamic nature of the transnationalism that feeds into conflict. We do so by examining the mechanisms that foster militancy throughout the whole refugee cycle (from pre-flight via exile to post-return), as well as the ways in which the relations between exiles and others (whether friendly or hostile) affect violence. The systematic application of a mechanisms-based framework, while empirically demanding, does give us a better understanding of the dynamism of the processes that yield political violence.

5 Rebels without a cause? Transnational diffusion and the Lord's Resistance Army, 1986–2011

HANS PETER SCHMITZ

In October 2005, the International Criminal Court (ICC) unsealed arrest warrants for five leaders of the Lord's Resistance Army (LRA). From the late 1980s and early 1990s onward, the LRA committed widespread atrocities against civilian populations in the border regions of Sudan and Uganda. During the past decade, the rebel group – estimated to number a few hundred to possibly several thousand fighters – committed similar acts of violence in the Democratic Republic of Congo (DRC) and most recently in the Central African Republic (CAR). Led by Joseph Kony, the LRA has evaded several high-profile military operations by the Ugandan, Sudanese, and Congolese military and has participated in several peace negotiation efforts without ever agreeing to a settlement ending the bloodshed. Thirty years of violence have resulted in an estimated 100,000 deaths, more than 30,000 children abducted, and many more displaced, often for decades forced into refugee camps (Okiror 2007).

While a long list of celebrities and state leaders have taken up the cause of the victims turned into child soldiers and sex slaves, the international community is not getting closer to ending this violence. The military has pushed the LRA out of Northern Uganda (in the early 1990s), out of Southern Sudan (in the early 2000s), and now out of the DRC (around 2008), but this response has been ineffective in protecting scores of civilians in these border regions from atrocities. At the same time, non-military efforts such as the ICC indictments and subsequent direct peace negotiations between the LRA and the Ugandan government from 2006 to 2008 have fallen short of creating the right incentives for LRA leaders to lay down their arms. What explains this particular pattern of violence, in particular its persistence as well as changes in the use of certain strategies, including committing atrocities against civilians and abducting children and adults?

To understand better new forms of post-Cold War violent conflict, a growing body of research focuses on the transnational dimensions of

120

these struggles. Many of the recent quantitative studies addressing such questions have highlighted the role of diaspora support or the ability of rebel groups to retreat across state borders. But most of these studies are content with claims that such factors matter for outbreak and perpetuation of violence without showing *how* they specifically play into the mobilization of resources, changes in framing the violence, and choices of targets and strategies (see Checkel, this volume). Such analyses also largely fail to look at the interactions between transnational mechanisms and other, more locally driven factors that may mediate or even render external influences ineffective. Finally, rarely do studies explore the interaction between transnational mechanisms sustaining the violence and countervailing transnational efforts designed to end it.

The LRA is a compelling and "hard" case for understanding the effects of transnational influences because its leadership deliberately limits any exposure to external influences. While it is impossible to assess the extent of many transnational ties that may have shaped the actions of the LRA (see also Bakke, this volume), Joseph Kony consciously avoided sustained and complex interactions with the outside world, even during the 1990s when the rebel group relied heavily on military support by the Sudanese government. Existing research on the LRA has frequently been preoccupied with its extraordinary violence against civilians as well as the perceived lack of a rational explanation for its goals and strategies. This type of scholarship views the LRA as a post-Cold War movement that no longer has a clear political agenda such as attaining some form of independent rule or seizing national power. However, more recent ethnographic studies of the LRA reject such claims of irrationality and have provided more contextual and historical accounts for its actions.

The present chapter adds to this reassessment a specific focus on transnational mechanisms and their impact on shifts in the levels of violence, the LRA leadership's framing of the struggle, and choices regarding targets and strategies. While greater attention to local context has helped us better understand the ineffective nature of international responses (Autesserre 2009), an added focus on transnational mechanisms sheds light on how shifts in a rebel movement's environment are equally relevant to developing more effective interventions.[1] The continued international military response reflects a limited grasp

[1] Thanks to Matt Evangelista for discussions on this point.

of both the local and the transnational dimensions of this conflict. As a result, the international community time and again fails to develop effective strategies to protect civilians. President Obama's October 2011 decision to deploy an additional 100 US armed forces personnel to eliminate the LRA (Obama 2011) represents a continuation of such failed external efforts.

I proceed in the following manner: the next section summarizes specific shifts in the LRA's behavior and how transnational mechanisms provide important insights into those changes. The three empirical sections that follow are organized around the topics of framing and the justification of violence, strategies used, and resource mobilization. The first empirical part focuses on how transnational mechanisms affected the initial framing of violence; the second explains how shifts in the use of violent means are a result of emulation and social adaptation, each of which operationalizes the broader category of transnational diffusion (Checkel, this volume); the third looks at shifts in resource mobilization over time, especially the relational diffusion of material and immaterial resources mobilized by external supporters and opponents.

The fourth section returns to the topic of framing and explains why the indictments of the ICC in 2005 and the peace negotiations from 2006 to 2008 have failed to adequately address the violence. The dominance of an international approach devoid of efforts to build meaningful transnational relations with those seeking to end the violence at the local level continues to give the advantage to the LRA and its efforts to exploit transnational opportunities for its own goals.

Transnational mechanisms and non-state violence

Research on social movements has focused particular attention on three aspects of domestic activism that may be shaped by outsiders through transnational mechanisms (see also the chapters by Adamson and Bakke in this volume). This chapter examines competing explanations accounting for: (1) shifts in the goals; (2) the framing, targets, and collective means used; and (3) the mobilization of resources. It not only investigates how external supporters of a rebel movement can shape such shifts, but also includes the often ambiguous effects of international efforts to end the violence, in particular, through global human rights mobilization. The analysis provides a broader understanding of how different and often uncoordinated international actions interact over time – including early missionary teachings in the region, the activism of the Acholi diaspora community, the emulation and learning of tactics and strategies from other rebel movements in neighboring nations, the impact of transnational human rights mobilization, and the practice of East African governments to use rebel groups to engage in forms "proxy warfare."

Tracing the process of how transnational mechanisms shape the goals, strategies, and resources of rebel movements creates challenges with regard to the availability and reliability of data.[2] Thanks to the work of local and international relief agencies, information about shifts in the targeting and strategies of the LRA is relatively reliable since episodes of abductions and violence are well documented. The main difficulty in assessing shifts in framing is over the authenticity of any written or spoken statements made on behalf of the LRA. Similar challenges arise when attempting to assess the amount of resources the LRA received from external sources at any given point in time.

The chapter's empirical evidence shows that transnational mechanisms play an important, but not necessarily overwhelming role in shaping behavior and outcomes. They are mitigated by pre-existing local conditions and their significance varies not only across the issues of framing, resources, and strategies, but also over time. Following the Nome and Weidmann and Bakke chapters (this volume), I argue that processes of relational diffusion – that is, the transfer of information or resources through personal networks and social bonds – are more robust. Indeed, efforts relying on targeted, non-relational diffusion – where people in one locale learn from people elsewhere through television, the radio, newspapers, and the internet – are not only less effective, but also often counterproductive. While diaspora mobilization was more prominent during parts of the conflict, its effects were much less important in this case than in Adamson's study of the conflict between the PKK and the Turkish government (Chapter 3, this volume). Table 5.1 summarizes the core claims about the relative importance of transnational mechanisms in accounting for significant shifts in the key activities of the LRA with regard to goals, strategies, and resource mobilization.

---

[2] On how to define and observe mechanisms, see the introductory chapter by Checkel.

Table 5.1 *Transnational mechanisms and shifts in framing, resources, and repertoires*

	Observable shift to be explained	Transnational mechanisms at work	Competing accounts
Framing and justification of violence (section 1)	1987–1995: Development of a loosely Christian ideology and "spiritualist" movement 1995–2003: LRA manifestos emphasize secularism and political goals	*Relational diffusion* *Non-relational diffusion* ("shaming" by human rights groups) and *relational diffusion* by diaspora	Incoherent "cult;" "rebels without a cause" Manifestos are not authored by LRA leadership/ represent mere "window-dressing"
Repertoires of violence (section 2)	Early 1990s: Increased use of atrocities against civilians, including own Acholi population Late 1990s: More limited use of atrocities, but continued abductions	*Emulation* and *situational learning* in the context of the civil war in Southern Sudan *Non-relational diffusion* ("shaming" by human rights groups)	Irrational behavior of a "cult" and its leader Material rewards for not targeting civilians
Resource mobilization (section 3)	1990s–2002: LRA moves to camps in Southern Sudan and gains military support by Sudanese government 2002–2005: LRA loses the material support from the Sudanese government; moves to camps in the DRC 2005–today: LRA participates in peace negotiations mediated by Southern Sudanese government; LRA moves to CAR after failed talks end in 2008	*Relational diffusion* to supply small arms by Sudanese government and/or private dealers; lack of government control over border regions *Relational diffusion* to supply small arms by private dealers; lack of government control over border regions Lack of *relational diffusion* and international capacity to address grievances; *non-relational diffusion* dominates international approach focused on prosecution, not protection	Self-sufficient strategy based on abductions and looting Self-sufficient strategy based on abductions and looting; Amnesty offers deplete force Military pressure; LRA faces defeat
Frames of global justice and peace (section 4)	2003–today: Increasing dissent within LRA following amnesty offer and ICC indictments	*Non-relational diffusion* (threat of prosecution by ICC); *relational diffusion* during peace negotiations	Material incentives and concessions in the context of negotiations; military pressure

Framing and justification of violence, 1987–2003: LRA manifestos and the transnational dimensions of the uprising

This section provides evidence on the role of transnational mechanisms in shaping two shifts in the framing of LRA violence. I first describe how taking up arms against Museveni's new government as well as the LRA's own Acholi population was rationalized in the late 1980s; second, I discuss how increased diaspora and international human rights activism caused a more defensive framing of violence in the mid to late 1990s. A third shift in framing following the ICC indictment of five LRA leaders in 2005 is discussed in the final empirical section.

Many external observers have been drawn to this conflict because of the extent of atrocities committed as well as the difficulties of establishing clear motives and justifications. Unlike the Chechnya case (Bakke, this volume), religion as a transnational force plays a more subtle role in the framing efforts of the LRA, and a number of external forces – in particular, governments of the region engaged in a "proxy war" (Prunier 2004) – shaped both resource availability and framing. While a majority of journalistic as well as academic coverage of the LRA tends to focus exclusively on the atrocities, this section will highlight in what ways attention to a combination of local grievances and transnational mechanisms enables an understanding of the significant shifts in the LRA's behavior and framing of the violence over time.

The main obstacle to tracing shifts in frames used by rebel groups such as the LRA is the limited access to documents such as manifestos or other forms of self-representation. Many websites posting information about the LRA were shut down after September 11, 2001 when the US government added the rebel group to its list of terrorist organizations. The dearth of first-hand information has led to significant distortions in the "official discourse" (Finnström 2008, 99) prevalent in the international media and among scholars claiming that public statements are useless and the LRA leadership is irrational. The media regularly portrays the LRA "as a barbaric and insane cult" (Allen 2006, 25) and even more experienced researchers claim that "the LRA has no political program or ideology, at least none that the local population has heard or can understand" (Gersony 1997, 59).[3]

---

[3] This view continues to dominate the current representation of the LRA by the Enough Project, a leading transnational activist group with the goal of "ending

More recently, a number of scholars have defied this mainstream view (Bevan 2007; Allen and Vlassenroot 2010) and offered more detailed analyses of LRA manifestos and shifts in how its leadership framed its violent struggle. These challenges to the "myth of madness" do not excuse LRA atrocities, but find current accounts unsatisfactory because "we need to pay attention to the power relations and structural circumstances that promote such persons' positions" (Finnström 2008, 129). While the authenticity of many LRA statements is contested, scholars with extensive field experience maintain they can be traced back to its leadership; moreover, the origin of the manifestos is less important than how they were used (or ignored) by local and global audiences (Finnström 2008, 120).

The dominant narrative that emerged in the mid 1990s was driven primarily by major human rights organizations, the Ugandan government, and international media, and focused almost solely on the atrocities and abductions of minors (Amnesty International 1997; Human Rights Watch/Africa 1997). Dolan notes that Amnesty International corrected its initial bias in a follow-up report two years later (Amnesty International 1999) "concentrating on government violations" (Dolan 2009, 229), but most of the attention by Northern publics remained focused on the LRA and its leader Joseph Kony.[4] Moral outrage about the welfare of children proved to be an effective tool in mobilizing Western audiences, but crowded out other important local grievances and interests. Western audiences found comfort in their preconceived notions about the continent, concluding that "the conflict is bizarre, but Africa is simply like that" (Ehrenreich 1998, 84). Aligned with the political interests of the Ugandan government, the aid community active in Northern Uganda during the 1990s followed an "inverse relationship between ... organizations' level of operations, scale and capacities in terms of funding and staffing, and their willingness to speak up about those aspects ... which involved criticism of the Government of Uganda" (Dolan 2009, 228). Local NGOs were most critical, national ones less so, and international NGOs as well as UN agencies almost entirely "laid the blame for all suffering at the feet of

genocide and crimes against humanity." On its website, it claims: "The LRA has no clear political agenda." See www.enoughproject.org/LRA (accessed July 31, 2010).

[4] It took Human Rights Watch until 2005 to publish a more comprehensive report on the violence in Northern Uganda (Human Rights Watch 2005).

the LRA" (Dolan 2009, 229). The idea of "rebels without a cause" resonated with Northern publics' perceptions of Africa and served the political and economic interests of the Ugandan government and many NGO and human rights activists.

Following the military victory of the NRM/A, local populations in the northern and north-western parts of the country quickly became concerned about their diminished role in national politics and the lack of development compared to the prospering southern parts (Omara-Otunnu 1992). The NRM government ended the long-standing northern domination (Acholi and Langi) of the Ugandan army and state (Omara-Otunnu 1987) and southern elites now took control of national politics. After decades of violence and civil war under the dictatorial regimes of Idi Amin (1971–1979) and Milton Obote (1981–1985), the NRM/A under the leadership of Yoweri Museveni decisively defeated government forces in late 1985 and gained control of the capital, Kampala. Significant insurgencies organized by military personnel of prior regimes persisted in many parts of the country until the early 1990s. Joseph Kony and his rebel movement differed from other violent rebellions during this time by combining local grievances about the marginalization of Northern Uganda with the use of elaborate religious rituals designed to challenge the traditional dominance of local Acholi chiefs and convince individual fighters that they were invincible (Behrend 1999; Cline 2003). When a rebel group called Holy Spirit Movement (HSM) led by Alice Auma (Lakwena) was beaten by NRA forces in 1988, Kony became the only remaining rebel leader capable of organizing violent resistance. Until the mid 2000s, the LRA regularly attacked Northern Uganda and close to 2 million Ugandans were forced into what the Ugandan government "euphemistically calls ... 'protected villages'" (Branch 2007, 181). This persistent state of insecurity left Northern Uganda economically devastated which regularly pushed young males into the arms of rebels and created more violence and insecurity.

Framing the uprising: missionary teachings, marginalization, and the crisis of traditional societies

The marginalization of Northern Uganda, going back to the colonial period (Mamdani 1984), provided the initial and most enduring frame justifying the violent struggle against the Museveni government in

Kampala since the mid to late 1980s. British colonial rule gave preferential treatment to the Southern Baganda and the "the northern region served mainly as a reservoir for cheap labor, from which Britain recruited its soldiers" (Van Acker 2004, 341). After independence, this imbalance led to the establishment of consecutive military regimes under Idi Amin and Milton Obote solidifying the idea of "competitive retaliation on an ethnic basis" (Van Acker 2004, 340).

Successive leaders of rebel movements in the North frequently gave meaning to the long-standing grievances by adding mystical and religious overtones to support their peculiar claims to leadership. Many observers have used the frequent biblical references as a reason to dismiss them as fundamentalist (Adam et al. 2007) or "millenarian" (Chabal and Daloz 1999, 86). Yet, the logic of this frame actually "echoes more than one century of missionary teaching" (Finnström 2008, 108) and confirms the importance of transnational processes of relational diffusion that show in what ways "this kind of terror ... might prove to be linked to the logic of the world system and, as such, to be less exceptional than hoped" (Doom and Vlassenroot 1999, 7). While the grievances of the Acholi people after the NRM/A victory were primarily local and national, the framing of the particular response developed by the LRA leadership was derived from a global structure of values that had been diffused into the Ugandan polity for a century using mechanisms of socialization, reward, and severe punishment. Many aspiring new leaders emerged in the North during that time and shared similar visions as those expressed by Kony and the LRA. For example, "Alice Lakwena's Holy Spirit Movement was the outcome of elements of missionary Christianity interacting with indigenous cosmology" (Van Acker 2004, 346).

Instead of understanding the unique combination of local grievances and transnational religious ideas, Western perceptions were primarily informed by pictures of the abducted and maimed. Finnström details how popular books and even feature films about the conflict perpetuated the contrast between a "dark continent" and the help provided by non-Africans, including the popular story of European nuns searching for 30 girls abducted from the Aboke missionary school (de Temmermann 2001; Finnström 2008, 110). The point here is not to question the good intentions of external actors willing to act, but to elaborate how ignoring the larger, transnational context reproduced problematic assumptions about the conflict. President Museveni and his government promoted this particular perspective of Africa, portraying his regime as modern and rational and declaring that his enemies in the North were "intoxicating poor peasants with mysticism and incredible lies" (Museveni 1992, 115). Internally, Museveni used the violence in the North to consolidate his power base by presenting himself as the leader guaranteeing peace (for the South) and protector "from the Acholi and other wild northerners" (Allen 2006, 48). Museveni skill-fully reinforced Western perceptions of an unresolvable conflict while also falling in line with US-driven global security interests focused on military solutions to terrorist threats (Schmitz 2006).

The most promising peace negotiations between the Ugandan government and the LRA during this time period took place in 1994, when the Acholi Betty Bigombe, a minister of state in Museveni's government appointed in 1988 to end the rebellion in the North, met directly with Kony on several occasions. Against much male prejudice, Bigombe built crucial trust among the Acholi prior to initiating the peace talks, which followed shortly after "Operation North," the first major military action by the Ugandan army, failed to defeat the rebels in 1992 (O'Kadameri 2002, 35). In a response to a letter sent by Bigombe, Kony indicated that he would need to "receive guidance by the Holy Spirit" and by October 1993 pre-negotiations on security questions took place. During a meeting with Bigombe and Acholi representatives in January 1994 in Gulu, Kony blamed the Acholi community and its elders for the violence because they abandoned the LRA (O'Kadameri 2002, 40). The talks soon deteriorated, with LRA leaders accusing government officials of humiliating them and the government suspecting the LRA of establishing contacts with the Sudanese government. Museveni visited Gulu in February 1994 announcing that the army would defeat the LRA if it did not lay down its arms within seven days.

Defensive framing: early human rights mobilization and diaspora activism

Following the breakdown of the first peace negotiations and the sub-sequent increase in violence, the diaspora community in collaboration with Acholi civil society groups initiated in 1996 the "Kacoke Madit" (big meeting) process, intended to champion peace and reconciliation. As the global human rights community began to take note of the atrocities and began to publicize the systematic attacks on civilians, a second shift in framing the violence took place. The LRA now supplemented its demands for greater political participation with a denial of abuses and a rhetorical emphasis on universal human rights. For the first time, the conflict became the subject of widespread discussion beyond the region and diaspora community.

At the first Kacoke Madit meeting held at the University of London,[5] James Obita claimed to represent the LRA/M and defended the refusal to surrender, arguing that those being offered amnesty in the past were killed by Museveni's troops (Obita 1997). Obita portrayed the emergence of the LRA as a rightful act of self-defense against the aggression of the Ugandan military, although his use of the term "NRA-Tutsi army" exposed his own ethnically biased discourse. The speech listed several political demands, including the immediate restoration of multiparty democracy, Museveni's resignation, formation of a government of national reconciliation, ending gross human rights violations, and economic prosperity for all Ugandans. While he acknowledged the suffering of Acholi civilians, the speech only admitted to "instances of indiscipline" on the part of the LRA while lamenting a failure to adequately investigate atrocities committed by government troops. Obita claimed that the LRA leadership took harsh measures against anyone in the organization who may have "reportedly taken people against their will or committed atrocities. Disciplinary measures, including even execution by firing squad of LRA fighters who have grossly abused civilians have taken place in our camps." Obita also claimed that investigations of atrocities were currently under way, but there is no subsequent record about their outcomes. With regard to mutilations, Obita emphasized that "no official policy of carrying out such atrocious acts" exists and he blamed government soldiers "masquerading as LRA/M" for several such incidents reported in 1996.

In 1997, a LRA manifesto demanded multiparty politics and constitutional federalism, expressed support for human rights and anti-corruption, and demanded a separation of the military from the judiciary and the executive ("From LRA/M to all Ugandans," cited in Finnström 2008, 122). Recalling how previous rebel movements

---

[5] Two subsequent meetings in 1998 (London) and 2000 (Nairobi) were attended by lower-ranking representatives of the Ugandan government, Acholi community members, and civil society groups. See www.km-net.org.uk (accessed November 20, 2010).

disappeared without accomplishing their goals, a 1999 statement – responding to an amnesty offer – insisted that "[w]e are not going to lay down our arms as long as Museveni is still in Uganda as president" (LRA letter, cited in Finnström 2008, 120). During this time, the LRA not only committed the majority of its atrocities in Northern Uganda, but simultaneously released the most detailed manifestos with a distinct new framing based on an emphasis on secularism and global values. The blatant gap between the violence against the civilian population and the claims in the manifestos widened as the written statements increasingly responded to criticisms of LRA atrocities and added explicit denials of the official discourse about their alleged motives. Finnström cites an 18-page political manifesto circulated in late 1999 which criticized the Ugandan army's recent military actions in the DRC, demanded multiparty elections, and claimed that structural adjustment programs had the most adverse effects on local populations in the periphery of Uganda (Finnström 2008, 125–126). The manifesto also outlined "brief descriptions of LRA/M's economic programs and proposed policies on education, agriculture, health, land and natural resources, infrastructure, commerce and industry, and defense" (Finnström 2008, 123). Other issues raised regularly included demands for national unity by promoting inter-tribal marriages and language instruction, education for all, an independent judiciary, the formation of an ethnically balanced national army, and policies to "end the use of witchcraft and sorcery by promotion of the Ten Commandments" (cited in Allen 2006, 43).

Along with promoting a broader political agenda largely ignored by the Ugandan government and external observers, the manifestos also explicitly denied that the LRA was motivated by fundamentalist Christian ideology. Finnström cites now defunct websites accessed in 1999 as well as written materials circulated under Kony's name stating that "I would like to strongly deny that these members [of the LRA, HPS] are or in any way have the intentions of becoming Christian Fundamentalists" (Finnström 2008, 124). At the height of the propaganda campaign in early 1999, the LRA broadcast daily for one hour on a station called Radio Free Uganda until the signal was blocked by the government. The program "belies the claim that the LRA lacked any political position" (Dolan 2009, 85) and consisted primarily of political attacks against the government. Topics discussed included excessive military expenditures, lack of democratic accountability, and the encouragement of mob justice by government officials (Dolan 2009, 84–85). The program was also used to refute claims circulating among the local population that the LRA was involved in slave trade and resorted to cannibalism. Most importantly, the broadcast denied claims by the government that the LRA was on the brink of military defeat. In October 2002, the Ugandan government prohibited another radio station in Gulu from airing any LRA statements after several call-ins by Joseph Kony and other rebel leaders during live broadcasts.

The LRA's intensified public relations efforts in the mid to late 1990s coincided not only with greater exposure of the atrocities in Western media, but also with increased military pressure by Uganda forces as well as greater international efforts to put an end to the violence. By 1999, Northern Uganda had experienced almost one year of peace as the Ugandan army was able to push the LRA deep into Southern Sudan. In December, the Carter Center facilitated a peace accord between Sudan and Uganda (Neu 2002), although the preceding negotiations excluded representatives from the LRA or the Sudan People's Liberation Army (SPLA). In January 2000, the Ugandan parliament adopted the Amnesty Act, offering a blanket amnesty to all rebels willing to lay down their weapons. While the top leadership of the LRA rejected the offer, many in the second or third tier left the rebel group, often citing the amnesty as the most important factor for their decision to return to civilian life (Conciliation Resources 2006). Dolan reports that the number of LRA members taking advantage of the offer increased from 1,086 in 2002 to 3,601 in 2004 before dropping to less than 100 in 2007 (Conciliation Resources 2010, 8).

The peace agreement between Sudan and Uganda as well as the amnesty put significant pressure on the remaining LRA fighters who responded with an increase in violence. Public statements now became rare, and no more manifestos emerged until after the ICC indictments and the commencement of the Juba peace talks in 2006. By December 2001, the US government had added the LRA to its "B" list of "other terrorist organizations" and by March 2002, the Ugandan government had passed its own Anti-Terrorism Act, effectively retracting the amnesty offer (Dolan 2009, 53). Following the peace accord with Sudan, the Uganda army received permission for a one-month military campaign to destroy LRA camps in Southern Sudan (Human Rights Watch 2006). Aided by US-sponsored training efforts, "Operation Iron Fist" commenced in March 2002, but once again failed to fully defeat the rebel group. LRA soldiers now pushed back into Northern Uganda, where insecurity increased.

By 2003/2004, the number of internally displaced in Northern Uganda had increased to about 1.7 million, from an estimated 400,000 in 2000. The number of humanitarian NGOs operating around Gulu had risen from five in 1996 to more than 60 (Dolan 2009, 239). In the meantime, Kony and his rebels had established new camps in Garamba National Park in the eastern part of the Democratic Republic of Congo. After repeated failures to defeat the LRA militarily, Museveni now called on the newly established ICC to investigate the LRA leadership for its atrocities. Following the ICC indictments in 2005, a third shift in the framing of the conflict occurred, which is discussed below following the sections on resource mobilization, and targets and strategies.

Transnational mechanisms help explain shifts in the framing of LRA violence that go unnoticed by alternative accounts that typically reduce the rebels to an irrational "cult." The initial shift in framing took place as Kony and other aspiring rebel leaders combined a desire to challenge the marginalization of Northern Uganda with a claim to be the true representatives of an Acholi community morally weakened and misled by traditional elders. The justification for attacking Acholi civilians had roots in missionary teachings and was understood as a necessary "cleansing" of a failed community. The active translation of a Christian ideology into the local context through processes of relational diffusion allowed Kony to construct a rationale for violence, recruit fighters, and turn them against their own ethnic group.

In the mid to late 1990s, a second shift of framing took place when the LRA was increasingly challenged on its human rights record and use of fundamentalist Christian terminology. The framing now became more directly driven by the influence of external actors without a direct presence in the region, pushing the LRA into defensive statements and a denial of responsibility for atrocities. This non-relational diffusion of ideas produced a response of written statements and manifestos projecting a secular character and a mainstream political agenda with frequent references to human rights and democracy.

The main challenge to including such transnational mechanisms into the analysis of LRA violence is captured by the idea of "rebels without a cause" and the claim of a new type of non-ideological, "chaotic warfare" spreading across Africa after the end of the Cold War

(Reno 2009, 9). But these claims cannot account for the shifts in framing identified here because they reject the possibility of any significant changes in the behavior and motives of Kony. In this view, the manifestos are not authentic or represent mere "window-dressing" and changes in framing are solely driven by military imperatives and material incentives on the ground.

While local grievances and conditions clearly shape much of the conflict, transnational mechanisms take a central place during crucial shifts in framing, strategies, and resource mobilization. Understanding their impact is imperative for scholars and policy-makers interested in shaping a strategy designed to exploit the political opportunities offered by a rapidly changing situation. This insight is confirmed by the deliberate efforts of the Ugandan government not to end the violence and protect civilians and instead to cast the rebels as "backward" and isolated. And while the manifestos were erased from the official discourse about the conflict, Finnström's work shows that they were common knowledge among the local population and shaped their views of the rebellion. One may even argue that despite the glaring gaps between the rhetoric of the manifestos and the actions of the LRA, the manifestos accomplished the goal of reminding the local population of the failures of the government (Finnström 2008, 129). Finally, if changes in the framing of the violence during the 1980s and 1990s had been taken more seriously by many international observers, it may have helped in anticipating better how the LRA would respond to the 2005 ICC indictments. The subsequent Juba peace process exposed significant internal divisions within the LRA, marking a third shift in the framing of the violence (discussed in the final empirical section below).

Repertoires of violence: changing levels of atrocities

Taking seriously the shifts in the framing of the violence by the LRA exposes the persistent disconnect between frequent demands for human rights and democracy and the atrocities committed. The main empirical puzzle for this section is to assess the importance of transnational mechanisms shaping the targeting and strategies of the LRA, in particular its use of abductions and atrocities committed against local residents of attacked villages. Apart from regularly engaging military forces, the LRA used the attacks on villages to steal food supplies and forcibly recruit new fighters. While activists and international media have almost exclusively focused on the LRA's abduction of children, more recent studies based on interviews and surveys (Allen and Schomerus 2006) have shown that such a view often "infantilizes the movement, suggesting a lack of accountability and making it appear a less than viable partner in peace negotiations. This has been a problem during the Juba peace talks" (Schomerus 2007, 16). Child abductions played a relatively minor role in the overall strategy and success of the LRA and the main recruits were young adults capable of receiving effective military training (Blattmann and Annan 2010).[6] Children were frequently "released after having done duty as porters" (Schomerus 2007, 16). The LRA was successful because it had a strong, centralized command, a virtually unlimited supply of weaponry (see section on resource mobilization below), and enough recruits to sustain a military campaign across four nations for almost 25 years. While child abductions were important for the LRA, focusing exclusively on them inhibits an analysis of the significant shifts in the strategies of the LRA, in particular, the rise in atrocities early in the military campaign and the apparent abandonment of some of the worst atrocities in the late 1990s.

Ignoring the political and social agenda of the rebels allowed activists to avoid the complexity of the situation and mobilize moral outrage. As a result, even well-informed observers concluded that the LRA was "not motivated by any identifiable political agenda, and its military strategy and tactics reflect this" (International Crisis Group 2004, 5). In this view, the rebel group not only lacked rational goals, but its selection of targets and strategies was largely random. In contrast, this section will elaborate why and how we can observe particular shifts in the targeting and strategies used by the LRA and which transnational mechanisms redirected strategizing and enabled different levels of organized violence. Two questions are central to the inquiry. First, why did the LRA turn against the population in Northern Uganda which it claimed to defend? How did it adopt practices of torture and maiming in its brutal campaign against civilians in Northern Uganda and three other nations? Second, while the LRA used

---

[6] Scholars with field experience interviewing former rebel fighters point out that NGOs and international media trumped up the issue of child abductions, when such actions were actually "a lesser part of a far larger pattern of adult abduction and a degree of voluntary recruitment" (Dolan 2009, 90).

abductions consistently throughout its entire military campaign, why were mutilations of civilians most prevalent between 1991 and 1996 (Dolan 2009, 79), and later on played a much less significant role?

Lack of governmental control over borders and the ability of LRA fighters to move easily across them enabled a strategy of increased brutality against the local population. But the crucial transnational mechanism was not simply crossing a border, but what the LRA fighters learned and emulated while being exposed to an ongoing civil war while establishing camps in southern Sudan in the early 1990s. Similar to Bakke's emphasis on transnational insurgents shaping the strategies of Chechen rebels (Bakke, this volume), LRA fighters learned some of their tactics after they were forced to flee northern Uganda and were thrown into a decades-long, brutal civil war in southern Sudan.

One Sudanese politician said that she felt the LRA changed its behavior after moving to Sudan, partly because they were encouraged by Khartoum to commit atrocities, but also because the already brutal environment increased the spiral of violence. She said, "They [the LRA] kill people and hang them up, so when local people come, they don't touch anything. I think the LRA learned these things from southern Sudan" (Schomerus 2007, 20).[7]

But it would be short-sighted to look only as far back as the late 1980s in accounting for the origins of these atrocities. The violence experienced and reproduced by the LRA can be traced back to British colonial policies which had given preferential treatment to ethnic groups in the South and reduced Northern Uganda to a recruitment pool for foot soldiers. At independence in 1962, Milton Obote, a Langi from the North became the first President, immediately relying on the military strength created by the British among his own ethnic group. One of his generals, Idi Amin, would dispose of Obote in 1971 and expand military rule, leading the nation into more than a decade of bloodshed and civil war ending only in 1986. While Obote came back to power in 1980 and temporarily reinstated the North's role in national politics, Museveni's military victory in 1986 signaled a profound crisis of Acholi identity and opened up opportunities for new leadership developing violent strategies.

Alice Auma and Joseph Kony relied on a mix of spirituality and references to religion to offer the Acholi a form of redemption and

---

[7] The quote is from an unnamed government official based in Juba/Sudan, who was interviewed by Schomerus in November 2006.

return to their identity following their "near destruction through using modern methods and structures" (Jackson 2002, 49). Both developed complex rituals and introduced a world of "spirits" to heal and cleanse individuals, including preparing fighters for battle. And each insisted that war was a form of healing and that "Acholi society had to be purified by violence" (Allen 2006, 40). While Auma's Holy Spirit Movement did not attack civilians during its brief military campaign from 1986 until its defeat in 1988, the LRA turned against its own population as a result of the particular framing of the crisis of Acholi society and its violent experience in southern Sudan. Kony is cited defending such practices during the 1994 peace negotiations:

If you pick up an arrow against us and we ended up cutting off the hand you used, who is to blame? You report us with your mouth, and we cut off your lips. Who is to blame? It is you! The bible says that if your hand, eye or mouth is at fault, it should be cut off. (Allen 2006, 42)

As the LRA was engaged in military combat by Ugandan forces, the practice of brutal attacks on civilians was further reinforced. Starting around 1991, mutilations became a way of deterring local collaboration with the government troops and many recruits were forced to commit atrocities in order to make it "difficult for them to return home" (Allen 2006, 42). Once the LRA received substantial material support from the Sudanese government and was also militarily strong enough to regularly raid villages and trading centers for supplies, support by the local population became less crucial and abductions served as a main recruitment strategy. The LRA abducted younger adolescents "because not only were they easier to indoctrinate, but Kony had given up on the adults. The youngsters were to form the core of a new Acholi identity" (Jackson 2002, 49).

Why did the LRA then begin to limit the practice of regularly mutilating civilians after 1996? Throughout its entire military campaign, the LRA consistently relied on raids and abductions to meet its material needs and resupply its ranks of fighters. The rebels also continued to regularly kill civilians indiscriminately during their raids. But some of the particularly gruesome attacks on civilians began to diminish in the mid 1990s and reports about the activities of the LRA contained fewer references to maiming and torturing, while continuing to highlight abductions and looting. Concomitant with the changes in framing discussed above, the increased exposure to human rights mobilization as well as the stepped-up activities of the diaspora community in the mid 1990s represent a form of weak transnational "shaming" transported largely through indirect mechanisms of non-relational diffusion. As the LRA found decreasing support from the Sudanese government in its proxy war against Uganda, the rebels' strategic freedom diminished. And after the ICC indictments signaled a success of the human rights mobilization, local actors such as the South Sudanese government, but also international relief organizations were able to offer material rewards to the LRA in exchange for not targeting civilians.

Transnational mechanisms offer unique insights into the LRA's strategic behavior, in particular, why it turned against civilians, committed atrocities, but then also dropped some of these tactics again from its repertoire. Processes of learning and emulation in the context of the southern Sudanese conflict played an important role in the initial shift of increased brutality against the local population in northern Uganda. While Kony had developed a rationale for why targeting his own ethnic group was necessary, the atrocities intensified only after the LRA moved to Southern Sudan. The geography of the border regions offered options for retreat and encouraged abductions, thus clearly establishing an observable effect of transnational mechanisms largely neglected in the literature. Throughout the conflict, the LRA behaved opportunistically in targeting civilians and frequently moved across borders, initially from northern Uganda to Sudan in the mid 1990s, back to Uganda in 2002, to the DRC in 2005, and again to southern Sudan and, most recently, to the CAR in 2008.

A second shift in the LRA's strategic use of violence occurred in the mid 1990s after the Acholi diaspora became more active in promoting a peaceful solution and the first major human rights reports and news about atrocities reached Western audiences. Abductions and raids continued, but some of the methods of maiming civilians became less prevalent. It would require additional research to determine if the mechanism at work here was more direct relational diffusion through personal networks between rebels and diaspora groups or if this change in repertoires of violence was caused by the more indirect influence of human rights mobilization focusing on the LRA. No matter if either or both mechanisms were at work, the external engagement was in many ways counterproductive to the goal of ending all violence against children and adults. Indeed, viewing the LRA as an irrational "cult" undermined more promising efforts at relational diffusion, which would have taken seriously the underlying grievances of the local population.

Resource mobilization: governmental interests and small arms diffusion

In the evolution of the LRA and its violent struggle, different resource streams and varying financial support shaped strategies and goals. But access to weaponry and other resources never limited the LRA and its military strength. From the early 1990s until about 2002, the rebel group received resources and training from the Sudanese government, but it could also rely on some support from members of the Acholi diaspora community. Moreover, its regular cross-border raids and abductions of children, youths, and adults made it quite self-sufficient. Over time, the LRA relied on a wide array of external resources and supporters, but looting villages and abducting civilians to carry the supplies back to its camps represented a key activity ensuring survival (Dolan 2009, Annex A: Testimony of LRA soldier). After 2006 and the beginning of the Juba peace talks, the LRA also temporarily received official humanitarian aid delivered by the Catholic charity Caritas and others, while local governments paid the LRA not to attack their territory (Human Rights Watch 2006). As recently as May 2009, the Ugandan Army reported intercepting trucks driven by Belgian nationals in southern Sudan carrying high-tech supplies for the LRA into the DRC (Egadu 2009).

Research on diasporas has long explored the material and ideational support these communities can provide in supporting violent rebellions (Adamson 2004; Lyons 2006). But this kind of support was likely less relevant in the case of the LRA. Diaspora resources may have been part of the arms supply and other material support, but most observers agree that the links between the leadership fighting on the ground and the often self-appointed political representatives were tenuous at best.

It is difficult to obtain reliable information on the extent of resource support for any given rebel group, especially looking back at almost 25 years of violent conflict. The most important resource – access to weapons and ammunition for combat – was never an issue for the LRA or any other rebel group operating in this area. A survey completed by Nairobi-based Larjour Consultancy in 2001 found that an AK-47 sold for about USh 25,000 (approximately USD 12) in the border regions (cited in Van Acker 2004, 345). This means that relational diffusion expressed in small arms supply by private dealers was sufficient to allow the LRA to continue the violent struggle.

The first significant shift in resource mobilization took place when the LRA relocated to southern Sudan in the early 1990s and began receiving military equipment from the Sudanese government. The weapons supply became more sophisticated and "the UPDF often fell behind in the quality of their equipment" (Schomerus 2007, 41). Until 2005, the Sudanese government used the LRA and its military capabilities in its war against the SPLA, but also in the Darfur region. LRA fighters would regularly fight alongside regular Sudanese forces against the SPLA and their camps were based in the Juba area close to army installations (Vinci 2007, 340). Kony and other commanders regularly visited Khartoum and this resource support allowed the LRA to engage in the kind of cross-border raids into Northern Uganda described above (Schomerus 2007, 24; Dolan 2009, 82). While Kony's particular framing of the conflict offered a rationale for attacking civilians in Acholi land and elsewhere, transnational geographical opportunities and the transnational diffusion of resources enabled implementing those violent strategies.

Stockpiles were easy to hide in the border regions and for its communications the LRA used radio equipment and satellite phones supplied by supporters. The supply of arms in the region was so plentiful that the LRA did not have to engage in large-scale arms trafficking, but frequently traded weapons to locals for valuable intelligence or money. Moreover, although the atrocities committed by the LRA eventually ended the support by the Sudanese government and also limited its ability to raise resources among the diaspora (Schomerus 2007, 13), there is no indication that any of these issues adversely affected its military strength.

After the Carter Center brokered a peace agreement between Sudan and Uganda in 1999 explicitly calling for an end to support of rebel groups, official supplies likely still reached the LRA, which continued to operate from southern Sudan until 2002. While the Carter Center had succeeded in getting a peace accord between two governments, the negotiations failed to include any of the rebel groups such as the LRA (Dolan 2009, 97). When the Sudanese government in 2002 allowed the UPDF to pursue the LRA on its territory ("Operation Iron Fist"), the violence was pushed back into northern Uganda, the number of internally displaced increased dramatically, and the LRA leadership ultimately found another safe haven in the Garamba National Park in the DRC. As one security expert interviewed in 2006 put it: "Why is the UPDF in Sudan? To make sure the LRA is not destroyed" (Schomerus 2007, 29). The other reason was (as was the case in the DRC in the late 1990s) that UPDF control over this territory allowed for Ugandan soldiers to profit from the exploitation of natural resources such as teak.

While some members of the Ugandan government and military developed an interest in sustaining a low-intensity conflict with the rebel group, the key resources for the LRA were increasingly no longer related to the *presence* of those sustaining the violence (e.g. Sudanese government support), but the *absence* of policies and capacities at the international level to effectively protect civilians and address the underlying local grievances. The LRA atrocities became a public relations resource for Museveni distracting from his dismal human rights record and abuses of power. Knowing that the LRA was never a real threat, his regime simply had to ensure that it "bolstered an appearance of doing the right thing" (Dolan 2009) while perpetuating an image of Kony as an insane cult leader.

The resource base of the LRA shifted after the Sudanese government ended its support and again after the opening of the Juba peace negotiations in 2006. What carries over from the earlier period is the LRA's emphasis on autarky and its continued use of raids and abductions for survival. The supply of small arms also remains largely in place, with no discernible decrease in the availability of such weapons. With the commencement of peace negotiations, what does change is the introduction of material rewards offered by local governments and channeled through international humanitarian groups. Since 2005, government officials in southern Sudan regularly paid off the LRA in exchange for not attacking their territory and population. The LRA was also regularly "paid" to attend peace negotiations (Johnson 2009) and even complained in 2007 about "not being granted USD 2 million for consultations in northern Uganda." These rewards play a highly ambiguous role in actually accomplishing the goal of ending violence because they simultaneously constitute "an incentive to keep the process going and a disincentive to streamline it" (Schomerus 2008, 96). Similarly, aid provided by NGOs also injects new resources into conflict zones. Lack of coordination across NGOs and humanitarian principles of neutrality offer rebel groups additional "opportunities . . . to exploit these resources" (Reno 2009, 12).

The supply of small arms and support by the Sudanese government played an important role in the context of lawless border regions. But the LRA stands out as a rebel group sustained primarily by a self-sufficient strategy of mobilizing resources using looting and abductions. Its military power was certainly significantly diminished after 2002, but not necessarily its ability to create widespread insecurity and displacement of civilian populations. As the conflict progressed, the importance of resources directly made available to the LRA diminished while the knowledge, capacities and resources *absent* at the international level become increasingly relevant in sustaining the cycle of violence. By not addressing underlying grievances and the complex motives of individual fighters, the ability of the LRA to sustain its violent campaign only diminished marginally. Only after the amnesty offer went into force and the ICC indictments were announced did the incentives for the rebels change – and the most recent shift in the framing of the conflict occurred.

Frames of global justice and peace, 2003–2011: ICC indictments and Juba negotiations

Museveni's 2003 decision to involve the ICC and the 2005 warrants issued for five LRA commanders fundamentally altered the framing of the conflict. While transnational human rights activists defend the indictments as a necessary step against impunity, many observers with field experience in the region tend to be critical of the indictments and argue that they undermine negotiations for a peaceful settlement of the conflict (Allen 2005; Branch 2007). Since the establishment of the ICC, scholars have debated vigorously the actual impact of the prosecutorial approach on ongoing conflicts as well as post-conflict political developments (Kastner 2007; Vinjamuri 2010).

The ICC proceedings against the LRA were preceded by two decades of transnational human rights mobilization, including the emergence of child soldiering as a new major cause for global human rights activism. In these campaigns, the violence in the DRC/Sudan/Uganda region became a prime argument for the establishment of the ICC and activists insisted that such a court would deter future crimes of this magnitude. For Yoweri Museveni, these global campaigns offered another opportunity to advance his own political agenda, following on the peace deal with Sudan in 1999, the never fully implemented Amnesty Act of 2000 and "Operation Iron Fist" in 2002 which had failed to capture Kony. In its referral application to the ICC, the Ugandan government denied that the LRA was a legitimate belligerent under humanitarian law (Government of Uganda 2003, 22); it was thus "befitting both from a practical and moral viewpoint to entrust the investigation and prosecution of these crimes to the Prosecutor of the ICC" (Government of Uganda 2003, 14). The document reinforced the dominant discourse, claiming that "the LRA has not had a coherent ideology, a rational political agenda, or any form of popular support" (Government of Uganda 2003, 6). By referring the situation to the ICC, the Ugandan government continued a deliberately incoherent approach of alternating between offering amnesty and reconciliation with new military operations and other threats (Dolan 2009, 100).

When the ICC announced the indictments in 2005, international reaction was overwhelmingly positive, while skepticism prevailed in Uganda. Save the Children/Uganda issued a statement expressing concern that "the LRA leadership might apply even more strict discipline to prevent witnesses from escaping" and predicted that the intervention would lead to "even more suspicion and distrust" (Allen 2006, 83–84). The indictments yet again raised the profile of the conflict in the international media and provided the backdrop for the extensive peace negotiations that took place from mid 2006 until 2008.

As a result of the 2002–2003 military "Operation Iron Fist" in southern Sudan, the LRA was now on the move again, filtering back into northern Uganda and leaving hundreds of thousands displaced (Allen 2006, 72). As the humanitarian crisis worsened, international attention and pressure for a negotiated settlement increased. In January 2004, the US Congress passed the Northern Uganda Crisis Response Act, which for the first time implicitly criticized the Ugandan government and military for its own human rights violations and lack of serious effort to negotiate an agreement. A national referendum held in Uganda in July 2005 led to the reintroduction of multiparty politics and Museveni's political space diminished as he was preoccupied with winning the elections in February 2006.

Pressure not only mounted on Museveni, but also the LRA and its leadership (Schomerus 2008, 94). The military campaign had taken its toll, visible in a significant jump in the number of LRA soldiers accepting the amnesty offer in 2003 and 2004. Several reception centers run by international NGOs such as World Vision reported receiving about 5,000 former abductees and fighters by late 2004. Around the same time, members of the diaspora succeeded in mobilizing donors and Betty Bigombe was brought back to Sudan to facilitate talks once again. The 2005 Comprehensive Peace Agreement between the Sudanese government and the SPLA led to the formation of the semi-autonomous government of Southern Sudan and the LRA was faced with three options: "withdraw from Sudan, declare war on the SPLA, or engage in negotiations" (Schomerus 2007, 34).

After a series of meetings, the Vice President of the new South Sudanese government, Riek Machar, brought both parties to the negotiation table in July 2006. Before the talks had begun, Machar was filmed handing US$20,000 to Kony; he was quickly accused of bribing the LRA to remain peaceful and show up. With the advent of the Juba peace talks, the LRA/M established a more professional information policy, expressing demands ahead of the negotiations and denying responsibility for attacks (Schomerus 2007, 16). In its opening remarks, the LRA/M delegation insisted once again on having a political agenda, stating: "Your Excellency, over the years, it has been suggested ... that the LRM/A has no political agenda ... Failure of the LRM/A to have access to the mass media to express its political agenda in intellectual form does not mean the lack of it" (Finnström 2008, 127). A month before the first Juba talks, Kony had granted rare interviews to international media where he claimed that LRA manifestos were widely available in Uganda and elsewhere. After being asked why the LRA had failed to get its political demands disseminated more widely, Kony replied: "All things [all information comes] from Museveni's side or from some other people, because I do not have proper propaganda machineries" (Schomerus 2007, 14). In the same interview, Kony acknowledged atrocities by stating that "I cannot say that we are fighting clean war [or that] Museveni is fighting dirty war, that one is difficult to say. Because a clean war is known by God only" (Schomerus 2007, 15). But in another interview with a BBC reporter, he flatly denied being responsible for any atrocities (Farmar 2006). At a parallel meeting between LRA leaders and a large delegation of Acholi civil society leaders from northern Uganda and southern Sudan, Kony and others apologized for atrocities committed.

The initial agenda of the negotiations covered the establishment of a ceasefire, political solutions, justice/accountability, and demobilization and reintegration. While a Cessation of Hostilities agreement, signed on August 26, guaranteed safe passage for LRA soldiers to designated assembly areas (Government of the Republic of Uganda/Lord's Resistance Army/Movement 2006, section 5), both sides violated the agreement and attacks between the UPDF and LRA remained common. Comprehensive written agreements emerged on all issues, including "political solutions to the situation in Northern Uganda" (May 2007), "accountability and reconciliation" (June 2007) and the most difficult issue of "disarmament and demobilization" (February 2008). During the entire time period, LRA leaders repeatedly demanded an end to the ICC investigations. In December 2006, Kony stated:

The international justice system is that if you are weak, the justice is on you. For the time being, they think me, I am weak … Same with Taylor, when he was in power nobody thought of justice. If you want to remain safe from the ICC, you must fight and be strong (translated into English from Luo, cited in: Schomerus 2008, 95).

The agreement on "accountability and reconciliation" signed by the LRA and the government on June 29, 2007 sought to assure LRA fighters that criminal and civil proceedings would take place in Uganda before a special War Crimes Division to be established at the High Court (Otim and Wierda 2010). Despite the significant progress in negotiating the separate parts of the peace agreement, the negotiations ultimately exposed deep divisions within the LRA's military wing. While Kony appointed all of the LRA/M representatives in Juba, significant divisions existed not only between diaspora representatives and the rebel group, but also within the leadership of the LRA. When Kony's second-in-command, Vincent Otti, apparently pushed in 2007 for a greater commitment on the part of the rebels, he was executed and the negotiations further delayed (Otim and Wierda 2010, 5).

Despite the significant upheaval within the LRA ranks, the final agreement was ready for signature in March 2008. In April and September 2008, Kony twice failed to appear at a scheduled signing ceremony for the Final Peace Agreement, citing both times the ICC warrant as a reason. However, the ICC indictment only served as a cover for deep divisions among those negotiating in the name of the LRA. First, and most importantly, those speaking for the LRA "were not the key decision-makers" and "things said in Juba would be interpreted differently in the field or in Garamba Park" (Conciliation Resources 2010, 18, interview with Julian Hottinger). Second, the Ugandan government had been pressured into the talks and its commitment to a peaceful solution was limited. Museveni and his military commanders were content with keeping the LRA physically out of northern Uganda. Third, the negotiations exposed the lack of capacities at the United Nations level, where a department with no mediation experience (UN Office for the Coordination of Humanitarian Affairs, UNOCHA) was put in charge of the process (Conciliation Resources 2010, 19, interview with Jan Egeland).

The Juba process ended without Kony's signature and by mid December the militaries of Uganda, southern Sudan and the DRC – under the direction of the US military command AFRICOM – launched "Operation Lightning Thunder" (Johnson 2009; Schomerus and Tumutegyereize 2009; International Crisis Group 2010). At the same time, the situation in northern Uganda improved markedly, and no major incidence of violence has been reported since the Cessation of Hostilities agreement in 2006. About one million of those forced into camps for the past two decades were able to return to their homes, while another million remained in the camps for the internally displaced or were transitioning into temporary facilities (Justice and Peace Commission of the Archdiocese of Gulu 2008). In May 2009, Kony moved his rebel group north from Garamba National Park to the Central African Republic (CAR), extending violence into yet another border region (International Crisis Group 2010).

The intervention of the ICC has significantly altered the conflict and the incentives for the participants involved. Both the "shaming" pressure of transnational NGOs and the threat of prosecution have had an impact on the LRA and especially the individual fighters. During 2003 and 2004, low-ranking members of the rebel group took advantage of the amnesty offer, while the LRA experienced significant internal strife as it participated in the peace negotiations. But this indirect effort to target the LRA through principled mobilization and prosecution fundamentally failed to engage effectively with the local realities not only of many fighters, but also the communities affected by the violence. Effective socialization to end the violence would require a more relational approach that abandons the dominant frame of viewing the LRA as a cult. Instead, efforts of the international community were uncoordinated and often contradictory, including bribery, threats of prosecution, and a prevailing rhetoric of military power.

Conclusions

Understanding the significant shifts in the goals, strategies, and resource mobilization of the LRA requires an in-depth analysis of how violence is shaped by external influences and the transnational mechanisms facilitating interactions between the local and the global. The framing and justification of LRA violence shifted as a result of many, and often hegemonic external efforts to foster learning and emulation. The evidence suggests that social adaptation in the context of the Southern Sudanese conflict provides a compelling explanation for why heinous attacks on Acholi civilians increased during the early 1990s. Subsequent efforts by international human rights organizations to "shame" the LRA for its atrocities as well as an increased effort by the diaspora community to end the violence preceded an almost complete stop in the deliberate use of maiming and other extremely violent practices. But these socialization efforts based on non-relational diffusion mechanisms had little to no effect on continued abductions and the wanton pillaging of villages. The primary reason for this failure to end the violence was the reliance of human rights activists on abstract norms at the expense of a more meaningful engagement with local grievances.

In the context of resources, transnational mechanisms came in many different forms. Small arms supply by private sources was important throughout the conflict, except during the time the Sudanese government directly supported the LRA during the 1990s. Its strategy of self-sufficiency made the LRA independent from external pressures, although diaspora and other resources likely expanded its military capacity. The major shifts in the resource supply did affect the rebel movement, but often those shifts were countered by the availability of alternative sources, preserving the basic disruptive capacity of the LRA. For example, when the Sudanese military support ended and the LRA began to access very different resources in return for sitting at the negotiating table, it had no major impact on its military strategy and attacks on civilians, which resumed as soon as the negotiations were over.

Against the prevailing views of the LRA as an incoherent and irrational "cult," this chapter showed how a largely isolated rebel group interacts in sophisticated ways with its transnational environment through specific social mechanisms of relational diffusion, emulation, and situational learning. But the conflict was most effectively perpetuated not by the *presence* of any of the mechanisms discussed here, but by the *absence* of an effective strategy based on relational diffusion, which would have addressed the root causes of this conflict. The dominant frame of viewing the LRA as irrational not only privileged non-relational approaches and prevented any sustained efforts to engage directly with the group, but also played well into the Ugandan government's political interests of sustaining a low-key violent conflict in the region. Without greater coordination of different external efforts and by not taking seriously local grievances and the transnational mechanisms at work, the international community is perpetuating its repeated failures and neglecting a more promising effort that would shift attention to the effective protection of civilians and the resolution of the conflict.

6 Transnational advocacy networks, rebel groups, and demobilization of child soldiers in Sudan*

STEPHAN HAMBERG

Introduction

In 2001, the Sudan People's Liberation Army/Movement (SPLA/M), while still fighting a war against the Khartoum government, demobilized what they claimed was their entire population of child soldiers (International Crisis Group 2002 and UNICEF 2001a; see also Singer 2004). Why? Did transnational activists shame the SPLA/M into demobilizing their child soldiers? Did the SPLA/M demobilize child soldiers because they were losing the war, and such demobilization would improve their moral position in future peace negotiations? Alternatively, were they winning the war, and thus could afford to reduce the number of soldiers in their ranks? Did the international community, with the US in the driver's seat, threaten or promise the SPLA/M something in return for demobilizing the child soldiers? These are all potential rival explanations and mechanisms for why a non-state armed group would demobilize soldiers while fighting a war.

This chapter takes a different starting point to many of the empirical studies in this book. Rather than focusing on the influence of diasporas on rebel groups (Adamson, this volume), or how transnational insurgents influence rebel groups (Bakke, this volume), my chapter focuses on whether transnational human rights networks impact rebel groups. As Checkel (this volume) points out, the literature on transnational advocacy networks (TANs) has focused on peaceful transnational dynamics, but has rarely examined whether such networks are successful in reducing human rights violations during violent civil conflict. This literature has also focused almost exclusively on how TANs can influence state behavior, thus neglecting how transnational actors can

* Thanks to Jeffrey Checkel, Kristian Berg Harpviken, Kristin Bakke, Andrew Bennett, Matthew Evangelista, Scott Gates, Elisabeth Wood, Martin Austvoll Nome and the other project participants for their many helpful comments on the chapter.

influence other non-state actors (both domestic and transnational). It is these gaps my chapter addresses. More specifically, it seeks to examine if and how transnational human rights advocacy networks can influence the behavior of rebel groups fighting in civil wars.

Rebel groups violate human rights on a daily basis by targeting civilians, using rape as a weapon and recruiting child soldiers. Some of the most serious human rights violations today are committed by non-state armed groups (Policzer 2006). As most rebel groups do not have formal legal and political status, the international community lacks many traditional tools when trying to reduce human rights violations by them. However, transnational human rights advocacy networks have during the last decade increased efforts to change rebel group behavior. Naming and shaming is the preferred tactic TANs use when trying to influence state and rebel group behavior. However, few efforts have been made to assess the efficacy of this tactic when it comes to the behavior of rebel groups. In this chapter, I use the SPLA/M's decision to demobilize thousands of child soldiers in 2001 to test, among other alternative explanations, the power of TANs and naming and shaming as a mechanism to induce rebel groups to change behavior.

Even though child soldiers have been used in wars throughout history, only recently has this phenomenon received attention by policy-makers, non-governmental organizations (NGOs), international organizations (IOs), media, and academics. NGOs and networks of NGOs and IOs – so-called transnational advocacy networks – are primarily responsible for the recent attention being paid to the issue of child soldiers. Thus, TANs have been successful in bringing attention to a problem they care about. They have also been successful in pushing for the creation of international rules and conventions against the use of child soldiers.[1] These advocacy networks have been so successful that we now speak of a norm against the use of child soldiers. However, despite the attention the subject has received, the new international rules and conventions against the use of child soldiers, and the more informal norm against their use, the number fighting in ongoing conflicts remains high. Indeed, the main explanation for why the total number of child soldiers we observe is lower today than some years ago is that many wars involving significant numbers of them have recently ended (Gates

---

[1] See Achverina and Reich (2009) for a list of all international rules and conventions against the use of child soldiers.

and Reich 2009). This raises an interesting puzzle: why, despite the considerable effort by transnational advocacy networks, do we not observe that rebel groups involved in civil wars demobilize child soldiers? And more specifically, why did the SPLA/M demobilize child soldiers in 2001?

The answer is that transnational advocacy by US and Southern Sudanese civil society actors towards US politicians and the SPLA/M led the rebel group to demobilize child soldiers to secure financial and political support. What emerges from the empirics is a modified boomerang pattern (Keck and Sikkink 1998), in which Southern Sudanese church organizations linked up with US religious organizations, which in turn put pressure on key US policy-makers to not only get involved in the Sudanese civil war, but to explicitly support the SPLA/M's cause. Rather than a traditional boomerang pattern, where domestic groups seek international support to name and shame human rights violators, this case shows that the New Sudan Council of Churches (NSCC) pressured the SPLA/M from below, while simultaneously securing support for the rebel group from the US government.

The remainder of the chapter is divided into three sections. First, I discuss four different approaches to explaining the SPLA/M's decision to demobilize child soldiers; I elaborate the causal mechanisms at work and discuss specific testable implications for each. Second, I test which explanation best explains SPLA/M's decision to demobilize their child soldiers. I conclude in the final section.

Rebel groups and child soldiers

Why does a rebel group choose to demobilize child soldiers? Any attempt to understand whether transnational factors played a role, must first examine whether domestic or internal reasons explain the outcome of interest.

Most of the literature on child soldiers refers to demobilization as any instance of a former soldier leaving the army, either voluntary or not. However, if a soldier, whether a child or not, leaves an army without the consent of his or her officer, he or she has not been demobilized; rather, they have deserted.[2] Demobilization, as used in

---

[2] Desertion is normally associated with untrustworthy soldiers not committed to fighting. Though this is often looked upon with negative connotation, I imply no

this chapter, refers to a decision by the top leadership of a military organization to discharge soldiers from the unit and let them rejoin society as civilians. In other words, demobilization only occurs if the leadership decides that some troops can leave the armed group, and not when soldiers leave without its consent. By defining a demobilized soldier as any soldier who has left an armed group, we are likely to overestimate the effect naming and shaming has on rebel groups, as we would count both soldiers who have been asked to leave by the leadership, as well as soldiers who have escaped an armed group they have been forcefully recruited to join.

Conceptualizing demobilization as a decision by the leadership in armed groups to discharge soldiers has several benefits. First and as suggested above, it will increase the accuracy of the numbers of soldiers who are actually demobilized by armed groups. Second, if one wants to understand whether international pressure impacts rebel group behavior, one needs to look specifically at the leadership's behavior and not an individual soldier's decision to desert or not.

Though we lack precise data on the child soldiers that serve, or have served, in armed non-state groups, we know the number runs to several thousands. It is also clear that the number of children serving as soldiers increased significantly in the latter half of the twentieth century (Singer 2006). As transnational advocacy groups began to campaign against the use of child soldiers, scholars responded by trying to explain the causes of child soldiering. Any attempt to explain their demobilization must consider the causes of child soldier recruitment. For example, if the cause of the increased number of child soldiers is poverty, then a reduction in the number of child soldiers might be caused by a reduction in poverty. Thus, it is necessary to examine the mirror image of the causes of child soldier recruitment. The latter literature can be divided into explanations focused on the supply of children and those examining the demand for them. To date, most research has focused on supply-side arguments.[3]

Several supply-side explanations can explain the increase in child soldiers during the last 20–30 years. Summarizing qualitative research

such thing here. Many soldiers, and especially child soldiers, have been forcefully recruited and desertion in this case is more accurately described as legitimate escape.

[3] To my knowledge, Andvig and Gates (2009) are the first to separate the cause of child soldiering into demand- and supply-based explanations.

on child soldiers, Ames (2009) distinguishes three categories of causes. First are grievance factors: poverty, loss of parents, lack of economic opportunity, abuse at home, ethnicity, and political beliefs. Second are inducement factors: improved income opportunities, glory, and promises of future payoffs. Third are solidarity factors such as group cohesion, village networks, and friends (Ames 2009, 15). Peter Singer (2006, 37–56) argues that the increase in child soldiers can be explained by high poverty levels, large numbers of orphaned boys, new weapons technology, and increased availability of small arms, especially after the end of the Cold War and the break-up of the Soviet Union. Achverina and Reich (2009) propose an additional supply-side explanation. They argue that Singer's explanations fail to explain why some states and rebel groups have fewer child soldiers than others, and argue that variation in child soldier recruitment is better explained by whether armed groups have access to weakly secured refugee camps. According to Achverina and Reich, it is "the degree of vulnerability of children in refugee/IDP camps that ultimately explains their participation rates" (2009, 57).

This list of factors all focus on the supply-side. Children with more economic opportunities do not become child soldiers, secure refugee camps reduce the opportunity armed groups have in terms of recruitment, and fewer small arms make children less useful as soldiers, etc. It is clear that all of these factors can, and probably do, explain the increased number of child soldiers the world experienced in the last three decades. However, and this is the key point, none of these factors can explain variation in demobilization of child soldiers. For example, better protected refugee camps can explain why we do not see new recruitment of child soldiers, but it cannot explain why armed groups choose to demobilize child soldiers. To examine whether the causes of child soldier recruitment mirror the causes of child soldier demobilization, one must look at demand-side explanations.

Compared to the literature on supply-side explanations, relatively little has been written on the demand-side. Demand-side explanations assume that child soldiers and adult soldiers are substitutable goods (Andvig and Gates 2009). With technological innovations in small arms and a large amount of AK-47 machine guns available on the market, children are relatively efficient soldiers, and thus armed groups might prefer child soldiers if they are cheaper to recruit and maintain than adult soldiers. Andvig and Gates (2009) write that child soldiers can be beneficial to armed groups in several ways. Children are easier than adults to recruit – both forcefully or voluntary – and indoctrinate (see also the socialization mechanism discussed in Chapter 1). They require less monetary benefits to fight, are more likely to obey orders, desert less often, and are often less fearful than adult soldiers. As rebel groups are relatively poor, we should expect these groups to use the cheapest form of soldier. Andvig and Gates use the example of Mozambique and the Renamo rebel movement to show this dynamic. As long as Renamo was supported by South Africa, the group could pay adult soldiers to fight for them, but as South Africa withdrew its support, Renamo significantly increased its use of forced recruitment and of child soldiers (Andvig and Gates 2009, 85). Whereas supply-based explanations cannot be used to explain demobilization of child soldiers, these demand-based explanations and market-based mechanisms can.

As Andvig and Gates (2009) show in the case of Mozambique, support from outside actors can decrease a group's demand for child soldiers. In the case of demobilization, one can argue that a group might demobilize child soldiers if it receives financial support from outside actors. An armed group may also acquire new and larger revenue streams through access to natural resources or aid. Following the logic of this argument, one would expect that rebel groups who increase their revenues would demobilize their child soldiers.

Demand for child soldiers can also vary depending on dynamics on the battlefield. If an armed group is winning the war, its demand for soldiers will decline and we should expect them to demobilize soldiers – child or not – regardless of age. This is particularly true for insurgencies that need the support of the population after the war; demobilizing child soldiers might improve their image both at home and abroad. If battlefield dynamics and the need to improve their image explain SPLA/M's decision to demobilize child soldiers, we should expect to see them go to great lengths to publicize their actions.

How might transnational human rights mobilization affect these demand-side dynamics focused on material support and image? Here, a natural starting point is Keck and Sikkink's (1998) boomerang model, in which they argue that domestic rights organizations link up with international human rights groups, which – in turn – put pressure on the violator from the outside. This pressure takes the form of persuasion and socialization, that is, "reasoning with opponents, but also bringing pressure, arm-twisting, encouraging sanctions, and shaming" (Keck and Sikkink 1998, 17). Persuasion through reasoning can certainly take place, but the key to the boomerang model is to increase the material cost to the human rights violator, either through material sanctions or moral leverage. On the latter, shaming plays an important role; it insures the behavior of the violator is publicized and thus "held up to the light of international scrutiny" (Keck and Sikkink 1998, 23). The logic behind shaming is that governments, even those who are serial violators of human rights, "value the good opinion of others" (Keck and Sikkink 1998, 23). Being viewed as a pariah state is costly, not only in moral currency, but also materially. The goal of shaming campaigns is to increase both the material and moral cost of human rights violations.

Several studies have shown that the boomerang model in general, and naming and shaming more specifically, successfully explain positive changes in human rights behavior (Keck and Sikkink 1998; Risse, Ropp and Sikkink 1999a; Klotz 1995).[4] Yet, as Keck and Sikkink point out, certain conditions increase the likelihood of success. In particular, success is more likely when shaming is about issues that involve "bodily harm to vulnerable individuals, especially when there is a short and clear causal chain" (Keck and Sikkink 1998, 27).

The use of child soldiers is a human rights issue that has received significant attention during the last two decades; it also seems exceptionally well suited for a naming and shaming campaign as it is specifically about bodily harm to vulnerable individuals. Thus, testing whether the boomerang model in general and naming and shaming in particular can explain the SPLA/M's decision to demobilize child soldiers is imperative.

If the boomerang model and naming and shaming explains SPLA/M's decision, we should expect to see several things. These include domestic civil society groups linking up with international or transnational advocacy groups; consistent shaming over time of the SPLA/M; shaming campaigns directed at the SPLA/M's use of child soldiers specifically; and transnational advocacy groups calling for material sanctions on the SPLA/M.

---

[4] For a dissenting view, see Hafner-Burton 2008; 2009; Hafner-Burton and Ron 2009.

One potential explanation that has received relatively little attention in the literature on human rights advocacy is the use of promises or concessions (Hafner-Burton 2009; Katzenstein and Snyder 2009). Whereas the boomerang model and the naming and shaming mechanism focus on increasing the cost of certain behaviors, using promises or concessions would reward changes in behavior. Even though these might seem to be similar or just different sides of the same coin, they are in fact quite different. Most rebel groups fighting in civil wars have little to lose. After all, they are willing to risk their lives for some more or less specific purpose. Thus, being threatened with sanctions or moral shaming has limited effects on their cost-benefit calculations. Promises or concessions on the other hand, as long as they increase the chances for an insurgency to achieve its goals, can significantly improve the group's expected utility without imposing many costs. If the SPLA/M demobilized child soldiers because they were promised something, we should observe that the child soldiers are demobilized after the promise has been put forward, but before any actual concessions.

In sum, to assess which of the explanations best explains the SPLA/M's decision requires that we carefully examine the testable implications of each mechanism. Table 6.1 summarizes the alternative explanations and the observable implications associated with each one.

The Sudanese Liberation Army's decision to demobilize child soldiers in 2001

In October 2000, in a letter to Carol Bellamy, the Executive Director of UNICEF, the SPLA/M committed to demobilize all child soldiers from its ranks; by August 2001, the SPLA/M had done so. This is the only time a rebel group has demobilized most of its child soldiers while still fighting a civil war. Considering the amount of effort human rights organizations have put into reducing the use of child soldiers, this is an excellent case to assess whether their work has paid off.

To assess which of the alternative explanations best explains the SPLA/M's decision, I collected both primary and secondary data, including personal communication with policy-makers, scholars, and civil society activists. What emerged was a narrative that provides important confirming evidence for the concessions mechanism. Interestingly, the empirics also suggest that a modified boomerang model best explains

Table 6.1 *Alternative explanations and testable implications*

Explanation/mechanism	Observable implication I	Observable implication II	Observable implication III	Observable implication IV
Resource availability mechanism	Did the SPLA/M get access to new resources PRIOR to demobilization of child soldiers?	Did the SPLA/M substitute child soldiers with adult soldiers?		
Battlefield dynamics/ winning war improve image	Was the SPLA/M winning the war?	Did the SPLA/M publicize their decision to demobilize internationally?		
Boomerang/shaming	Did domestic human rights groups link up with international groups?	Did human rights organizations consistently shame the SPLA/M?	Were shaming campaigns directed at the SPLA/M's use of child soldiers specifically?	Did transnational advocacy groups call for material sanctions targeting the SPLA/M?
Concessions/promises	Did someone promise concessions to the SPLA/M in return for its demobilization of child soldiers?	Did the SPLA/M demobilize child soldiers prior to receiving any concessions?		

how the SPLA/M was able to secure promises of financial and moral support from the US government in return for a better human rights record. Indeed, it was a process in which transnational advocacy, information sharing, and persuasion played an important role. However, where the boomerang model predicts that naming and shaming will be the key mechanism behind behavioral change, my empirics indicate that they in fact played little role in the SPLA/M's decision to demobilize child soldiers.[5]

In what follows, I first give a brief overview of the civil war in Sudan, and the origin of the SPLA/M and its use of child soldiers. I then show how transnational advocacy, information sharing, and moral persuasion convinced US religious organizations and policy-makers to back the SPLA/M in their war against the Sudanese government. I also show that US policy-makers indirectly provided promises of material and moral support to the SPLA/M in return for a better human rights record.

The SPLA/M emerged in 1983, shortly after the beginning of the second civil war in Sudan. The movement published its manifesto in 1983, but to understand its demands and goals, we need to examine the underlying causes of the conflict. Both civil wars in Sudan have generally been classified as a war between Arabs and Africans, Muslims and Christians, or a war between North and South Sudan, but as Johnson (2003) shows, these labels are simplistic. He argues that the war(s) have been caused by the interaction of several factors. First, there are the patterns of governance established in Sudan long before independence. These patterns established "an exploitative relationship between the centralizing power of the state and its hinterlands or peripheries, mainly through the institutions of slavery and slave raiding, creating groups of peoples with lasting ambiguous status in relation to the state" (Johnson 2003, xviii). It is clear that these exploitative relations have taken place between Khartoum in the North and South Sudan, but the patterns have also been replicated in the North between Khartoum and Eastern and Western Sudan. Thus, it is not only a North vs. South question.

Second, there has been the recurring introduction of particularly militant brands of Islam and attempts to Islamize all of Sudan (Johnson

---

[5] Schmitz, this volume, similarly finds that naming and shaming had a limited effect on the behavior of the Lord's Resistance Army.

2003, xviii). These attempts to introduce Islam and sharia to the entirety of Sudan have severely limited the rights of non-Muslim citizens. Third, the first two factors have led to great inequalities in economic, educational, and political development between the center, Khartoum, and other regions, especially Southern, Western, and Eastern Sudan. Finally, these combined factors have led to a "failure to obtain a national consensus in either the North or the South concerning national unity, regional development, and the balance of power between the central and regional governments" (Johnson 2003, xix).

The interaction of these factors led to the first civil war that lasted from the early 1960s to 1972, and the second civil war that began in 1983, and hopefully ended with the signing of the Comprehensive Peace Agreement between the government in Khartoum and the SPLA/M in 2005.

The use of children or very young men as soldiers in Sudan has a long history. As early as the 1870s, the Turco-Egyptian army enslaved young boys, who at the ages of seven to ten, would work as "gun-boys" for the army. These "gun-boys" started out by carrying the guns for the soldiers, but, as they grew, they became soldiers themselves (Johnson 1992, referenced in Human Rights Watch [HRW] 1994). According to Johnson (1989), this practice has continued until recent times and includes the SPLA/M.

Reports about the SPLA/M's recruitment of child soldiers began to appear in the early 1990s (Amnesty International 1991; HRW 1994). According to these sources, the SPLA/M encouraged children to leave for refugee camps in Ethiopia, where they would receive education. On arrival, boys would quickly be separated from the other refugees and housed in separate buildings, where they received both regular education and military training. In 1994, HRW reported that:

there were some 17,000 boys in these camps, where, according to SPLA/M officers and the children themselves, they were given military training as well as education. They were removed from the camps for military service when the needs of the SPLA/M demanded.[6] (HRW 1994, 7)

As with most literature on child soldiers, no exact number exists on how many young people have fought for the SPLA/M. However, there

---

[6] On the militarization of refugees in civil war, see also Harpviken and Lischer, this volume.

is no doubt that the number is in the thousands. Indeed, the Coalition to Stop the Use of Child Soldiers reported in 2008 that the SPLA/M had demobilized nearly 20,000 child soldiers in the 2001–2006 period (Coalition 2008, 319).

In October 2000, UNICEF Executive Director Carol Bellamy met with the SPLA/M leadership in Sudan. During this meeting, the deputy chairman of the SPLA/M, Salva Kiir Mayardit, guaranteed in writing that the organization would no longer recruit soldiers under the age of 18, and that they would demobilize all soldiers under the age of 18. According to UNICEF, Salva Kiir told Bellamy that "for the good of our country we want all the children of southern Sudan out of the military" (UNICEF 2000). In the period February 23–27, 2001, the SPLA/M demobilized a total of 2,600 child soldiers ranging from 8–18 years of age (UNICEF 2001a). By August 2001, nearly 3,500 former child soldiers had been repatriated to their home communities with the help of UNICEF (UNICEF 2001b). In the following five years, another 17,000 child soldiers were demobilized by the SPLA/M (Coalition 2008).

In 2000 and 2001, the civil war was still ongoing, and prospects for peace, or victory by either side, seemed bleak. The SPLA/M's decision to demobilize child soldiers, and thus weaken their own fighting capability is a puzzle in need of an answer.

The answer is that the SPLA/M was promised US financial and moral support if they improved their human rights record. In May 2000, in a Senate Foreign Relations Committee hearing, Senator Sam Brownback stated that he would work to get the US government to provide Southern Sudanese opposition groups with non-lethal and humanitarian aid, provided they "have developed procedures to comply with verifiable international human rights standards" (US Senate 2000, S Hrg 106–662, 46).[7] However, Brownback's statement of support raises several important questions. Why would a US Senator publicly voice his support for a rebel group with a very questionable human rights record? And even if he did provide public support for the SPLA/M, did the SPLA/M know that they had supporters in the US

---

[7] The hearing was about the US Commission on International Religious Freedom's (CIRF) annual report, which listed a series of recommendations on how to improve religious freedom in Sudan. One of the recommendations was to support South Sudanese opposition forces in their fight against the Sudanese government; it is this recommendation Brownback supports and publicly promises to address.

Congress? And did this somewhat vague statement of support lead the SPLA/M to demobilize child soldiers? The answers to these questions are all related to transnational mechanisms of diffusion; indeed, the empirical evidence suggests that a boomerang effect – without a focus on the naming and shaming of the perpetrator – was key.

The first observable implication of the boomerang model is the presence of a domestic civil society that works to change the behavior of human rights violators. These domestic groups also need to link up with international actors to put pressure on the perpetrators from above. The evidence clearly shows that this was the case in Southern Sudan. Early on in the conflict, the SPLA/M worked hard to avoid the establishment of any independent civil society organizations, domestic or international. While there was a massive need for humanitarian assistance in the mid to late 1980s the SPLA/M did not allow any NGOs to establish bases in South Sudan (Rolandsen 2005, 30).

However, the SPLA/M's view of civil society changed towards the end of the 1980s and the early 1990s. In 1989, a large number of churches formed the New Sudan Council of Churches (NSCC). This group worked tirelessly for peace, justice, and human rights in Sudan (Brown 2008). Even though the SPLA/M originally was against the establishment of any independent civil society organization, they accepted the NSCC for instrumental reasons – as a sign of tolerance, to help them improve their standing internationally, and to increase Western states' willingness to provide aid (Rolandsen 2005, 76). The key goal of the NSCC was not to weaken the SPLA/M; rather, they worked against the "excesses and abuses conducted by the SPLA/M" (Brown 2008, 205). However, the NSCC's success was limited. Indeed, when the SPLA/M split into several groups in 1991, human rights abuses against the people of South Sudan reached new heights and the NSCC began to look outwards for support and increased leverage. In the US, they found a group of religious activists who were more than willing to help put pressure on the US government to get involved in the Sudan conflict.

NSCC's effort to link up with US activists led to a broad coalition of religious and anti-slavery human rights organizations. In turn, this coalition sought to influence US policy-makers and members of Congress, and pressured the US government to increase its involvement to end the Sudanese civil war. The coalition viewed the war there as between Islam and Christianity, as African versus Arab and as slave-owning versus slaves; it saw the Sudanese government as the perpetrator of grave human rights abuses, and almost uniformly supported the cause of the Southern Sudanese, if not the SPLA/M itself.[8] Key individuals in the coalition and amongst the policy-makers kept in close touch with the SPLA/M leadership, as well as with decision-makers in the Clinton and later the Bush White House; they sought to push President Bush into a policy of engagement and international mediation between the government in Khartoum and the SPLA/M (Hertzke 2004).

In retrospect, the shifts in US policy towards Sudan and the ongoing civil war are both surprising and counterintuitive. Whereas the Clinton administration had shown significant interest in Africa and peacemaking efforts, President Bush was expected to concentrate on domestic politics and certainly not to focus on the African continent. Indeed, the incoming Bush administration had made it clear during the campaign that it was reluctant to get involved in peacemaking or peacekeeping missions (Woodward 2006, 113). However, in the context of Sudan, their roles were reversed. The Clinton administration initiated sanctions against the Khartoum government, froze diplomatic relations, and finally bombed the Shifa pharmaceutical plant in August 1998. The Bush administration would follow a very different and surprising strategy towards the conflict in Sudan. Rather than isolating the government in Khartoum and continuing in the footsteps of Clinton, it engaged with both the government and the SPLA/M. It also set in motion a protracted peace process that ended in the Comprehensive Peace Agreement between the government in Khartoum and the SPLA/M (Woodward 2006).

To understand why the Bush administration pursued peacemaking in Sudan, we need to understand how the network of Christian human rights organizations and key legislators came together to put pressure on it.[9] President Bush was influenced by religious groups prior to taking office in 2001. Franklin Graham, a prominent Christian evangelical and the president and founder of Samaritan's Purse, a Christian relief and development organization with a long-standing commitment to Southern Sudan, met with presidential candidate Bush two days

---

[8] This is contrary to Uganda where, at least at the beginning of the insurgency, the LRA was seen as the villain and the Ugandan government as the savior (Schmitz, this volume).

[9] In the remainder of the chapter, I refer to this group of organizations and individuals as the US coalition.

prior to the 2000 election. In the meeting, Graham implored Bush to help bring peace to Sudan. According to Samantha Power, Graham told Bush, "[w]e have a crisis in Sudan. I have a hospital that has been bombed. I hope that if you become President you'll do something about it" (quoted in Power 2004).

Though Graham was an influential actor, he was not alone. A wide variety of religious groups, from all denominations had become interested in Sudan in the early to mid 1990s, and the groups were well connected in Washington DC. They linked up with both Republican and Democratic legislators and framed the debate about Sudan as one about religious freedom and modern slavery (Hertzke 2004).[10] Indeed, they participated in congressional hearings and hosted members of the NSCC, who themsleves participated in public events about the Sudanese civil war, met in private with key members of Congress, the State Department and the National Security Council.[11]

A large number of legislators joined the cause, but three individuals were particularly important: Senator Bill Frist, Senator Sam Brownback, and Congressman Frank Wolf.[12] All three had been interested in Sudan for several years prior to the election of Bush, but by combining their efforts with the religious movement, and by appealing to President Bush's ideas of compassionate conservatism, they now saw an opportunity to make some headway on the issue.

Of the three senior politicians, Frank Wolf had the longest ties to South Sudan. Wolf made his first trip there in 1989, where the SPLA/M arranged a celebration for his entourage, which included other US Congressmen; they left with newfound respect for John Garang, the leader of the SPLA/M (Press 1989). Between 1989 and 2001, Wolf traveled to Sudan 11 times, and was instrumental in passing the Sudan Peace Act. However, Wolf was not the only one traveling to South Sudan. Bill Frist traveled there several times in the late 1990s. In 1998, he went with Franklin Graham to visit Samaritan's Purse hospitals, where Frist, a surgeon, performed surgery in a bush hospital bombed

---

[10] For other examples of framing as a key transnational mechanism at work in civil war, see the chapters by Bakke, Schmitz, and Adamson, all in this volume.

[11] For example, the Institute on Religion and Democracy – a Washington-based NGO – hosted a number of NSCC members (personal communication, Faith McDonnell, IRD, December 3, 2010).

[12] These were the three most important individuals, but they got support from a range of Democrats both in the House and the Senate (Hertzke 2004).

by government troops (McGrory 2001). During his time in Sudan, he met John Garang several times, and subsequently called him a close friend (Frist 2009). In his memoirs, Frist writes that though he did not condone the behavior of the SPLA/M at all times, he certainly supported their cause (Frist 2009).

The story of Sam Brownback is not much different from that of the two others. Brownback visited South Sudan for the first time in 1997, and just as Frist, he called John Garang a friend (Brownback 2007). Frist, Brownback, and Wolf, together with other legislators, policymakers, and religious organizations were instrumental in putting pressure on both the Clinton administration in its later years and the Bush White House.

That the US coalition supported the cause of South Sudan and the SPLA/M is clear, and it is reflected in several pieces of legislation. In 1999, the US Congress passed its first resolution in six years regarding Sudan; it called for increased support for SPLA/M controlled territories, and condemned the government in Khartoum (Woodward 2006, 120–121). In December 2000, seven months after Brownback's public statement of support for the SPLA/M, and four months after its commitment to demobilize child soldiers, President Clinton signed legislation, sponsored by Senator Brownback, which allowed the US to give humanitarian aid to the SPLA/M directly (Public Law 106–570, Title V). In addition, the Sudan Peace Act passed the Senate in 1999, but was not signed into law before 2002. This was perhaps a sign that the coalition had more leverage on the Bush administration, which assumed power in early 2001.

In addition to public statements and legislation passed to support the SPLA/M, the Sudan Peace Act most clearly shows how the US coalition supported South Sudan and the SPLA/M. The Act requested the president to take an active role in resolving the conflict between the government in Khartoum and the SPLA/M. Perhaps most significantly, it stipulated a list of measures to punish the Sudanese government unless it participated faithfully in future peace negotiations. However, if the SPLA/M declined to participate or negotiate in good faith, there were no repercussions, except for the fact that the Sudanese government would not be penalized (Sudan Peace Act, 2002).

The evidence clearly shows that the NSCC worked to change the SPLA/M's behavior by linking up with international human rights actors. It also shows that these actors put pressure on the Sudanese government, through threats of sanctions and naming and shaming (Wolf 2001; Shea 1998), while offering SPLA/M promises of support if it improved its human rights record.

However, it is not clear whether US support for the South Sudanese people and the SPLA/M influenced the group to demobilize its child soldiers. Was the decision to demobilize a concession to religious human rights organizations and US supporters, in return for US financial and moral support during future peace negotiations? Answering this question requires that we show the SPLA/M was aware of the US offer of support.

Again, the empirics indicate that the SPLA/M was well aware of what was happening in the US at the time. For one, members of the NSCC, who discussed these issues directly with US policy-makers, also had direct contact with the leadership of the SPLA/M. According to Brown, by the late 1990s, the leaders of the NSCC "were granted personal access to Garang and his closest advisors and regularly utilized that ability to convey messages of personal accountability and immediate implementation of human rights and good governance" (Brown 2008, 210). In addition, the SPLA/M had representatives in Washington who were kept informed about US efforts as well. Indeed, according to Ted Dagne, a congressional staffer, the SPLA/M was even queried on the drafting of some legislation.[13]

In addition to the NSCC leadership's communication with the SPLA/ M, and the rebel group getting information directly from US policy-makers, several members of the US coalition also remained in close contact with the rebel movement. Deborah Fikes, the spokesperson for human rights in the Midland Ministerial Alliance, kept in close touch with John Garang (Brown 2008, 233). After the peace negotiations began in Kenya in 2002, the US coalition sent a message to Garang reminding him "that failure of the negotiations on grounds that leave room to assign blame for the failure on the SPLM could sharply undermine our capacity to maintain the support of the administration and the United States Congress on your behalf" (quoted in Brown 2008, 234). This letter was sent long after the SPLA/M's decision to demobilize its child soldiers, yet it shows how transnational communication and pressure took place between the US religious coalition and the SPLA/M.

---

[13] Ted Dagne, personal communication, December 1, 2010.

In sum, the empirics demonstrate that transnational advocacy took place between the NSCC, the US Church Alliance for Sudan, US policy-makers, and the SPLA/M. For sure, there is no "smoking gun" evidence that the SPLA/M's decision to demobilize was a direct response to US offers of support in exchange for an improved human rights record. However, it is clear that the US offered support in return for an improved human rights record, and that the SPLA/M knew about this offer. In addition, we know that Senator Brownback stated his support for such legislation on May 16, 2000, and that the SPLA/M committed – in writing – to demobilizing its child soldiers in October 2000. Thus, the key observable implication for the concessions mechanisms is satisfied, namely, that the offer was given prior to the SPLA/M's decision.

However, if the SPLA/M wanted to improve its human rights record, why did it choose to focus on child soldiers? I argue this decision makes sense for three reasons. First, it was something the SPLA/M leadership could do as it did not require the rank and file to change their behavior. As I discussed above, demobilization is an elite driven process. Even without complete command and control of its forces, the leadership of a rebel group can still make a decision to demobilize child soldiers and then follow through on that commitment. This does not mean that low-level officers will refrain from continuing to recruit or even re-recruit child soldiers; rather, it means the elites can control their soldiers enough to collect the children and demobilize them. Second, demobilizing child soldiers had symbolic value which could be verified at the time it occurred. Indeed, when the SPLA/M demobilized the first several thousand child soldiers, they did it in an official ceremony with both UN officials and news media present (UNICEF 2001a).

Third, the SPLA/M leadership knew that child soldiers were being frowned upon by the international human rights community. Increasingly during the 1990s, conventional human rights advocacy organizations had put a spotlight on child soldiers, by naming and shaming rebel groups and governments that recruited them.

On the last point, however, we need to assess the degree to which transnational advocacy networks specifically shamed the SPLA/M's use of child soldiers. Was the SPLA/M's use of them singled out? Did advocacy networks call for sanctioning the SPLA/M because of its use of child soldiers? There is in fact very limited evidence that naming and shaming played a direct role in the SPLA/M's decision. This is not to say that the SPLA/M was not shamed by international human rights organizations. They clearly were. Yet, this shaming has been sporadic and much of it came well before and after the SPLA/M's decision to demobilize its child soldiers.

The first report mentioning recruitment of child soldiers in Sudan was by Amnesty International in 1991 (Amnesty International 1991). It deals mainly with human rights abuses by the Sudanese government; human rights violations by the SPLA/M are given one page, and its recruitment of child soldiers, one sentence. In subsequent reports, Amnesty rarely discussed the SPLA/M's use of child soldiers. Human Rights Watch (HRW) has been more active in reporting on the SPLA/M's use of child soldiers. Out of 17 reports on Sudan from 1990 to 2001, the issue of child soldiers and the SPLA/M was mentioned in nine of them. Some of these reports were dedicated almost entirely to the issue of the SPLA/M and child soldiers (Human Rights Watch 1994, 1996). However, most were about human rights violations in general in Sudan; these would often include sections on the SPLA/M and child soldiers.

There was thus clearly some naming and shaming of the SPLA/M and its use of child soldiers in the mid 1990s, but other rebel groups have received much more attention in this regard.[14] In 1998, five international NGOs created the Coalition to Stop the Use of Child Soldiers, and much of the naming and shaming of states and rebel groups has since taken place through it. In the beginning, the Coalition sent out press releases and newsletters, and in 2001 it published the first of three global reports on the use and recruitment of child soldiers. In this first report, the SPLA/M was praised for demobilizing over 3,000 child soldiers in 2001, but was also criticized for having more than 7,000 child soldiers remaining in its ranks (Coalition to Stop the Use of Child Soldiers 2001).

Human rights organizations and the Coalition also pushed the UN to take a stronger stand on the issue. In 1997, the UN General Assembly passed a resolution which requested that the Special Representative of the Secretary General for Children and Armed Conflict submit annual reports to the General Assembly on how children are affected by armed

---

[14] Especially the Lord's Resistance Army in Uganda, the Revolutionary United Front in Sierra Leone and the LTTE in Sri Lanka. However, see Schmitz, this volume, for an assessment of how little shaming influenced the LRA's behavior.

conflict around the world (UN General Assembly 1997). In 1999, the Security Council passed resolution 1261, where it condemned the use and recruitment of child soldiers. The resolution urged relevant parties to demobilize them, and further urged UN agencies to make sure their personnel were trained and equipped to deal with war-affected children. Finally, the resolution requested the Secretary General to submit a report by July 31, 2000, on the implementation of the resolution.

In addition to Resolution 1261, the Security Council has passed five resolutions specifically dealing with the issue of child soldiers (UN Security Council 2000, 2001, 2003, 2004, and 2005). The most important of these are resolutions 1379 and 1460, which request the Secretary General to submit a report to the Security Council detailing which groups and states use and recruit child soldiers and to what degree these groups have made progress in demobilizing them. Looking at the timing of these resolutions, most were passed after the SPLA/M made its decision to demobilize child soldiers; it thus seems unlikely that any mentioning of the SPLA/M in reports from the Secretary General influenced its 2000–2001 decision to demobilize children.

Examining the UN's effort to name and shame the SPLA/M prior to 2000 reveals a rather weak effort. UN General Assembly Resolutions and notes by the Secretary General on the situation of human rights in the Sudan from 1993–2001 indicate that the UN largely focused on shaming the Sudanese government and only sporadically mentioned the SPLA/M by name regarding its use of child soldiers.[15] The first report on the human rights situation in Sudan by the Secretary General's Special Rapporteur was written in 1993 (UN 1993). It focused heavily on human rights abuses by the government of Sudan, but a brief section included SPLA/M abuses, including recruitment of child soldiers. Later reports by the Secretary General on the human rights situation in Sudan followed a similar pattern. In all the reports, the main focus is on human rights abuses by the Sudanese government, and only minor sections are related to the recruitment of child soldiers.

When recruitment of child soldiers is mentioned, it is almost always discussed as a problem relating to all parties in the conflict. For example, in the 1994 report, the Special Rapporteur wrote that:

---

[15] In 1993, the UN Commission on Human Rights asked the Secretary General to submit annual reports on the human rights situation in Sudan.

based upon his own findings and on information from several reliable sources, the Special Rapporteur considers the problem of unaccompanied minors and the use of children as soldiers by all parties to still be of great concern, despite repeated calls from the international community to put an end to this practice. (UN 1994, 14)

In terms of UN General Assembly Resolutions, the situation is very much the same. In all of the resolutions, the Sudanese government bears the brunt of the critique, and when the resolutions specifically deal with child soldiers the language is almost identical to that of the Secretary General's reports. As this shows, the shaming of the SPLA/M and its use of child soldiers by the UN has been weak and sporadic; the UN has mainly shamed the Sudanese government regarding its human rights record.

In sum, it is clear that the human rights advocacy networks successfully brought the issue of child soldiering to people's attention, and their work probably led the UN Security Council to pass several resolutions in the early to mid 2000s. However, neither the advocacy networks nor the UN consistently shamed the SPLA/M's use of child soldiers prior to its decision to demobilize them. Indeed, my analysis indicates that naming and shaming of the SPLA/M by mainstream human rights organizations played little or no direct role in its decision. In addition to the lack of consistent shaming by traditional human rights NGOs, South Sudan's supporters in the US never publicly named and shamed the SPLA/M for its human rights abuses, including the use of child soldiers.

Rather than name and shame the SPLA/M, the US coalition concentrated its energy on shaming the Khartoum government. Both publicly and behind closed doors, they focused on portraying the Sudanese government as the perpetrator of grave human rights abuses and the people of South Sudan as victims (Wolf 2001; Shea 1998). Indeed, they rarely publicly supported the SPLA/M. Instead they "focused on how to frame arguments to avoid getting bogged down in side battles that were hard to understand or justify, such as the nature of the SPLA/M" (Hertzke 2004, 274). However, the underlying sentiment was one of support and admiration for the SPLA/M and especially of John Garang (Belz 2001). Consider the following statement by one of the founders of the Church Alliance for Sudan, a key organization in the US coalition:

I was/am on the side of the SPLA/M, and loved and respected John Garang very much, as I do Salva Kiir, as well. I believe that they were fighting a righteous, just war to protect and defend the people of South Sudan and Nuba Mountains from jihad and the imposition of Shariah, annihilation of the black, African people of Sudan.[16]

The point was not that the US coalition was unaware of SPLA/M's human rights abuses; rather, they believed the Sudanese government's abuses were so much worse, that they focused exclusively on those.[17]

In a manner similar to the shaming argument, both the domestic level approaches discussed above also fail to explain the SPLA/M's decision to demobilize its child soldiers. In the period 1999–2001, the dynamics of the war are best characterized as a stalemate and the SPLA/M's financial situation had deteriorated rather than improved in the years prior to its decision.

The core claim with the battlefield dynamics argument is that insurgencies will demobilize child soldiers if they are winning the war. If this argument explains the SPLA/M's behavior, we would expect it to be doing well on the battlefield and to publicize its decision to demobilize child soldiers internationally and domestically. The situation on the ground in Sudan in 2000–2001 does not support this argument. By the early 2000s, the best description of the battlefield dynamics was a military stalemate, with the government having a somewhat stronger hand. In other words, the SPLA/M was neither winning nor losing the war when it made its decision to demobilize child soldiers. In addition, there is no evidence that the SPLA/M tried to publicize its decision to demobilize them. Except UNICEF press releases and NGO reports, I have not uncovered any news articles about its decision.

The second domestic explanation considers the financial strength of the rebel group. One would expect a rebel group to demobilize (relatively cheap) child soldiers when and if its financial situation improves, as this allows the group to recruit more efficient soldiers, even if they cost more. This was clearly not the case for the SPLA/M.

For the first 15 years of the conflict (1983–1998), the SPLA/M was financially supported by several of Sudan's neighbors. It maintained bases in Ethiopia and received support from both Eritrea and Uganda. According to Woodward, Eritrea, Ethiopia, and Uganda "felt

---

[16] Personal communication, August 27, 2010.
[17] Roger Winter, personal communication November 30, 2010. Winter is a former State Department and USAID employee. For more on him and his sympathies for the SPLA/M, see Griswold 2008.

threatened by the subversive activities of Islamists that they saw as sponsored by Sudan," and they were in a position to actively intervene (Woodward 2006, 94). All three countries were also encouraged by the US to support the SPLA/M in its fight against the regime in Khartoum. In 1996, the US sent $20 million in military aid to Eritrea, Ethiopia, and Uganda, and according to Woodward, it was expected that some of this money would end up with the SPLA/M (Woodward 2006, 98).

This support helped the SPLA/M improve its military position. Through major offensives in 1997–1998, people began to believe that the regime in Khartoum was nearing its end – but the SPLA/M did not manage to win the civil war. These hopes were further dashed when the war between Eritrea and Ethiopia broke out in 1998. At the same, the Ugandan government became increasingly involved with its own war against the LRA (Woodward 2006, 99). While the SPLA/M was losing financial and material support from outside states, the Sudanese government was able to increase its revenues through oil exploration. This improved its ability to fight the SPLA/M, while the latter retreated from places it had taken just years earlier.

Therefore, when the SPLA/M announced its decision to demobilize child soldiers in 2000–2001, it was much worse off financially than in 1997, and accordingly we would expect it to recruit child soldiers, not demobilize them. There is also no evidence that it recruited adult soldiers to substitute for the demobilized child ones.

Conclusion

The SPLA/M's decision to demobilize its child soldiers in 2001 was a major milestone. No armed group has demobilized the majority of its child soldiers while still fighting a civil war. The empirical analysis shows that transnational advocacy by US and Southern Sudanese civil society actors towards US politicians and the SPLA/M led the rebel movement to demobilize child soldiers to secure financial and political support from the United States. Southern Sudanese church organizations linked up with US religious organizations, which in turn put pressure on key US policy-makers to not only get involved in the Sudanese civil war, but to explicitly support the SPLA/M. Rather than a traditional boomerang pattern, where domestic groups seek international support to name and shame human rights violators, this case shows that the New Sudan Council of Churches pressured the SPLA/M from below, while simultaneously securing support for the rebel group from the US government.

The fact that the SPLA/M demobilized child soldiers to secure US support speaks to the importance that positive incentives played in its decision. Even though it is difficult to draw generalizations from this one case study, my findings support Katzenstein and Snyder's (2009) argument that human rights organizations need to pay more attention to the incentives that rights violators face. Naming and shaming can impose significant costs on actors, but for rebel groups or other non-state armed groups, these costs rarely outweigh the benefits of future violations.

7 | Conflict diffusion via social identities: entrepreneurship and adaptation*

MARTIN AUSTVOLL NOME AND
NILS B. WEIDMANN

The grand narratives of armed civil conflicts – through which participants explain their actions and observers identify the clashing interests – link them to social identities. In El Salvador, 1992, insurgents invoked the distinction between the propertied and the landless (Wood 2003, 1–2); in Cyprus, 1974, with a Turkish intervention looming, the leader of the Turkish-Cypriot community emphasized the indivisibility of Turkishness in Turkey and Cyprus (Markides 1977, 33); and in Chechnya, 2007, one insurgent leader described as paramount the opposing identities of believers and unbelievers (Bakke, this volume).

In the effort to understand the mechanisms that lead armed civil conflicts to diffuse from one country to another, it is therefore appropriate to give attention to conflict diffusion via social identities. How might particular social identities diffuse across international boundaries?

Social identities are social categories that can be characterized by several sorts of content. Abdelal et al. (2009, 19) argue that social identities may contain sets of goals shared by members of the group, particular views of other social identities, and worldviews or understandings of conditions and interests. We focus on a fourth type of identity content: its constitutive norms. Abdelal et al. (2009, 19) describe these as the formal and informal rules that define group membership. In other words, the constitutive norms of a social identity are its boundary-drawing properties. By defining the boundaries of social identities, constitutive norms should be of particular interest for students of conflict. By modeling the transnational diffusion of norms, we seek to capture one aspect of the diffusion of armed civil conflicts.

* For valuable comments on earlier versions of this chapter, we thank Andy Bennett, Jeff Checkel, Kristian Skrede Gleditsch, Matthew Hoffmann, Jay Lyall, Idean Salehyan, and the members of the Working Group on Transnational and International Facets of Civil War, Centre for the Study of Civil War, Peace Research Institute Oslo.

Diffusion is notoriously difficult to observe. The diffusion of conflicts, as the diffusion of other phenomena, is a process, not an outcome (Elkins and Simmons 2005). Armed civil conflicts have diffused, rather than merely occurred in sequence, when the onset of one conflict is a consequence of processes set in motion by conflicts elsewhere. As Checkel argues in his introduction to this volume, the emphasis on process suggests that diffusion is a large class of mechanisms linking one civil conflict with another. It is understandable then that the comparativist literature on conflict diffusion struggles with good measures, often settling for measures of its outcome, or for proxies of scope conditions. Diffusion is assumed.

In line with this book's ambition to examine transnational conflict processes, we offer an alternative way to explore mechanisms of diffusion, using agent-based modeling. This technique allows us to posit that particular mechanisms of diffusion are at work, to model them closely, and to assess the plausibility of such mechanisms by using computer simulation. If the results of these simulations resemble empirical patterns of conflict diffusion, then the underlying mechanisms are candidate explanations of diffusion.

As we develop our model, we begin from the understanding that conflict diffusion via social identities is a transnational process. The importance of transnational factors in civil wars is well established (Checkel, this volume). At the same time, a strong research tradition on transnationalism in international relations (IR) theory could contribute much to conflict research. We thus turn to this transnationalist literature, positing two alternative mechanisms of diffusion and compare how they perform. One mechanism involves norm-driven individuals who seek to behave appropriately in what they define as their social context. We observe the populations in two separate countries and the effect of transnationalizing the social context in which individuals interact. We call this mechanism "social adaptation." The other mechanism involves single individuals – norm entrepreneurs – who have the power to alter people's repertoires of imaginable behavior. Via this mechanism, norm entrepreneurs affect the latent norms in a society. We call this mechanism "norm entrepreneurship."

By using the technique of agent-based modeling, we are able to model social adaptation and norm entrepreneurship directly, and assess their consequences in an environment of norm-driven individuals. Rather than assuming their operation when observing the outcome of diffusion or its scope conditions, we know that these mechanisms operate at the outset, and then explore their effects. From a modeling perspective, our objective is simple. We seek to create an abstract heuristic model designed to explore some fundamental logics of diffusion. Our aim is to develop a model that generates macro-patterns that qualitatively match empirical patterns uncovered in this volume (and elsewhere). Anecdotal evidence suggests that both social adaptation and norm entrepreneurship are plausible mechanisms of diffusion.

One such anecdote leads into the remainder of this chapter: We begin the next section by briefly describing the spread of Kurdish nationalist contention from Turkey to Germany to illustrate the sort of diffusion we explore. In the same section, we review the mechanisms of social adaptation and norm entrepreneurship. The subsequent section makes the case for agent-based modeling, explains its basics and logic of inference. The final two sections present our model in full. First, we model the emergence of a norm in a single country. Second, we link two such countries: one source country from which norms can diffuse, and one recipient country that might be affected by developments in the source country. We present three scenarios: norm emergence in two closed polities, diffusion by transnationalized social adaptation, and diffusion by transnationalized norm entrepreneurship. We then discuss our observations by linking them to evidence from other chapters in the book, and by suggesting ways in which our model might add to the understanding of their empirics. We conclude by noting that norm entrepreneurship seems to be the more robust mechanism of diffusion, and by pointing to possible model extensions.

Conflict diffusion as identity diffusion

As an example of the phenomenon we explore, consider the immigrant communities in Germany with origins in Turkey. Up until 1996, Germany became a new arena of sometimes violent activism in the armed civil conflict between the Workers' Party of Kurdistan (PKK) and the Turkish state. This diffusion of conflict manifested itself in events such as large-scale demonstrations, hunger strikes, the targeting of Turkish-owned businesses for attack, and threats of violence against Germans in efforts to pressure the German government to promote the PKK's cause (Lyon and Ucarer 2001). Prior to this escalation of activism, the immigrant community from Turkey experienced a change in social identities in which many immigrants with some Kurdish ancestry began to view themselves as Kurdish and sympathize with Kurdish separatism. Lyon and Ucarer (2001, 932–933) characterize this change as a "development of the collective insurgent consciousness." This outcome was a consequence of the diffusion of social identity, including its constitutive norms. It involved a process where the social context of the PKK – Turkey conflict was transnationalized, and in which norm entrepreneurs were active.

By the time the recruitment of Turkish guest workers was halted in 1973, about 900,000 Turkish citizens had settled in Germany (Leggewie 1996, 81). Although many of them had some Kurdish ancestry, only a few called themselves Kurds (Leggewie 1996, 81). In a change away from economic migration, Kurds began in the 1980s to apply for political asylum in Germany. Their reasons for migrating were political to a larger extent than before, and among the immigrants were dedicated supporters of Kurdish separatism, as well as members of the PKK (Leggewie 1996, 81; Lyon and Ucarer 2001, 931). The political liberties in Germany allowed immigrants to discuss the Kurdish question openly (Leggewie 1996, 82); it was now "possible to explore and express Kurdish cultural and linguistic identity" (Lyon and Ucarer 2001, 933). Kurdish cultural associations became arenas where a transnationalized social context could manifest itself in the consolidation of Kurdish identity (Lyon and Ucarer 2001, 933). Research on the socialization of new group members suggests that individuals are more likely to adopt in-group norms when they have few prior ingrained beliefs, and when they interact with authoritative members of the in-group (Checkel 2001). When economic migrants of Kurdish origin were exposed to Kurdish nationalism in such small-group settings, one might imagine that they were likely objects of socialization into the norms of Kurdish nationalist identity. The norm entrepreneurs in this process were the PKK, who infiltrated cultural associations to spread their version of Kurdish nationalism (Leggewie 1996; Lyon and Ucarer 2001). In sum, the diffusion of social identities from Turkey to Germany was a consequence of the transnationalization of the social context of the PKK – Turkish conflict and of the activities of PKK norm entrepreneurs. In its wake, Germany experienced sometimes violent events in the conflict between the PKK and Turkey.

The diffusion of Kurdish nationalist activism from Turkey to Germany raises not only the question of diffusion mechanisms; the case also raises the question of how social identities and armed civil conflicts are linked. By modeling the diffusion of social identities' constitutive norms, we model the diffusion of rules that determine group membership. In other words, we model the diffusion of social identities' boundary-drawing properties. Work on how the boundaries of social identities relate to violent civil conflict is too extensive to review in full here. However, we need to make clear some basic assumptions.

Had violence in civil conflicts followed the fault lines of readily observable social identities, then the task for social scientists would have been an easy one. Our model depends not on a one-to-one association between social identities and the behavior of perpetrators and targets in civil wars. Rather, we assume that social identities provide the grand narratives within which violence unfolds and is perpetuated. These are narratives that elites, perpetrators, and victims take part in prior to, during, and after violence. By linking violence to social identities, both perpetrators and victims take part in the coding of armed civil conflicts. One must expect actors in civil wars to be influenced by prevailing interpretive frames that in turn are supplied by changing social identities (Brubaker and Laitin 1998, 428; see also the discussion of framing in Bakke, this volume). We follow Brubaker and Laitin (1998) when they argue that conflict and violence should be analyzed as separate phenomena.

That is not to say that social cleavages and violence are unrelated. By combining the concepts of cleavage and alliance, Kalyvas (2003) is able to link conflict and violence. To Kalyvas, a cleavage is "a symbolic formation that simplifies, streamlines, and incorporates a bewildering variety of local conflicts" (Kalyvas 2003, 486); it is the structure that links actors at the center with action on the ground. Actors at the center provide resources and a context of impunity that allow actors in the periphery to let a variety of local cleavages unfold in violence. Center and periphery are linked by alliance. As Kalyvas puts it "[the concept of] alliance allows us to see civil wars as concatenations of multiple and often disparate local cleavages, more or less loosely arrayed around the master cleavage" (Kalyvas 2003, 486). The constitutive norms that define the boundaries of social identities provide the raw material for such master cleavages. As such, particular social identities come close to being a necessary condition for armed civil conflict. Any account of the diffusion of civil conflicts must therefore include an account of the diffusion of social identities.

Social adaptation and norm entrepreneurship

Social adaptation and norm entrepreneurship are our two candidate mechanisms of conflict diffusion. Recalling Checkel's brief survey of the literature on causal mechanisms (this volume), social adaptation and norm entrepreneurship are pathways or processes by which the diffusion of social identities is produced (see also Gerring 2007b, 178); they are "relational and processual concepts ... not reducible to an intervening variable" (Falleti and Lynch 2009, 1149). By using agent-based modeling, we are able to closely approximate these relational and processual phenomena.

Social adaptation and norm entrepreneurship are by no means the only mechanisms of conflict diffusion. Bennett's (this volume) taxonomy of mechanisms is helpful in assessing the ground we do and do not cover. Bennett classifies social mechanisms along two dimensions that generate a reasonably exhaustive taxonomy. One dimension distinguishes mechanisms that are rooted in power, functional efficiency, and legitimacy. By focusing on the constitutive norms of social identities, we limit the paper at the outset by not considering explanations based on power or functional efficiency. Since norms are standards of appropriate behavior, they evoke notions of legitimacy. In Bennett's 12-quadrant property space it is only the top row that we are considering.

A second dimension of the taxonomy classifies mechanisms by their direction of interaction between structures and agents: agents interacting with agents, structures affecting agents, agents affecting structures, or structures relating to structures. As we conceive of them, social adaptation is a structure-to-agent mechanism, and norm entrepreneurship is an agent-to-structure mechanism.

Social adaptation is a mechanism by which individuals alter their behavior to conform with the norms of their social context. People are norm-driven. Individuals change their conduct once they have developed a notion of the standards of behavior in their society. As such it is a structure-to-agent mechanism. A society develops an intersubjective understanding of behaviors that are more and less desirable, and in turn, individuals adapt to these understandings. As Bennett (this volume) puts it in his taxonomy, norms work as an enabler and constraint on action. Norms that are constitutive of social identities are in this manner internalized or habituated in a process where norms bias choice. In the words of Abdelal et al. (2009, 21), "certain behaviors are consciously ruled out or discounted as inappropriate for one's identity."

By labeling this mechanism "adaptation," we wish to distinguish it from related mechanisms such as mimicking and emulation. Mimicking is the mechanism by which a novice copies the behavioral norms of a group as a reaction to uncertainty in situations where the costs of not fitting in are high (Johnston 2008, 45). In contrast, social adaptation is a mechanism not reserved for novices. We expect individuals that are well established in a society to continuously try to fit in. Emulation, in turn, is the "conscious and careful search for exemplars and success stories, a dissection of the reasons for their success, and the application of these lessons to the maximization of some specific expected utility" (Johnston 2008, 45–46). Where emulation is a search for methods, procedures, or tactics, social adaptation is a move towards appropriateness; where emulation emphasizes highly rational maximizing behavior, social adaptation involves less utility-maximizing processes of internalization and habituation.

In dictionary usage, adaptation is described as "adjustment to environmental conditions," or the "modification of an organism or its parts that makes it more fit for existence under the conditions of its environment" (Merriam-Webster), and as "the process of changing to suit different conditions" (Cambridge).[1] In ecology, adaptation is understood as "the adjustment or changes in behavior, physiology, and structure of an organism to become more suited to an environment."[2] In an analogous social environment, this is precisely the mechanism we seek to capture. Might social adaptation be a mechanism of the diffusion of social identities?

We ask the same question of norm entrepreneurship. Norm entrepreneurship is a mechanism by which individuals who wish to influence social identities, and who have some platform from which to propagate their views, attempt to affect the norms in a society. Norm entrepreneurship is an agent-to-structure mechanism. Individual agents, often with an institutional platform, attempt to influence the

---

[1] www.merriam-webster.com/dictionary/adaptation (accessed July 31, 2010); http://dictionary.cambridge.org/dictionary/british/adaptation (accessed July 31, 2010).
[2] www.biology-online.org/dictionary/Adaptation (accessed July 31, 2010).

standards of appropriate behavior that are held intersubjectively in a population.

One often associates norm entrepreneurs with Finnemore and Sikkink's (1998) work on norm emergence in the society of states. To Finnemore and Sikkink, norm entrepreneurs' methods of choice are persuasion and framing; they "attempt to convince a critical mass of states ... to embrace new norms" (Finnemore and Sikkink 1998, 895; see also Payne 2001, 38–39). Many scholars of transnationalism have found it useful to classify certain actors as norm entrepreneurs. Recent examples include Williams (P. Williams 2007, 255), who traces how several actors have engaged with the African Union to affect its range of legitimate policy options; Capie (2008), who recounts how international bureaucracies such as the United Nations Department of Disarmament Affairs and single states such as Canada and Japan have acted as norm entrepreneurs to affect the Association of Southeast Asian Nations' policies on small arms; Rushton (2008), who describes Boutros Boutros-Ghali as an erstwhile norm entrepreneur in his efforts to promote democratic governance when serving as General Secretary of the United Nations; Mantilla (2009), who analyzes efforts to affect the human rights practices of transnational corporations; and Saurugger (2010), whose work is on the participation of civil society in EU decision-making processes. This work may be varied, but the listing of recent applications of the norm entrepreneur concept suggests they are safely situated within the realms of international and transnational organizations. By modeling the activities of norm entrepreneurs in the context of conflict diffusion, we transpose norm entrepreneurship to the field of conflict research.

One might reasonably ask who these norm entrepreneurs are. Finnemore and Sikkink (1998, 896) describe them as "agents having strong notions about appropriate or desirable behavior in their community," whose motivations are "difficult to explain ... without reference to empathy, altruism, and ideational commitment" (898). A close analogy to norm entrepreneurs in the literature on conflict diffusion is Kuran's (1998) "ethnic activists," who are "self-motivated to promote public ethnic behavior among co-ethnics."

Where Finnemore and Sikkink's norm entrepreneurs target a society of states with a limited number of members, our norm entrepreneurs operate in societies of individuals whose numbers are much greater.

They have less of an opportunity to engage directly with people, and are therefore less able to use persuasion in an interactive process. Instead, our norm entrepreneurs have a one-directional impact. By propagating their views about social identities, they affect people's possibilities of action by altering the repertoire of imaginable behavior for individuals in the target audience. Norm entrepreneurs do not affect behavior directly. Rather, they introduce latent behavioral norms. By reaching some or all individuals in the target audience simultaneously, norm entrepreneurs create latent possibilities of action that are present in the entire group of receptive individuals. These possibilities of action only manifest themselves in people's behavior when they begin to observe an emerging norm. Through norm entrepreneurship, the mass of individuals is thus changed, but the change only manifests itself in behavior if people deem the new standard to be the most appropriate one. Therefore, in order to result in changed behavior, norm entrepreneurship depends on subsequent social adaptation.

We consider neither structure-to-structure nor agent-to-agent mechanisms. The former is most easily justified. The method of agent-based modeling precludes structure-to-structure mechanisms because it depends on specifying interaction on the micro level. True, agent-based models can link structural developments. These are the "emergent phenomena" in modeling language. However, agent-based models can only link structural developments via mechanisms that connect individual agents. Those with a commitment to methodological individualism would approve (see for example Coleman 1986; Hedström and Swedberg 1998). Rooted in Coleman's macro-micro-macro model of collective social action, Hedström and Swedberg (1998, 21–22) argue that social phenomena on the macro level can only be linked via three sorts of mechanisms: situational mechanisms through which a macro state influences individual actors; action-formation mechanisms that relate individuals to each other; and transformational mechanisms through which individuals' actions generate new macro states. To Coleman and Hedström and Swedberg there are no structure-to-structure mechanisms. Whether one agrees with them or not, it remains true that agent-based modeling is only compatible with notions of social life in which individual actors hold prominence.

The fact that we leave out agent-to-agent mechanisms has less of a methodological rationale. Agent-to-agent mechanisms such as persuasion, socialization, complex learning, and coercion, are probably important micro processes when social identities spread from one country to another. They are mechanisms that should be explored in agent-based models of norm diffusion. However, we exclude them from the present model primarily to retain its simplicity and replicability. By starting with the most simple model and then adding features step by step, it allows us to incrementally make it more complex and not lose sight of its foundations. In this chapter, we add a second country to a base model of only one country. This move allows us to introduce two features. We transnationalize the social context in which social adaptation occurs, and we turn norm entrepreneurs into transnational agents of norm diffusion. In order to improve the explanatory value of the model, there is little doubt that we should add agent-to-agent mechanisms in future work.

The case for agent-based modeling

In a volume that arguably privileges empirical work, how might agent-based modeling contribute to an understanding of conflict diffusion? Agent-based modeling has advantages because diffusion can be difficult to observe, and because it forces the modeler to carefully specify and operationalize possible mechanisms of diffusion. Mechanisms are difficult to observe by any standard. Indeed, empirical researchers do not observe mechanisms directly, but at best their observable implications (Checkel, this volume; Hamberg, this volume, Bennett, this volume).

Some work on conflict infers diffusion from rather indirect proxies. Its focus is not on diffusion mechanisms as such, but their conditions, typically means of communication and determinants of receptivity. Thus Hill and Rothchild (1986) observe that domestic conflict is more likely when there is a certain level of conflict in the region (from which conflict can diffuse) and when there is a greater level of ethno-linguistic fractionalization (meant to suggest a latent sense of group identity), when the per capita number of radios is greater (indicating means of communication as a condition for diffusion), and when the country has experienced earlier domestic conflict (designed to indicate receptivity). Buhaug and Gleditsch (2008) observe that domestic conflict is more likely when there is an ongoing domestic conflict in a contiguous country, suggesting that it proxies a condition for diffusion because reference examples and media attention primarily focus on events in nearby states (Buhaug and Gleditsch 2008, 220). Finally, both Buhaug and Gleditsch and Forsberg (2008) find that domestic conflict is more likely when groups can be ascribed the same ethnic identity as cross-boundary groups in a conflict zone. Transnational ethnic ties would seem to be understood as a scope condition of diffusion, not an observable implication of any diffusion mechanism as such.

In short, the difficulties of observing mechanisms of diffusion lead some to measure conditions for diffusion, and not any observable implications of diffusion mechanisms. Agent-based modeling enjoys an advantage in this regard because it allows us to operationalize and measure specific mechanisms in a virtual environment.

By requiring the modeler to specify how individual agents interact, agent-based modeling has the added advantage of inducing the explicit theorization of diffusion mechanisms. After beginning deductively and developing an informal model of the workings of social adaptation and norm entrepreneurship as mechanisms of diffusion, we then develop an agent-based model by proceeding in four steps (Hoffmann 2008, 188–189). In general terms, we first create artificial agents – individuals in two virtual countries – endowing them with characteristics such as particular behavioral rules, the ability to perceive their environment, and the ability to take decisions and act on them. These characteristics are simply a conjecture about how social adaptation and norm entrepreneurship work on the micro level to generate the foundations of conflict on the macro level. We then define the social environment in which our agents interact. Third, we simulate histories in this world, and record these histories in real time – a process analogous to retrospectively gathering data from real-world histories. Finally, we analyze these histories by graphic means and statistical comparisons.

Generally speaking, the purpose of agent-based modeling is to understand macro-level patterns or processes by locating their generative social mechanisms (Cederman 2001, 17). In the metaphorical language of Epstein and Axtell, agent-based simulations are like "*laboratories*, where we attempt to 'grow' certain social structures in the computer – or *in silico* – the aim being to discover fundamental local or micro mechanisms that are sufficient to *generate* the macroscopic social structures and collective behaviors of interest" (Epstein and Axtell 1996, 4, emphasis in the original). Agent-based modeling looks at first glance like a purely quantitative method, since the agents' characteristics and behavioral rules are represented by numbers. However, as Hoffmann (2008, 188) emphasizes, agent-based modeling is at least as much a qualitative method. Its lack of reliance on closed-form analytical solutions and its possibility of generating many different simulation histories render it complementary to game-theoretic approaches and large-N statistical analyses. Thus, it is much better suited to represent notoriously fuzzy concepts such as emotions or norms, which have traditionally been the domain of qualitative researchers. By adding a level of higher theoretical precision to purely verbal accounts, the simulation allows us to examine more closely the implications of a theoretical framework.

The inferences one might draw from such a procedure are modest, but non-trivial. By beginning with an informal model of the workings of social adaptation and norm entrepreneurship, agent-based modeling offers a means to assess the logic of that verbal model (Hoffmann 2008, 196). Should we be able to grow the diffusion of social identities from our conjectures about the workings of the mechanisms, then we would have a "candidate explanation" of diffusion. Such candidate explanations could be a useful theoretical starting point for subsequent empirical research.

A model of norm emergence

We present the model of the diffusion of social identities in two steps. In this section, we first describe how we model the mechanisms of social adaptation and norm entrepreneurship within one country. Neither mechanism is necessarily transnational, so for clarity we first describe how they work in a "closed polity" setting (Gleditsch 2007). In the next section, we then simulate how social adaptation and norm entrepreneurship might work as mechanisms of diffusion by transnationalizing the context in which they operate. It is by adding a second country and linking the two societies with our candidate mechanisms that we can assess how social adaptation and norm entrepreneurship might work to diffuse social identities.

To model the emergence of the constitutive norms of social identities in a single society, we need a social environment in which agents are norm-driven. Hoffmann (2008) provides such an environment. We adopt his model of norm emergence in single societies as a foundation for developing our model of diffusion. Hoffmann applies his model to exploring Finnemore and Sikkink's (1998) theory of the norm life cycle among states in the international system. In other words, Hoffmann conceives of his agents as countries. In contrast, we think of the agents as individuals. Let us describe how we replicate Hoffmann's model for any one country.

The essential conjecture of the model is that agents are norm-driven. Via social adaptation, agents seek to behave appropriately according to a standard that is set intersubjectively, that is, by the collective behavior of their society at any one time. In our computer simulation, agents make their behavior known to all other agents by picking a number between 0 and 100. This is not a random pick. Agents are limited at any one time by an individual repertoire of imaginable behavior. This repertoire is operationalized as a set of three norms, or rules. Representing the repertoire by exactly three rules is a modeling choice we adopt from Hoffmann (2008) – there is no theoretical reason to use this number, and others are possible. These three rules come from a universe of seven rules, where rule 0 limits behavior to the range 0–10, rule 1 limits behavior to 15–25, rule 2: 30–40, rule 3: 45–55, rule 4: 60–70, rule 5: 75–85, and rule 6: 90–100. For example, if an agent at a particular time has a repertoire of imaginable behavior that consists of rules 2, 4, and 5, it means that the number representing its behavior can only come from the ranges 30–40, 60–70, or 75–85. Agents select their behavior from only one of their three rules. Because they seek to adapt to their environment, this is the rule that has proven to be closest to the collective behavior. Agents keep the other two rules private – that is, they do not reveal them to the remaining agents in their society.

The model's logic of social appropriateness posits that agents choose their behavior in line with the behavior they observe in the population. Since agent behavior in the model is driven by rules, agents choose their rules based on how well they match observed collective outcomes in the agent population. That is, rules that have proven successful in keeping the agent close to the behavior of the population are retained, whereas others are suppressed. The model incorporates this by letting agents keep "success scores" for each of the three rules they currently have in their repertoire. Agents reward or penalize each rule – both the public and the private ones – according to how close the rules turn out to be to the collective outcome, which is simply the average behavior across all agents (the mean across all chosen behaviors, each in the

[0,100] interval). From time step to time step, agents behave according to the rule with the best score, and at set intervals they replace the worst performing rule with a fresh rule from the universe of seven rules.[3] In this way, social identities change or are habituated in a process where norms bias choice. That is, certain behaviors are discounted as inappropriate for one's identity (Abdelal et al. 2009, 21).

In Hoffmann's model, however, perception of the collective outcome is not perfect. That is, agents do not use the true average behavior of the population, but a slightly blurred value of it. This implementation is meant to capture the uncertainty that surrounds agents' perceptions. Hoffmann presents two arguments for why this imperfect social perception is likely to occur: First, lack of information, since some agents may be wrongly perceived or not at all, and second, the complexity of the social environment which makes it difficult for agents to assess the predominant behavior (Hoffmann 2008, 193). When people develop an image of the society in which they live, they do so based on clues from selective sources, and then aggregate up. This process of aggregation leads to truer images in less complex societies and distorted images in more complex societies. Systematic distortion such as media bias and censorship contribute to complexity. The level of noise is implemented in the model as a confidence interval around the true population behavior: if noise is high – and the interval large – agents perceive a randomly chosen value from within this interval, rather than the true outcome.

When norm entrepreneurs are present, that is, when certain agents seek to define social identities in particular ways, they enter the model by proposing a rule that agents adopt with a certain probability, and privately. For example, if a norm entrepreneur promotes rule 6, some agents adopt the behavioral range 90–100 as one of their two private rules. This has no immediate impact on collective behavior, but a norm that is latent for some agents from that point can emerge via social adaptation. Norm entrepreneurship thereby involves the simultaneous altering of agents' repertoires of imaginable behavior. Agents behave

---

[3] The fact that we program our agents to keep "success scores" and follow rules according to how well they perform is not intended to suggest they are instrumentally rational. Our agents are norm-following. We simply need some way to operationalize the difference between more and less appropriate behavior. Following Hoffmann in attaching scores to the different rules is a sensible way of operationalizing appropriateness.

according to the new rule – and thereby make it public – only if they expect it to be the best approximation of collective behavior.

As an illustration of norm entrepreneurship, consider an example from Russia's Tatarstan, where the Tatar Public Center (TOTs) promoted the revival of Tatar language (Giuliano 2000). Formed in 1988, TOTs acted as a norm entrepreneur in trying to elevate Tatar as the appropriate language among urban, Russian-speaking Tatars. Some Tatars equated the loss of the Tatar language with the cultural death of their nation, suggesting that they considered language as an important constitutive norm of their Tatar social identity (Giuliano 2000, 305). In the end, TOTs was unsuccessful in its norm entrepreneurship. Tatarstan experienced no wholesale revival of Tatar. Instead, urban Tatars continued adhering to an existing and competing constitutive norm of an alternative social identity, speaking Russian as a marker of higher social status (Giuliano 2000, 306). TOTs' nationalist program failed, in part because its norm entrepreneurship only resonated with a small portion of its target audience (305–306). It is a reminder of an important element in the way we model norm entrepreneurship: the reach of entrepreneurs may be limited, and we cannot take for granted that norm entrepreneurs reach all individuals in the population and affect their latent norms in the same way. As we model norm entrepreneurship, we therefore vary the receptivity among the population, and examine how this affects the success of the mobilization effort.

By implementing the model of social adaptation and norm entrepreneurship as we have so far described it, one would simply replicate Hoffmann's (2008) model of norm emergence in a single society. Social adaptation and norm entrepreneurship would operate in a closed polity. The model would capture neither transnational relations nor cross-border diffusion. To explore transnational diffusion, we add to Hoffmann's model by letting two societies evolve side by side. We add a second country and transnationalize the context in which social adaptation and norm entrepreneurship are at work.

The transnational diffusion of social identities

How can constitutive norms of social identities spread from one country to another? As described above, Hoffmann's (2008) model simulates the emergence of norms among a set of agents in only one country. In this section, we describe a simple extension to the model that introduces different mechanisms of norm diffusion across national boundaries. In a stylized setting of two countries – each following the Hoffmann model – we ask in what particular ways norms can spread from one country to another. We designate one country (the *source* country) to be the origin of a behavioral pattern, and a second country (the *recipient* country) to be the potential follower of this pattern. Once we transnationalize the mechanisms of social adaptation and norm entrepreneurship, either mechanism might generate outcomes that are observationally indistinguishable: the emergence of a norm in the recipient country following the emergence of the same norm in the source country. However, since we can control the mechanisms behind this convergence, we can examine how and under what conditions convergence is reached.

In our stylized model, norms move, but people do not. Even though our model treats the populations of the two countries as separate, it also applies to cases where migration creates overlaps between the two populations. For example, in the case of the PKK in Germany discussed above, migration from Turkey into Germany led to a diffusion of ideas across borders simply by means of the individuals holding these ideas. Similarly, Harpviken and Lischer (this volume) explain post-return violence as the result of refugees being socialized in a violence-breeding context abroad, and bringing home the corresponding norms and ideas. In short, migration could partially explain why the population in the recipient country adopts norms from the source country, or why norm entrepreneurs in the recipient country advocate these norms. We acknowledge the importance of migration as a diffusion mechanism. However, in this chapter we take advantage of agent-based modeling to explore the much harder-to-observe diffusion of norms when people do not cross borders.

Hoffmann's base model allows for collective behavior along a dimension between normal and extreme. Whereas normal behavior at the center of the 0–100 scale is most frequent because of the averaging of agents' behaviors, there are occasional instances of extreme behavior at the upper and lower ends. We set up our model such that the source country converges to extreme behavior, and examine how this behavior can spread to the recipient country. The reason for focusing on extreme behavior is twofold. First, theoretically, the aim of our paper is to explain how a non-normal behavior – strong group antagonism – can spread between countries. Diffusion is defined such that the origin of this process (our source country) must show this behavior before it can travel to the recipient country. Second, methodologically, the Hoffmann model's natural tendency towards normal outcomes at the center of the scale would not allow us to attribute the occurrence of this behavior in both countries to the mechanisms we are examining, since they may simply be due to independent normal outcomes in both countries.

We generate extreme behavior in the source country by inserting a norm entrepreneur into the population that advocates an extreme rule at the lower end of the scale (rule 0, 0–10). This leads to a convergence to this rule in the source country. In the following, we explore social adaptation and norm entrepreneurship, either of which might lead to the recipient country adopting this norm, which corresponds to a diffusion of extreme behavior across national borders. We proceed in three steps. First, we describe a baseline setting in which the two countries have no links with each other, which makes diffusion impossible. Second, we transnationalize the context of social adaptation by linking the agent populations in the two countries, which can lead to the spread of extreme norms by mass-driven diffusion. Third, we examine the elite-driven mechanism of norm entrepreneurship that might generate the spread of norms. In our artificial world, we examine the impact of these diffusion mechanisms under two conditions: a scenario of perfect social perception (low noise level) and a scenario of fuzzy perception (high noise).

Countries without linkages

Our first baseline test illustrates the model setup for a pair of disconnected countries. We do so to provide a contrast against which to compare the diffusion models. It also allows us to illustrate the impact of variation in noise levels, independent of the diffusion mechanisms. We create two countries, the source and the recipient country, and populate them with 10 agents each. In order to generate extreme behavior in the source country, we insert a norm entrepreneur who advocates rule 0 (0–10). As a result, most of the model runs lead to a norm between 0 and 10 in the source country. Since we do not specify any linkages between the two countries, we expect the outcomes in the two countries to be unrelated to each other. In particular, there will be no convergence of the recipient country norm to the extreme source country outcome. Figure 7.1 illustrates this baseline model for two sample runs, under the low and high noise scenarios.

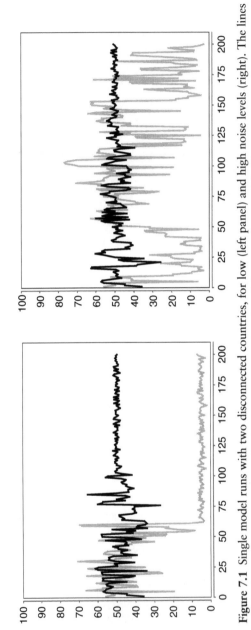

Figure 7.1 Single model runs with two disconnected countries, for low (left panel) and high noise levels (right). The lines show norm emergence over time in the source country (grey) and the target country (black).

Table 7.1 *Number of runs (out of 50) with successful norm convergence in the baseline model*

Low noise	High noise
4	0

The grey line in the left panel shows that following a period of unstable norms, the source country converges to an extreme norm, as advocated by the norm entrepreneur. The recipient country is not affected by developments in the source country. It quickly stabilizes around normal behavior (around 50). In the high noise scenario (right panel) the outcome is the same for the recipient country. However, fluctuations are much higher for the source country, where – as shown in Hoffmann (2008) – deviations from the norm proposed by the entrepreneur are more drastic and occur frequently when noise is high.

The plots above show results only for single model runs. However, in each agent-based model, a number of probabilistic moves are made. In our model, for example, agents do not perceive the true collective behavior, but rather a noisy estimate of it. This noise is essentially random; we only control its magnitude using the noise parameter. In order to make sure that these random outcomes do not determine the outcome in the single runs, we repeat the model for different sequences of random numbers. Since we cannot easily eyeball all these runs to check for convergence, we need to define a criterion so that the computer can calculate whether in a particular run, the norms in the source and recipient country have converged. We therefore define norm convergence to have occurred once the difference between the true collective behaviors in both countries is 15 or less for 200 consecutive time steps. This threshold is arbitrary, but changing it within certain limits does not alter our conclusions. Each model run ends when convergence is reached, or otherwise, is terminated at time 3,000. Table 7.1 reports the number of model runs (out of 50) where we observe convergence.

The table shows that when both countries are disconnected, there is very little if no convergence at all. For the low noise scenario, there are a few runs with seemingly successful diffusion, but these are due to the fact that neither the source nor the recipient country is hard-wired to extreme or normal behavior. For example, rather than settling on a norm around the center, the population in the recipient country – while completely disconnected from source country – can settle on an outcome close to 0, which our model counts as convergence. However, these instances are rare and do not challenge our general approach.

Transnationalized social adaptation

We are now ready to apply our first diffusion mechanism to the baseline model. Given our theoretical considerations, we argue that one route by which norms spread is via transnational intra-group networks where, in effect, the social context of social adaptation is transnationalized. We translate this to our model by letting recipient country agents base their assessment of their society's norm in part by observing the population in the source country. In other words, the individuals in the recipient country rely on information from the source country to determine which rule in their repertoire of imaginable behavior is the most appropriate.

The social contexts to which agents adapt are transnationalized once networks and means of communication cross national boundaries. For example, Haider (2005) describes how the transnational context of Xinjiang's Uighur population was transnationalized when the Karakoram Highway opened in 1982, linking Kashgar, Xinjiang with Islamabad, Pakistan. Uighurs are predominantly Muslim, and therefore share faith with the majority Pakistani population. Many Uighurs traveled to Pakistan to study in religious schools well into the 1990s. Their time in Pakistan contributed to instilling in them a "strong, moderate Muslim identity" (Haider 2005, 529). As the Islamic awareness grew among the Uighurs, one might expect that this process involved the adoption of the constitutive norms of Muslim identity. Much like the emergence of Kurdish identity among Turkish immigrants to Germany depended on the relative liberties of German society, the emergence of a stronger Muslim identity among Uighurs occurred at a period of liberalization in China. Transnational relations with Muslims in Pakistan were facilitated by the greater economic freedoms, the encouragement to trade with neighbors, and the greater cultural and religious liberties in China of the 1980s (Haider 2005, 525).

This underlines another assumption in our model: there is no strong state or other third party that by means of coercion can control agents' actions. The Karakoram Highway was to some extent conducive to conflict between Uighurs and China. Some Uighurs who traveled to

Pakistan took part in the violent resistance against the Soviets and in turn the US in Afghanistan (Haider 2005, 529). Upon their return to Xinjiang, they took part in the violent resistance against China as part of the nationalist movement (Haider 2005, 530). Recent unrest in Xinjiang testifies to the continuation of social conflict. Xinjiang's social cleavages continue to manifest themselves in the constitutive norms of social identities – some very particular. As Haider describes one norm, "feelings of alienation remain strong, with some Uighurs shunning Han restaurants because they serve pork, while looking down on those Uighurs who do eat at Han establishments" (Haider 2005, 527).

The opening of the Karakoram Highway was one manifestation of the transnationalization of a social context. In our model, this incorporation of transnational information is guided by a single parameter, *transnational impact*, which controls the extent to which the source country collective behavior affects agents in the recipient country. This impact parameter takes values between 0 and 1. For example, if transnational impact is set to 0.4, the recipient country agents' perception of the appropriate collective behavior will be the weighted average of the source country behavior (40%) and the behavior in their own country (60%). The baseline model as described above is a special case of this one with transnational impact set to 0. Figure 7.2 again shows the norm trajectories in both countries, for two selected runs of the model.

The left panel in Figure 7.2 shows the quick effect of transnationalized social adaptation under low noise conditions. Already after a small number of time steps (about 50), the dominant norm in the recipient country converges to the extreme outcome in the source country. Yet, there is no perfect overlap. Because of the model's natural trend towards the center, norms in the recipient country turn out to be somewhat closer to the center than the extreme outcomes in the source country. The disparity between the points at which source country and recipient country converge suggests that local conditions are important in determining the outcome of diffusion. Whereas the extreme outcome in the source country is driven by a norm entrepreneur, this entrepreneur promotes a rule that is not adopted without alteration by the recipient country population. Instead, the emergent norm in the recipient country has its own local flavor. The imperfect convergence echoes Schmitz' (this volume) argument that local factors shape the impact of transnational mechanisms. Schmitz analyzes how one insurgent organization adopted a transnational (Christian) ideology – "a global

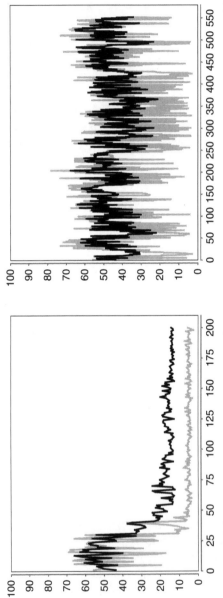

Figure 7.2 Diffusion by transnationalized social adaptation, for transnational impact set to 0.4, under the low and high noise scenario.

structure of values" – and put it to work to address local grievances stemming from economic and political marginalization.

An analogy in IR work on transnationalism is the phenomenon of norm localization (Acharya 2004). Acharya defines localization as "the active construction ... of foreign ideas by local actors, which results in the former developing significant congruence with local beliefs and practices" (Acharya 2004, 245). One should be careful not to belabor this analogy. We do not explicitly model norm localization. Instead, our recipient agent society settles around a norm that is influenced by a very generalized natural attractor. Still, Acharya's work on norm localization and the literature that has emerged in its wake (see, for example, Williams 2007 and Capie 2008) point to some ideas that could well be incorporated in subsequent agent-based models. Such ideas include dynamics of contestation between outside and inside entrepreneurs, the distinction between inside and outside initiatives for diffusion, and the connection between social identities and institutions in the recipient country. We return to some of these ideas in the conclusion.

In Figure 7.2, the picture changes once we introduce noise. The recipient country norm follows the lead given by the source country, but because of the fluctuations due to noise, convergence does not occur. This result suggests that diffusion by social adaptation can only occur once a stable norm has emerged in the source country that agents in the recipient country can follow. If this is not the case, reliance on a volatile example set by the source country can even disturb the modest norm emergence in the recipient country that would have occurred had there been no transnational linkages.

Again, we examine the success rate of norm diffusion on a larger set of cases. We run the model for different levels of transnational impact (0.1, 0.2, 0.4) and count the number of successful diffusions under low and high noise. We intentionally keep the level of impact low (at least below 0.5), because we believe that the domestic dynamics carry much more weight in the norm emergence process than outside influences. Table 7.2 reports the results. Two findings stand out. First, diffusion by social adaptation can only be successful under low noise conditions. Very few runs in the high noise scenario exhibit norm diffusion. Second, there is a non-linear effect of the transnational impact parameter. Low values of transnational impact are insufficient to generate diffusion. However, as we increase this parameter to 0.4, all of our

Table 7.2 *Number of runs (out of 50) with successful norm diffusion for different levels of transnational impact*

Transnational impact	Low noise	High noise
0.1	0	0
0.2	3	1
0.4	50	3

model runs exhibit successful diffusion. Clearly, small shifts in the transnational impact parameter can dramatically change the effect of social adaptation.

Transnationalized norm entrepreneurship

Next, we consider norm entrepreneurship as a mechanism of diffusion. As we argue in the theory section above, entrepreneurs can be key actors for the collective establishment of norms, as they actively propagate a certain norm. Recall that in Hoffmann's model, an entrepreneur's suggestion only affects the agents' set of private rules. There is no guarantee that this suggestion will eventually become the rule by which all agents behave. Hence, the norm emergence that the model generates is the result of a constant shaping of the agents' repertoires of imaginable behavior and subsequent social adaptation. In the following, we examine how this shaping can account for the diffusion of norms between the two countries.

In the previous section, we modeled diffusion purely by transnationalizing the context in which agents adapt, with no norm entrepreneur present in the recipient country. We now implement a simple entrepreneur-driven mechanism of diffusion by introducing a norm entrepreneur into the recipient country. This entrepreneur advocates the predominant norm from the source country whenever agents update their norm repertoire (on average at every 25th time step). It is important to note that as mentioned above, agents only add this rule to their existing repertoire, from where it may be activated only if evaluated favorably. In addition, norm entrepreneurs might be limited in their success in changing agents' repertoires, which is what we observed in the Tatarstan example. We therefore introduce a receptivity parameter into our model, which captures the probability

Table 7.3 *Number of runs (out of 50) with successful entrepreneur-driven norm diffusion*

Receptivity	Low noise	High noise
1	21	20
0.9	28	20
0.8	20	16
0.7	16	14
0.6	12	8
0.5	12	3

that an agent incorporates the norm promoted by an entrepreneur into his or her own repertoire. For example, with receptivity set to 0.8, on average only 80 percent of the population would include the proposed rule, whereas the remaining 20 percent would simply ignore it.[4]

This extremely simple implementation shifts the locus of diffusion from the population as in the previous experiment to the norm entrepreneurs in the recipient country. Do we observe norm diffusion, even though the agents themselves have no direct perception of the happenings in the source country? Figure 7.3 shows the results of two model runs using our entrepreneur-driven mechanism, under the low and high noise scenarios and with receptivity set at 100 percent.

With little noise present, the recipient country converges to an extreme norm quickly and remains there, even though the source country is undergoing some initial fluctuations before settling on the same outcome. In essence, norm entrepreneurship seems to work, similarly to social adaptation as shown above. What if we now impose high noise on agents' perceptions? Whereas high noise largely eliminates diffusion by social adaptation, this does not seem to be the case for norm entrepreneurship. High noise introduces larger fluctuations during the beginning of the simulation, but does not impede the recipient country's convergence to the extreme behavioral norm 0–10. Still, we need to examine if these findings are robust even if entrepreneurs are only partially successful, which is why we examine a larger set of runs that vary both receptivity and noise level. Table 7.3 reports the

---

[4] Since – in the model – we are interested only in the recipient country dynamics, the success rate is only applied to the entrepreneur in that country.

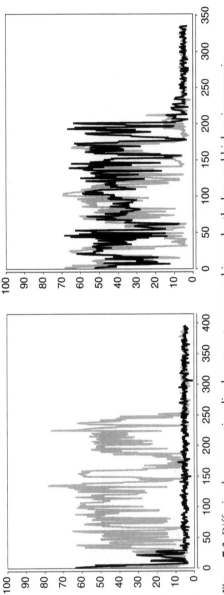

Figure 7.3 Diffusion by transnationalized norm entrepreneurship, under the low and high noise scenario.

number of successful diffusions in a set of 50 runs with different random number sequences.

The results in Table 7.3 support our initial conclusions. In contrast to our above findings for transnationalized social adaptation, entrepreneur-introduced norms from the source country can successfully be established in a significant number of runs, regardless of whether we apply low or high noise. These results hold even if we assume that entrepreneurs are only moderately successful (receptivity at 0.6–0.7). In other words, whereas perfect social perception (low noise) is a precondition for social adaptation, entrepreneur-driven diffusion is much more robust to varying levels of noise and works almost equally well under both conditions, even if entrepreneurs have only limited reach.

Discussion and conclusion

The importance of norm entrepreneurship is supported by at least two empirical contributions to this volume: Bakke's (this volume) study of goals, tactics, and resources in the Chechen wars, and Adamson's (this volume) work on diaspora mobilization in the PKK – Turkey conflict.

Bakke describes training camps in Chechnya as sites of the transnational diffusion of goals and tactics. A central piece of evidence involves one transnational agent of diffusion, Khattab, setting up a training center in Chechnya in which young recruits were trained in religion and military tactics by foreign teachers (Bakke, this volume). These transnational insurgents sought to instill their beliefs in the young recruits, or to convey ideas from foreign ideologues, and in this we see norm entrepreneurship at work.

Adamson analyzes how the social identity of Turkish immigrants in Germany changed into a Kurdish insurgent consciousness. She argues that PKK activists worked to promote a particular Kurdish identity in a way that closely resembles our understanding of norm entrepreneurship. In our agent-based model, norm entrepreneurs affect people by making available new norms that could influence subsequent behavior. Similarly, when PKK activists promoted particular constitutive norms such as language and customs, they "carved out a *publicly available alternative identity category*" to either "German" or "Turkish" (Adamson, this volume, emphasis added). In other words, political entrepreneurs formulated "political categories and ideologies that presented individuals with *identity options* that countered both German and Turkish national identities" (Adamson, this volume, emphasis added). Adamson thus describes the diffusion of a separatist social identity from Turkey to Germany through a process where norm entrepreneurship was important.

At the same time as Bakke and Adamson's contributions lend empirical plausibility to the mechanism of norm entrepreneurship, our agent-based model suggests extensions to their work that could be explored in future research. Recall that we model norm entrepreneurship not as a stand-alone mechanism, but as a sequence of transnational norm entrepreneurship and *domestic* social adaption. The norm entrepreneur in the recipient country is a transnational agent because he or she promotes the current norm from the source country. However, for that norm to translate into behavior in the recipient country, it depends on a process of social adaptation within the boundaries of the recipient country.

As a possible contribution to Bakke's work, our computer simulations suggest social adaptation as a mechanism that could account for the dynamics of training centers such as that established by Khattab in Chechnya. A presumably transparent social setting of young recruits would be conducive to social adaptation. Norm entrepreneurship would work in sequence with social adaptation where transnational insurgents sought to instill their beliefs in the young recruits. Indeed, our simulation suggests that the product of such training centers need not only be a change in the framing of an insurgent movement, as Bakke argues, but a more fundamental change in its social identity.

Our model of transnational norm entrepreneurship could contribute to Adamson's account of identity change by adding social adaptation as an account of how these alternative identities might emerge inter-subjectively in a population. As a stand-alone mechanism, norm entrepreneurship is an insufficient account of identity change. It misses important social dynamics that are involved when new identity norms arise. Instead, a sequence of norm entrepreneurship and social adaptation capture a more complete process of identity change.

To summarize, our agent-based model suggests that both social adaptation and norm entrepreneurship are candidate explanations of diffusion. When the social context to which agents adapt is transnationalized, norms that constitute social identities can diffuse from one country to another. Alternatively, norm entrepreneurs who work as transnational agents can promote norms from a source country to a recipient country audience, leading to diffusion. Either mechanism can operate in societies that are both more or less complex. Herein lies the difference. Norm entrepreneurship leads regularly to diffusion irrespective of the level of social complexity. Social adaptation leads to diffusion only in more transparent societies. In short, norm entrepreneurship is the more robust mechanism of diffusion.

As the process of diffusion is currently operationalized, it is meant to be a simple base model for norm diffusion in a transnational context and leaves ample room for extensions. For example, an interesting question to explore is the interaction of social adaptation and norm entrepreneurship. What if the two mechanisms complement each other, and what if they compete? Similarly, another form of competing diffusion mechanisms could occur between norm entrepreneurs in different locales. Work on norm localization points to processes where outside and inside norm entrepreneurs contest each other (Acharya 2004). Implementing this process would require us to introduce entrepreneurs that target the recipient country population both from within and from a source country. Finally, our model could be extended to include abstract representations of political institutions in the recipient country, in an effort to understand how norms shape these institutions, but also how institutions affect the emergence and diffusion of behavioral norms.

PART III

Theory, mechanisms, and the study of civil war

8 | Causal mechanisms and typological theories in the study of civil conflict*

ANDREW BENNETT

Introduction

Most political scientists are rightly focused on their empirical and theoretical research and its policy implications, but this has often left them out of date in their understanding of debates in the philosophy of science. Many political scientists have continued to espouse ideas from scholars like Carl Hempel, Thomas Kuhn, and Imre Lakatos that have long been considered deeply problematic among philosophers of science. A recent survey of American scholars in the international relations subfield, for example, found that approximately two-thirds identified themselves as "positivists" (Maliniak et al. 2011, 454), even though the philosophical schools of thought most closely associated with this label fell out of favor among philosophers of science decades ago. Other notions still common in political science but long since discarded by philosophers include explanation by reference to "covering laws" (Waltz 1979), self-styled Kuhnian "paradigm" wars in the international relations subfield (Maliniak et al. 2011), and efforts to construct theoretical schools of thought as Lakatosian "research programs" (for critiques see Elman and Elman 2003; Sil and Katzenstein 2010b).

The epistemological challenge for political scientists is that the remnants of these earlier philosophies of science are at odds with an increasing focus on explaining complex phenomena via reference to "causal mechanisms." The idea of explanation via reference to causal mechanisms builds on the work of "critical realists" like Roy Bhaskar (1975) and more contemporary "scientific realists" like Colin Wight (2006, 2007; on the differences between scientific and critical realism, see Chernoff 2007). One need not take recent versions of scientific realism as unproblematic – indeed, they are not (Chernoff, 2002) – to

* I thank the contributors to this volume, and particularly its editor Jeff Checkel, for insightful comments on several drafts of this chapter.

argue that scientific realism offers important improvements over earlier philosophies of science and that it has pragmatic value for a discipline focused on explaining, understanding, and to the extent possible predicting and influencing the complexities of political life. This chapter explores the costs and benefits of explanations that reference causal mechanisms, pointing out how the mechanism approach to explanation differs from earlier philosophies of science. It draws upon the empirical chapters in this volume, as well as on the broader literature on civil war, to illustrate the benefits of focusing on explanations that invoke hypothesized causal mechanisms.

The chapter proceeds as follows. First, I define causal mechanisms and distinguish explanation via reference to causal mechanisms from both covering law explanations and post-modernist approaches to understanding. Second, the chapter addresses the relationship between the epistemology of explanation via mechanisms and common methods of political science research, focusing on the method of process tracing but including a brief discussion of statistical methods and formal modeling. The chapter then presents a taxonomy of some of the most commonly theorized mechanisms in political science including, but not limited to, the mechanisms invoked in this volume's empirical studies. I illustrate the value of this taxonomy by using it to classify the mechanisms theorized in the empirical chapters within this volume and to identify the important categories of mechanisms that these chapters leave out. This leads – finally – to a discussion of typological theorizing as a means of addressing combinations of mechanisms and the complexities this creates, with a focus on how to build such theories within the literature on civil war. I conclude that explanation via reference to causal mechanisms entails important costs, particularly a substantial loss of parsimony relative to most extant political science theories, but I argue this is the necessary price for improving our understanding of the complexities of political life.

Causal mechanisms – definitions and theoretical framing

In his introduction to this volume, Checkel borrows from John Gerring to define causal mechanisms as "the pathway or process by which an effect is produced or a purpose is accomplished" (Checkel, this volume, citing Gerring 2007b, 178). This is a good start, especially with Checkel's elaborations that causal mechanisms are "ultimately unobservable ontological entities that exist in the world, not in our heads." This distinction, easily overlooked, is critical, and deserves contextualization within the history of the philosophy of science. The appeal to metaphysical unobservables is precisely what the positivists wanted to avoid, but their efforts to elide this appeal created sharp contradictions (Salmon 1990). The positivists' conundrum can be summed up in the bumper sticker slogan that "observation is theory-laden." We cannot even take in the direct stimuli that our senses receive without filtering them through implicit or explicit theories that try to make sense of these stimuli.

Recognition of this problem led to a search for justifications of theories rather than observations as the bedrock of explanation. This motivated the attempt by Carl Hempel and Paul Oppenheim to justify theories by reference to "laws" or "covering laws," known as the "deductive-nomological" approach to explanation. In this view, to explain an outcome was to refer to a covering law, or an underlying regularity, of which the outcome was an instance. This effort at explanation foundered on the inability to find any independent warrant for covering laws – something Hempel and Oppenheim promised in a famous footnote (1948 [Hempel 1965, 273]), but ultimately failed to deliver.

Subsequently, the "scientific realist" school substituted the assumption of an ontological reality independent of our minds and our theories for Hempel's search for justification via "laws." Our theories, in this view, aspire to refer to this independent reality with as much verisimilitude as possible. This may not seem a very heroic assumption, but it presents six philosophical challenges that merit discussion in view of this volume's emphasis on explanation via reference to causal mechanisms.

First, by what standards can we judge whether one theory about causal mechanisms has greater verisimilitude than another? Imre Lakatos (1970) focused on this challenge of judging scientific progress. Lakatos dismissed as "naïve falsificationism" the idea that theories could be readily falsified by inconsistencies with observed "facts," as measurement errors and other problems could also account for failed predictions. Lakatos objected even more strongly to Kuhn's (1962) suggestion that the most relevant standard for progress was the consensus of the relevant scientific community, a view that Lakatos found too subjective. Instead, Lakatos argued that theories could be judged as progressive if over time they uncovered "novel facts" that were empirically verified. Later discussions (Elman and Elman 2003) clarified that two kinds of novelty are key: use novelty, or the ability of theories to predict facts that are independent of the evidence from which these theories were derived, and background theory novelty, or the ability of theories to predict facts that are inconsistent with alternative theories. Although other aspects of Lakatos's approach have undergone sharp criticism, these two kinds of novelty remain as useful albeit fallible standards for assessing whether our theories about how mechanisms work are progressive (Bennett 2003).

Second, what are we to make of the metaphysical appeal to ontological entities that are ultimately unobservable? In one sense, this is no more problematic than the positivists' reference to unobservable "laws." After all, most of what we "know" about the political and social world we learn not through direct observation but through reading, hearing, or seeing books, journals, and news reports. Some of these sources and their instruments of observation are more reliable and less susceptible to user biases than others, and we rightly do not treat all observations as being created equal.

It is useful here to think of a movable border or horizon between the observable and the unobservable worlds (George and Bennett 2005). As our instruments of observation improve, as in the introduction of public opinion polls or brain scans, we push back the border of the unobservable world. Yet ultimately there always remain more discrete or distant mechanisms that we cannot directly observe. Still, as scientific realists maintain, our theories about mechanisms often generate observable implications on what should be true if the posited mechanisms operate in the manner that we theorize. We can test these implications to assess the accuracy of our theories, even if we cannot observe mechanisms or causation directly or unproblematically assess how well our theories fit the observable evidence.

Third, how does explanation via reference to mechanisms differ from explanation via reference to "laws"? In some respects, the two seem quite similar: to explain an outcome in either sense is to show that it was to be expected under the circumstances. There is a crucial difference, however, in that deductive-nomological or covering law explanations admit as "causal" many relationships that a mechanism view excludes. The covering law model, for example, allows the readings on a barometer, which provide a strong correlation with the weather, to be accepted as an explanation of the weather. The problem is that this form of explanation readily adopts "as if" assumptions: in this view, it does not matter if entities acted as the theory suggests, it only matters that outcomes behave "as if" this were true (Friedman 1953). A mechanism-based approach to explanation, on the other hand, eschews "as if" assumptions and requires, in principle, that our theory about how underlying mechanisms work must be consistent with the finest degree of detail that we can observe.

Fourth, and related, does a commitment to explanation via causal mechanisms require all social scientists to become methodological individualists, or even neuroscientists? On the one hand, requiring that our theories must be consistent with what we can observe at lower levels of analysis does not mean that the interesting explanatory action, the most cost-effective means of theory testing, or the relevant policy levers are at these lower levels of analysis. If a social structure is so strongly confining and self-reproducing that all individuals in it behave the same, then the interesting explanatory leverage is at the level of the social structure, not that of an individual's brain chemistry. On the other hand, a commitment to explanation via mechanisms does make theories suspect if it can be shown that individual actors did not make the calculations or engage in the behaviors posited by structural theories. Ultimately, assumptions that are more accurate on the micro level should lead to more accurate structural or systemic models.

Fifth, is explanation via reference to mechanisms incompatible with constructivist or post-modern views of social and political life? The short answer is that the lines of thinking espoused by some construct-ivists and post-modernists are irreconcilable with explanation via mechanisms. At the same time, those constructivists who have embraced scientific realism (Wendt 1992) are comfortable with mechanism-based explanations. As Checkel makes clear in his intro-ductory chapter, scientific realism is open to all kinds of mechanisms that constructivists emphasize, including persuasion, learning, naming and shaming, framing, legitimacy, and appropriateness, as well as mechanisms involving material power and transactions costs.

Scholars who are skeptical of any possibility of causal explanation, however, will remain skeptical of mechanisms. This includes research-ers who believe that social agents and social structures are so inextric-ably mutually constituted "all the way down" to the finest observable slices of space and time that there is no sensible way of separating the two into causes and effects. Many constructivists and post-modernists are not unalterably opposed to aspirations to causal explanation, however, and leading interpretivists suggest in their writings that behavior can be explained and that some explanations are better than others (Hopf 2007). Scientific realists remind us that although observation is theory-laden, it is not theory-determined. The social world that exists independently of our minds can surprise us and force us to rethink our theories and explanations.

Sixth and finally, what other accounts of causation and explanation are consistent with or incompatible with explanation via reference to causal mechanisms? Henry Brady has very usefully summarized three approaches to causal explanation, which he terms neo-Humean regularity theory (focusing on constant conjunctions), counterfactual theory, and manipulation theory; these are in addition to the mechanism-based understanding presented here (Brady 2008).

My argument is that the mechanisms approach is compatible with all of these except the positivist variants of neo-Humean regularity theory. The counterfactual approach, which Brady associates with statistical methods and with efforts to establish and measure "causal effects," is fully compatible with a search for theories about the mechanisms that might account for such effects. It makes no sense to discuss effects that lack mechanisms or mechanisms that lack effects (see also Checkel's introduction to this volume). Similarly, a "manipulation" account of explanation and inference that emphasizes the role of experiments and the ability to manipulate potential causes is perfectly compatible with explanation via mechanisms. Experimentalists typically have in mind or would like to uncover theorized mechanisms that might account for the outcomes that result from the manipulation of specific variables.

These six issues are what led Alex George and I to adopt a definition of causal mechanisms that is more detailed than Gerring's but not incompatible with it. We defined causal mechanisms as "ultimately unobservable physical, social, or psychological processes through which agents with causal capacities operate, but only in specific contexts or conditions, to transfer energy, information, or matter to other entities," thereby changing the latter entities' "characteristics, capacities, or propensities in ways that persist until subsequent causal mechanisms act upon it" (George and Bennett 2005, 137). This definition places mechanisms on the ontological level. It also makes clear that theories about mechanisms may not be universal laws that operate in all times and places, but may instead be operative in some circumstances and not others, and that their operation is mediated by that of other mechanisms.

Mechanisms and methods

All of the three most common general methods in political science – statistical analysis, formal modeling, and case studies – can contribute to the development and testing of theories about causal mechanisms. Statistical methods can test whether any population-level observable implications of hypothesized mechanisms are borne out. Formal models can deductively drive a researcher to theoretical insights about, or testable implications of, hypothesized mechanisms that the researcher otherwise might have missed (see also the discussion in Nome and Weidmann, this volume). This chapter focuses mostly on case study methods for identifying and testing theories on causal mechanisms, particularly process tracing. Process tracing in individual cases provides a powerful means of using both induction and deduction to develop and test theories about hypothesized mechanisms. Case studies afford an opportunity to examine closely sequences of actions and events, and the details that emerge, often unknown even to experts on the case prior to its intensive study, provide many opportunities to test the observable implications of alternative explanations. The detailed analysis of sequences also provides some leverage over the issue of causal direction – that is, did A cause B or did B cause A?

As Checkel argues in his introduction, process tracing is the analysis within a single case of the sequence of events that intervenes between the starting point and outcome of the case as these are defined by the researcher. The researcher's prior choice of theories she or he deems to be relevant to the case drives much of the analysis, as it determines which intervening events are of interest, when to start and end the time period relevant to the case, which case(s) to study, what the "case" is, and what the phenomenon or population is of which it is a case. In addition to this largely deductive construction of the case and testing of the observable implications of alternative explanations within it, there can also be an inductive side to process tracing. This involves "soaking and poking" within a case and identifying new explanations of its outcome. These explanations may be based on theories that are fairly new or on theories that other scholars had already proposed but that the researcher had not thought to apply to the case prior to studying it.

Contrary to the common injunction that one cannot develop a theory from a case and test it against the same case, it is possible to develop a theory from a case and test it against *new observable implications* within that case that are different from and independent of the evidence that helped the researcher derive the theory. Such new implications can provide a check on confirmation bias and satisfy the criterion of "use novelty" discussed above if the researcher had not thought to look for them prior to developing the theory that predicts they should be found within the case. Detectives and medical diagnosticians as well as political scientists frequently engage in this kind of inference.

Several researchers have begun to develop explicit community standards for what constitutes good process tracing (see Checkel, this volume; Bennett and Elman 2006; Checkel 2006; Van Evera 1997; and Collier 2011). One criterion is that researchers should consider a wide range of alternative explanations, treat them fairly, and do sufficient process tracing to assess their roles. A second is that one should relentlessly pursue the most important observable implications of alternative explanations, or in Bayesian terms, the pieces of evidence that are most likely to update the prior probabilities assigned to the truth value of alternative explanations. A third criterion is that good process tracing anticipates and accounts for potential biases and gaps in the sources of evidence. Finally, to the extent possible, good process tracing explains each of the important potential turning points in the sequence of events leading from hypothesized causes to observed outcomes in the case.

From analytic eclecticism to structured pluralism: causal mechanisms and the cumulation of knowledge

What are the implications for the study of civil conflicts, and the study of politics more generally, that emerge from a shift toward mechanism-based explanations? As Charles King has pointed out, studies of ethnic and civil conflict have already begun to move toward a more micro- and mechanism-based approach (King 2004). Indeed, the latter is one of the three moves that Checkel advances to justify this book's value added, with the other two being an effort to draw on theories of transnationalism and an emphasis on measuring mechanisms in action (Checkel, this volume).

Yet there is a tension among these moves, as explanation via causal mechanisms, with its openness to many kinds of theory and its emphasis on interactions among different kinds of mechanisms, is at odds with the current division of the international relations subfield into paradigmatic "isms" (most prominently neorealism, neoliberal institutionalism, and constructivism) and the treatment of these isms as if they were internally complete and mutually exclusive explanations of phenomena. As Peter Katzenstein and Nobuo Okawara have argued (2002), the reification of the IR subfield into competing isms has obscured as much as it has revealed, and most scholars, when pressed to explain specific cases or phenomena, draw on more than one paradigmatic ism. The paradigmatic isms, in their view, are best thought of as rubrics helping scholars organize collections of hypothesized mechanisms that can be combined to construct explanations, rather than self-sufficient and complete grand theories of politics. Katzenstein and Okawara, and later Sil and Katzenstein (2010b), have thus argued for an "analytically eclectic" approach that brings together theories on mechanisms from different isms.

This is a clear improvement over formulating schools of thought in IR theory as if they were Kuhnian paradigms or Lakatosian research programs. Yet the "eclectic" label can easily be misinterpreted, as it can mean either borrowing from the best of various approaches, as Katzenstein and his co-authors clearly intend, or patchwork. This ambiguity is not merely linguistic, as a critical question regarding explanation via causal mechanisms is whether it provides a framework that allows scholars to research, explicate, and teach theories about politics in ways that are cumulative and progressive, rather than merely creating a collection of disparate explanations of different phenomena.

I argue that it is in fact possible to construct a taxonomy of theories on causal mechanisms that provides a framework for cumulative theorizing and a useful checklist to ensure we are not leaving out important mechanisms from our explanations. My taxonomy draws upon James Mahoney's (2000) typology of sociological explanations of institutions, which includes those rooted in power, efficiency, and legitimacy. This tripartite division usefully mirrors the three leading "isms" in the IR subfield – (neo)realism (power), (neo)liberalism (institutional efficiency), and constructivism (legitimacy) – but it does not reify these approaches into Kuhnian paradigms or Lakatosian research programs.

It is useful to think of the power and institutional mechanisms as involving the "logic of consequences," and the legitimacy mechanisms as embodying the "logic of appropriateness" (March and Olsen 1984; Ruggie 1998). The taxonomy also embodies different approaches to solving collective action problems and providing public goods. The "power" solution is that one or a few of the most powerful actors provide public goods largely or wholly by themselves. The incentive for these actors to do so is that they are sufficiently well endowed to substantially affect the amount of public goods provided and big enough to reap benefits from public goods that outweigh the costs of providing them (Olson and Zeckhauser 1966). The "legitimacy" solution involves creating shared identities that make free-riding in the provision of public goods socially inappropriate. The "institutional efficiency" solution involves creating institutions that increase transparency and lower transaction costs to make it easier for actors to provide public goods, share burdens in doing so, and identify and punish free-riders.

A second dimension of the taxonomy draws from constructivism (Wendt 1992) and structuration theory (Giddens 1984). It captures the four possible combinations of mechanisms through which agents and structures interact: agent to agent, structure to agent, agent to structure, and structure to structure.

These two dimensions form the core of the taxonomy in Table 8.1. For illustrative purposes, I have added levels of analysis, fields of study associated with particular agent-centered and structural mechanisms, and examples from the literature on civil war. The examples of hypothesized mechanisms in each box are meant to be illustrative rather than exhaustive, though it will become evident below that they include many of the mechanisms invoked in the empirical chapters in the present volume.

This taxonomy serves six purposes in fostering cumulative theorizing and knowledge about politics. First, it provides a checklist that scholars can use to make sure that they are not leaving out important alternative explanations of a phenomenon. As Checkel noted in his introduction to this volume, in his own work on evolving European citizenship norms, he omitted structural factors until critics brought

Table 8.1 *A taxonomy of theories on social mechanisms*

	Agent to agent	Structure to agent	Agent to structure	Structure to structure
Legitimacy: Constructivism, logic of appropriateness	Emulation socialization	Culture as enabler and constraint	Norm entrepreneurs, framing	Unintended evolution of social systems
Material power: (Neo) realism, logic of consequences	Hegemonic socialization	Resources as enabler and constraint	Revolution	Power transitions
Functional efficiency: Neoliberalism, logic of consequences	Emulation diffusions	Evolutionary selection	Functional competition, innovation	Moral hazard, adverse selection
Levels of analysis **Fields of study**	Individual, social Cognitive and social psychology	Systemic Economics Sociology Social psychology	Individual, social Economics Sociology Social psychology	System to system Economics Sociology
Examples in civil war literature	Principal-agent theory (Salehyan 2010)	Collective action (Lichbach 1998) Opportunity structures (Fearon and Laitin 2003) Lootable resources (Collier and Hoeffler 1998, 2004)	Framing (Gagnon 1994, Kalyvas 2006)	Demographic change as an input in civil and ethnic conflicts (Goldstone 2002)

this gap to his attention (Checkel, this volume). Using the taxonomy in its capacity as a checklist could have alerted him to the possible role of such factors – and before his critics did so.

Second, scholars can drill down deeper into any one of the boxes in the taxonomy, refining or adding new theories on the mechanisms in that category, or disaggregating theorized mechanisms into different sub-types. Much of Checkel's framing of this book's contribution and Wood's assessment in Chapter 9 focus on this kind of improvement, seeking more detailed explanation of the mechanisms behind the diffusion of practices in civil war. Third, researchers can develop increasingly comprehensive historical explanations of particular cases drawing on theories from any or all of the categories in the taxonomy. Fourth, using statistical methods, we can develop estimates of the magnitude of the causal effects of the variables specified by theories about how causal mechanisms work.

Fifth, researchers can refine the scope conditions of the theories in any of the categories, clarifying where and when or under what conditions they are strongest and weakest and specifying more clearly the populations to which they apply. The specified populations should ordinarily include "negative cases" that could have had the outcome of interest but did not (Goertz and Mahoney 2004).

Finally, and perhaps most important, we can use the taxonomy to develop typological theories about how combinations of mechanisms interact in shaping outcomes for specified populations. A typological theory is a theory that not only specifies individual independent variables and the hypothesized causal mechanisms that shape their effects, but provides "contingent generalizations on how and under what conditions they [these variables] behave in specified conjunctions or configurations to produce effects on specified dependent variables" (George and Bennett 2005, 235). Typological theories attempt to address complex causal relations, including non-linear relations, high-order interactions effects, and processes involving many variables. The taxonomy thus provides the building blocks of theorized mechanisms that can be brought together in specified conjunctions to develop typological theories on how combinations of variables behave.

The empirical chapters in this book illustrate each of these six kinds of contributions. Generally, as most of these chapters deal with one or a few cases, they collectively make more contributions in the first three of these areas than in the last three (cross-case generalizations, identification of theoretical scope conditions, and development of typological theories). I address each of these actual and potential contributions in turn.

This clarifies the mechanisms each author has studied and those they have either set aside or perhaps overlooked. Nome and Weidmann, for example, explicitly note that their agent-based modeling approach necessarily sets aside structure-to-structure mechanisms or emergent properties. Adamson indicates that her account de-emphasizes structural factors without entirely ignoring them. More generally, the empirical chapters emphasize agent-to-agent power/resource and legitimacy mechanisms, structure-to-agent power mechanisms, and agent-to-structure legitimacy mechanisms; they give less attention to institutional efficiency mechanisms and structure-to-structure mechanisms.

These relatively neglected mechanisms could have been used to address more fully issues such as how particular rebel leaders and ideas won out over more traditional leaders and concepts – as with Joseph Kony and the Lord's Resistance Army (LRA) in Uganda, the Kurdistan Workers' Party (PKK) in Germany, and the more radically Islamic rebel fighters in Chechnya. In part, these leaders and their ideas likely prevailed because they were functionally efficient in serving purposes for other actors, in addition to being able to gain legitimacy and control resources.

Most of the codings in Table 8.2 are fairly straightforward, involving terms used directly by the authors, but some reflect more implicit arguments. For example, Schmitz notes that lower-ranking rebels took up the amnesty offered by the Ugandan government, while top rebel leaders rejected the offer. He does not explicitly argue, however, that this process may have created an "adverse selection" effect by leaving the most committed and violent rebels in even greater control of the LRA, nor does he suggest that this might help account for the increase in violence that followed. Even though it works through individual choices first by Ugandan government officials and then by rebel leaders, the adverse selection going on here is a structure-to-structure mechanism: the amnesty policy constitutes an institutional rule, the outcome (a more violent LRA) is also a social structure, and that outcome is presumably not intended by the Ugandan government.

Table 8.2 reveals that framing, resources, and brokerage received considerable attention in the empirical chapters. Yet the chapters devoted less attention to the functional efficiency row and the structure-to-structure column. One exception is Hamberg's consideration as an

Table 8.2 *Locating the causal mechanisms invoked in the empirical chapters within the taxonomy*

	Agent to agent	Structure to agent	Agent to structure	Structure to structure
Legitimacy	Emulation **B** Socialization **A, B, S, HL** Learning **B, S** Teaching **B**	Adaptation **NW** Ethnic bidding **A** Shaming **S**	Norm entrepreneurs **NW, S** Framing **A, B, H, S** Ethnic/leadership bidding **A, B**	
Material power	Hegemonic socialization **B, H, S**	Resources as incentives **B, H, S** Resources enable **A, B, HL, S** Networks/ brokerage **A, B, H, HL, NW**	Agents change material power balance **A, B, HL**	Demographic change **A, HL**
Functional efficiency	Emulation of successful agents **B, S**	Evolutionary selection of efficient leaders or practices **A, B, HL**	Functional innovation **B**	Adverse selection **S**

Key: A = Adamson; B = Bakke; H = Hamberg; HL = Harpviken and Lischer; S = Schmitz; NW = Nome and Weidmann

alternative hypothesis whether the use of child soldiers became functionally less efficient for the Sudan People's Liberation Army/Movement (SPLA/M) than the use of adult soldiers. He concludes this was not a strong explanation in his case. The structural opportunities for rebellion emphasized by Fearon and Laitin (2003) get only passing references in the chapters as well.

Future research might usefully explore these dimensions and their underlying mechanisms more closely, addressing questions such as: do considerations of functional efficiency help explain why certain practices and leaders rise and fall? How do demographic change, economic change, and broad changes in information technologies and global discourses (such as the growing prominence of discussions on the "responsibility to protect") shape the structural context within which transnational actors operate? By seeking to assassinate leaders of transnational movements that oppose them, have states unintentionally brought younger and more radical leaders to power?

Regarding the second way in which the taxonomy can be used, the empirical chapters make several very helpful contributions by drilling down and disaggregating theorized mechanisms in one or another of its categories. Nome and Weidmann distinguish norm entrepreneurship from adaptation, emulation, and learning. Adamson differentiates frame bridging (the linking of two different frames) and frame extension (the extension of a frame to new issues or groups). Bakke clarifies the differences among mediated, relational, and non-relational diffusion (see also Wood, this volume).

The third kind of contribution – historical explanations of individual cases using a variety of theories on causal mechanisms – is the most readily identifiable in the volume's empirical studies. It is also an important form of knowledge accumulation that often gets overlooked in those social sciences that prize theoretical generalizations across cases over theoretical explanations of specific historical ones. With the exception of the chapter by Nome and Weidmann, each of the substantive chapters focuses upon an empirical puzzle and draws on a variety of theorized mechanisms to explain it. Why did the SPLA/M, in contrast to other rebellious groups, demobilize its child soldiers (Hamberg)? Why did the LRA (Schmitz) and the Chechen rebels (Bakke) shift the framing of their conflicts? How did Turks in Germany who could not even speak Kurdish come to think of themselves as Kurds and contribute to the PKK (Adamson)? Why did some refugees and not others engage in violence upon return to their home countries (Harpviken and Lischer)? The authors then proceed to explain these historical puzzles with the combinations of mechanisms identified in Table 8.2.

A fourth possible contribution of the taxonomy – improving our understanding and estimates of the magnitude of the causal effects of the variables in play – is under-utilized, which is understandable given that the qualitative methods used in most of the chapters do not allow estimates of causal effects in the way that regression analyses might. Nonetheless, contributors, on several occasions, do give assessments of which mechanisms might have greater, more lasting, or more robust effects than others. In particular, Nome and Weidmann use agent-based modeling to derive the result that the mechanisms involved in norm entrepreneurship are more powerful than adaptation mechanisms in the conditions they specify, including social complexity. Also, Hamberg argues that "naming and shaming" has not proved sufficient for the demobilization of child soldiers; indeed, he comes close to suggesting that outside actors' control of non-substitutable resources that rebel groups desire is a necessary condition for them to demobilize such soldiers. Similarly, Schmitz notes that the LRA's learning of reprehensible tactics in Sudan proved more powerful than the efforts of states, NGOs, and the International Criminal Court to persuade it to respect human rights.

The taxonomy's fifth contribution – the specification of scope conditions – also receives little attention, with the empirical studies only occasionally making claims regarding them, a point Wood (this volume) has also noted. Still, the chapters do at times make brief comparisons to other cases or use counterfactual analysis to suggest possible scope conditions. Harpviken and Lischer, drawing on their longitudinal analysis of refugees in Afghanistan and Rwanda, conclude that groups deeply socialized into adopting certain norms and practices will continue to use these to guide their behavior even when resources decline. In contrast, groups that adopt norms for the instrumental purpose of gaining resources will no longer follow these norms when resources decline. The accounts by Adamson and Bakke suggest that PKK militants and transnational jihadists would have had less success in Germany and Chechnya, respectively, if local elites had more independent resources or if imported identities had not resonated with pre-existing historical narratives and local actors' lived experiences of alienation.

This volume's focus on individual cases limits efforts at the cumulative development of theories that might apply across them. The empirical chapters at times make reference to additional positive or negative cases, but this is typically done to set the stage for the authors' chosen cases as particularly puzzling or interesting. An example is provided by Hamberg's analysis, where he claims the SPLA is the only successful case of getting a rebel movement to demobilize child soldiers.

Bakke's chapter arguably goes the farthest toward identifying generalizable and often structural factors that affect the ways in which mobilization mechanisms play out. She notes that these factors include the prevalence of conflict in the region, the strength of the target state (weak states present low opportunity costs for insurgents, strong states may push insurgents to seek havens and help across borders), the presence or absence of ethnic or ideological ties between insurgents and neighboring states, the existence or absence of brokers between local actors and diasporas, and the willingness of local fighters to accept foreign fighters and/or the (in)ability of locals to keep out foreign fighters. Still, neither Bakke nor the other authors move farther toward cumulative theorizing by identifying the population of positive and negative cases relevant to the phenomenon they study or discussing more than a few comparative cases.

An additional reason the empirical chapters do not attempt more ambitious cross-case generalizations is that the field has only recently begun to develop new ways of couching them, ones that allow for complex interactions among variables. Statistical analyses seldom model interaction effects beyond two variables. At the same time, qualitative analyses of one or a few cases, like those in this volume, rarely attempt to provide an empirical basis or a theoretical framework for generalizations, even contingent ones.

Case studies, causal mechanisms, and typological theories

The foregoing discussion brings us directly to the sixth type of contribution: using the taxonomy of mechanisms to help build typological theories. Constructing a typological theory involves both deductive and inductive reasoning. Deductively, the analyst defines the dependent variable of interest and uses prior theories – such as those included in the taxonomy – to identify the relevant independent variables. The analyst then creates a typological space (or what is known in logic as a "property space") that consists of all the possible combinations of the variables. Inductively, the analyst begins placing known cases into the typological space according to preliminary knowledge of the values of the variables in those cases. The analyst can then iterate between what was theorized a priori, what is known empirically, and what is learned from additional empirical study, refining the typological space and possibly re-conceptualizing variables to higher or lower levels of aggregation depending on the complexity of the space and the analyst's research goals (George and Bennett 2005, chapter 11; Elman 2005).

A study I did with colleagues on alliance burden-sharing in the American-led Desert Storm coalition in the 1991 Gulf War (Bennett, Lepgold, and Unger 1994) illustrates the potential value of typological theorizing. Most research on alliances up to that time had focused on only one or a few mechanisms that led to alliance contributions, including collective action dynamics, the domestic politics of potential allies, the security threats to potential allies, or the alliance security dilemma. In contrast, we developed a typological theory on how *combinations* of these variables might lead to or inhibit alliance contributions. We then briefly examined some states that contributed and other states that did not contribute to the Gulf War coalition, using this to refine our theory. We next selected a smaller number of cases for close study and process tracing to test our theory against more detailed evidence from the cases. At this point, even though we had partly constructed our theory on the basis of preliminary knowledge of the outcomes of the cases, our theory could still have proved to be wrong about the processes through which those outcomes arose.

One of the most striking findings, backed up by both the outcomes and the process-tracing evidence, was that Germany and Japan each contributed over $10 billion to the 1991 coalition because of the alliance security dilemma (in these instances, security dependence on the United States). This was true even though the variables for all the other three theories incorporated into our typological account weighed against Germany and Japan making large contributions. This finding limited the scope conditions of collective action theory, which had dominated the alliance literature and which wrongly predicted free riding by Germany and Japan. The typological theory we developed provided a useful framework that other scholars have built upon and applied to additional coalitions (Baltrusaitis 2009; Davidson 2011).

Like alliance burden-sharing, the transnational dimension of civil war is an enormously complex subject, and present space permits only a first cut at a typological theory on this topic. Even this preliminary effort, however, highlights the costs and benefits of typological theorizing.

To build an illustrative typological theory on transnational actors and civil conflicts, I examine whether rebel groups have external sanctuaries, as this is a critical factor in two ways. First, rebel sanctuaries in neighboring states are common, having played a role in more than half of the insurgencies since 1945 (Checkel, this volume; Salehyan 2009). Second, the presence or absence of cross-border sanctuaries strongly shapes the fighting and bargaining among the rebels' home state government, the rebels' host state, the international diaspora, third countries, NGOs, and rebel leaders. As Salehyan (2009) points out, cross-border havens lower the opportunity costs for rebels to mobilize, but they also complicate the bargaining problem between rebels and their home governments by intensifying information asymmetries and bringing an additional party – the host government – into the bargaining process. The presence or absence of cross-border rebel havens thus powerfully shapes the relationship between transnational actors and civil conflicts, and rebel havens are accordingly an important factor in the chapters in this volume by Adamson, Bakke, Hamberg, Harpviken and Lischer, and Schmitz.

To develop a typological theory on cross-border havens, I introduce three independent variables. The first of these concerns whether rebels control territory in their home state. If they do control home state territory, this gives them greater bargaining leverage vis-à-vis both the home state government and potential host governments.

A second variable is whether the government of a potential host state, a minority group in that state, or neither, supports the rebels' agenda. Government support can provide resources and a haven, while support from a minority group can provide a haven but can also put rebels at odds with the host state government if it fears any growth in the minority group's power. A loss of host government support can force rebel leaders to seek support from wider diaspora communities, third governments, NGOs, or homeland groups, and can force a return of the diaspora to its homeland. This is evident in the ups and downs of the various rebel-host relations documented in this volume: the LRA and Sudan; the Taliban and Pakistan; the Tutsis and Uganda; and the SPLA/M and Uganda.

A third variable is whether the potential host is a strong or weak state. If the host country has a strong state, it may use its resources to manipulate the rebels to serve the host's goals, as happened with the LRA in Sudan and the Taliban in Pakistan. If the host country has a weak state, the rebels will be able to pursue their own goals, and they could even become influential in the politics of the host state, as happened for a time with the Tutsis in Uganda.

The first of these independent variables (presence or absence of a rebel haven in the home state) is dichotomous, as is the third independent variable (strength or weakness of the host state). The second variable, support for rebels from the host government, a host state minority, or neither, is trichotomous. There are thus 2×2×3 or 12 possible combinations of these independent variables, or 12 types, in the typological space.

I define the dependent variable as the nature of the triangular relations and bargaining among the home government, the host government, and the rebels (for a similar approach, see Salehyan 2009). If rebels control territory in their home state, they will have more bargaining leverage and autonomy vis-à-vis both their home government and potential host governments. This presence or absence of a rebel haven in the home state then interacts with the six combinations that are possible between the second and third independent variables. These six combinations represent all of the possible mixes of three kinds of host state support for the rebels' agenda (government, minority, or neither supports the rebels) and two levels of host state strength (the state is either strong enough to expel rebels if it so chooses, or too weak to do so). I provide descriptive labels for each of these six combinations as follows:

1. A "meddlesome neighbor" arises when a strong host state supports the rebels against the home state.
2. A "cooperative neighbor" is when a strong host state opposes the rebels but needs home state help to keep them out because a minority in the host state helps the rebels.
3. No haven exists when the neighboring state is strong and neither that state nor a strong minority within it supports the rebels.
4. A "weak troublemaker" is when a weak host state backs the rebels.
5. An "eager junior partner" exists when a weak host state needs help from the home state to fight the rebels and their host state minority supporters.
6. A "weak partner" is when a weak state is unable to keep out rebels even though the rebels lack support from a minority in the host state.

Having developed the independent and dependent variables, the next step is to combine them into a typological space comprising all 12 possible combinations of these variables. This typological space is outlined in Table 8.3. Table 8.3 also represents the next step in the development of the typological theory: the categorization of the extant cases in the typological space based on a preliminary understanding of the values of the variables in each case. The table thus represents the typological theory sketched out above and places within the resulting typological space all the cases discussed in the chapters by Adamson, Bakke, Hamberg, Harpviken and Lischer, and Schmitz. I categorized the cases based on my reading of the chapters, rather than doing so based on dedicated measurements by the authors themselves or any expert independent knowledge of my own. In addition, some cases defy easy measurement, as I have simplified the typological theory by using dichotomous measures of variables that are in fact continuous. The case of Pashtun refugees in Pakistan, for example, is difficult to characterize in view of ambiguities in the Pakistani government's policies toward the Pashtun-dominated Taliban. The goal of the present exercise is to illustrate the potential value of typological theorizing rather than to categorize the cases definitively. Indeed, part of the value of such theorizing is that by making the categorization of cases explicit, it sparks useful discussions on the underlying concepts and the operationalization and measurement of the variables.

Four contributions flow from my effort at bringing together variables from different theories about causal mechanisms to construct this typological theory. First, it helps us see which cases should have similar processes and outcomes. According to Table 8.3, the Chechen rebels and the SPLA/M are the same type of cases, and they do indeed have arguably similar processes and outcomes. The Chechen rebels, lacking a secure home base or cross-border haven, were heavily reliant on the aid of transnational actors – in this case, a transnational radical Islamic movement that provided weapons, funds, and training in exchange for the Chechens' adoption of a more radical Islamic agenda. As Bakke notes, the Chechen case might have turned out differently if local leaders had been better able to push themes of nationalism and independence over those of jihad and sharia. However, the secular leaders lacked resources to win the framing fight. The other case in this type, the SPLA/M group in Sudan, displayed a similar dynamic. Hamberg recounts how the SPLA/M, lacking a secure base at home or abroad, was not convinced by normative pressures from NGOs to stop using child soldiers, but proved very open to US pressure to demobilize child soldiers in exchange for US material support.

Table 8.3 *A typological theory on triangular bargaining among rebels, home states, and host states*

Cases: Home/host, dates	Rebels hold territory in home state?	Host government, host minority, or neither support rebels (G, M, N)	Host state strong or weak?	Outcome: predicted nature of the triangular bargaining
– Tutsis in Rwanda 1990–present	Y	G	S	Meddlesome neighbor, rebels have leverage
– Hutus in Rwanda, 1996–present	Y	M	S	Cooperative neighbor, rebels have leverage
– LRA/Sudan, 1990–2002	Y	N	S	No haven; rebels vs. home government
– LRA/Democratic Republic of Congo, 2002–2005	Y	G	W	Weak troublemaker, rebels have autonomy
	Y	M	W	Eager junior partner, rebels have leverage
	Y	N	W	Weak partner, rebels have autonomy
	N	G	S	Meddlesome neighbor, rebels dependent on host
– Chechen Rebels 1999–present	N	M	S	Cooperative neighbor, rebels depend on minority in host
– SPLA/M	N	N	S	No haven; rebels vs. home government
– Tutsis/Uganda, 1961–late 1980s	N	G	W	Weak troublemaker, rebels depend on host
– Hutus/Zaire, 1994–1996				
– Pashtuns/Pakistan 1979–1989				
– Pashtuns/Pakistan 2001–present	N	M	W	Eager junior partner, rebels autonomous
– Turkish Kurds/Iraq 1991–present				
– LRA/Central African Republic 2005–present	N	N	W	Weak partner, rebels have autonomy but are vulnerable

Another set of parallels concerns the fates of the Rwandan Hutus and Tutsis. For some years in the 1960s through the 1980s, the Tutsis had a haven in Uganda. Similarly, the Hutus fled in 1994 to a haven in Zaire. While the governments of Uganda and Zaire were weak and willing to support or at least tolerate refugees from Rwanda, the militants among these refugees had relative autonomy. Harpviken and Lischer recount, for example, how Ugandan leader Yoweri Museveni drew on Tutsi support to take power in 1986. The Tutsis lost their leverage, however, when Museveni turned on the Tutsis in the late 1980s and forced them back into Rwanda. When the Tutsis lost their haven in Uganda, and when the Hutus later lost their haven in Zaire, each group was forced back into Rwanda, where the groups entered into zero-sum conflicts with one another as they lacked any cross-border haven into which they could retreat.

If cases in the same type have different outcomes from one another, or if any cases do not fit the predictions of the typological theory, these merit closer study to see if the outcomes might be due to variables omitted from the theoretical framework. There are no obvious anomalies in Table 8.3, but categorizing additional cases and placing them within the typological space could reveal some anomalies worth exploring.

Second, the typological theory helps identify "most similar cases" that differ in one independent variable and in the dependent variable, and that can thus be usefully compared. This allows the use of process tracing to help assess whether the independent variable that differs between the cases accounts for the difference in their outcomes. There are many pairs of cases in Table 8.3 that differ in one independent variable. The cases that have no base in the home state and have minority support in a weak neighboring state might be compared to those that lack a base in the home state but have support from a weak neighboring government (i.e., the NMW cases compared to the NGW cases). Cases lacking a home base but having the support of a weak cross-border government could also be compared to those that have both a home base and foreign support from a weak government.

Third, the theory facilitates the explanation of individual cases. Schmitz notes, for example, that the LRA's Joseph Kony avoids reliance on outsiders. However, he does not note that Kony's autonomy was in part an outcome of his structural position. Being able to retreat to either his base in Uganda or his cross-border bases made Kony autonomous from 1990 to 2005. In contrast, Kony's loss of cross-border bases since 2005 and the weakening of his influence inside Uganda have undercut his bargaining power vis-à-vis the Ugandan government and made him vulnerable. Similarly, although this bare-bones typological theory omits how rebel leaders framed their messages, adding this variable to the framework would provide a sharper focus on whether the changes in framing by Kony, the Kurds in Turkey, and the Pashtuns in Afghanistan were driven more by structural needs and opportunities or by leaders' ideological predilections. Pashtun refugees in Pakistan, for example, appear to have tempered their support for an independent Pashtun state in order to win support from or at least moderate the opposition of the Pakistani government.

Fourth, the typological theory advanced here provides an initial framework that scholars can expand by adding new independent variables. Most of the variables in this typological theory are drawn from structural theories about power mechanisms, but the theory could be expanded, albeit with a loss of parsimony, by incorporating additional structural or agent-centered variables. Additional structural variables might include the host state's international autonomy or dependence on other states with an interest in the conflict, the presence or absence of lootable resources, geographic terrain that provides rebel havens, rebels' social networks and legitimacy among potential followers and allies, and military and spying technologies that raise or lower the relative costs of government repression and rebel mobilization. Agent-centered variables could include the frames that rebel leaders choose, as well as their skills at negotiations and the use of force. Adding variables of course adds to the complexity of the theory, but researchers can pare back this complexity by controlling for some of the variables, thereby exploring only subsets of the full typological space in any one study.

Conclusions

The field of political science has moved increasingly over the last two decades toward mechanism-based explanations of complex phenomena. This shift is related to the development of variants of scientific realism in the philosophy of science, but it has been hampered by limited understanding among political scientists of how mechanism-based explanations differ from explanations built upon earlier philosophies of science. As Peter Hall has persuasively argued (2003), our ontological theories of how politics work, which increasingly embrace complexity, have outrun our epistemological notions of how to study politics, which still cling to the vestiges of forms of positivism that lost favor among philosophers decades ago.

A focus on explanation via reference to causal mechanisms offers one way of bringing our ontological assumptions, epistemological approaches, and research methods back into alignment. Yet political scientists have been hesitant to commit fully to this move because they have lacked a clear sense of the philosophical costs and benefits of mechanism-based explanations. The present chapter has argued that although mechanism-oriented explanations are not without their own drawbacks, they are an improvement over Kuhn's concept of "paradigms" and Lakatos' notion of "research programs." Whereas Kuhnian paradigms and Lakatosian research programs both foundered, in different ways, on the difficulties of justifying large sets of partially testable interrelated ideas, the concept of theories about discrete causal mechanisms allows for middle-range theories that are more localized, if also, more complex.

At the same time, political scientists need assurance that explanation via mechanisms does not entirely lack the key attraction of paradigms or research programs: a structured discourse that provides a framework around which we can organize cumulative research findings. Why should we move away from the "isms" – realism, liberalism, and constructivism in the IR subfield; rational choice, historical institutionalism and other "isms" in the study of American and comparative politics – and toward causal mechanisms if the latter contribute only to a hodgepodge of discrete explanations of individual cases? Here, the taxonomy of causal mechanisms introduced above shows how extant paradigms and research programs have implicitly relied on causal mechanisms all along and can be mapped onto an approach that focuses on explanatory mechanisms without reifying them into grand schools of thought.

This volume's empirical chapters demonstrate how the taxonomy allows cumulative research along many dimensions: identification of the mechanisms invoked and overlooked in particular explanations; differentiation of subtypes of mechanisms; explanations of historical cases using a variety of theorized mechanisms; assessment of the relative strength of alternative mechanisms in cases; delineation of the scope conditions under which theorized mechanisms operate; theories that cut across small groups of cases; and, finally, typological theories that provide contingent generalizations about populations of cases. As the empirical studies largely focus on one or a few conflicts, the first three of these contributions are stronger than the last three. Yet even here it is possible to demonstrate the potential contributions of constructing a typological theory of civil conflict, which examines how combinations of mechanisms interact in different structural circumstances and among mixes of actors with varying endowments of power, legitimacy, and institutional access.

Mechanism-oriented theorizing poses important costs, particularly a loss of parsimony compared to extant paradigms and research programs. Still, researchers using this approach to theory-building can choose different tradeoffs along the spectrum between parsimony and complexity. In the end, there is a strong philosophical basis for rooting the study of politics in theories about causal mechanisms. More important, it is possible to do so without losing a structured discourse and cumulation of research findings – as this book's cases and their extension suggest (see also Wood, this volume).

9 | Transnational dynamics of civil war: where do we go from here?

ELISABETH JEAN WOOD

Introduction

The transnational aspects of conflict are a pervasive theme in news reports. Revolutionary uprisings spread from Tunisia to many countries of the Middle East and North Africa in 2011, led in many cases by activists who had trained with activists from other countries. Afghan insurgents retreat across the Pakistan border to relative safe havens. Kenyan troops cross into Somalia to fight against the al-Shabab insurgency, itself responsible for attacks in Kenya, where some 500,000 Somali refugees have sought refuge from drought and violence. Transnational drug supply routes finance non-state actors in Colombia, both rebels and narco-paramilitary groups. US drones target members of al-Qaeda in Yemen, including US citizens – themselves transnational insurgents – as well as in Pakistan. Many Tamil emigrants from Sri Lanka contributed regularly to the Liberation Tigers of Tamil Eelam (LTTE), often under the threat of violence from LTTE sympathizers in the diaspora.

Although these examples may suggest that the transnational dimension of civil conflict is increasing, transnational flows of various kinds have supported actors engaged in conflict since well before the end of the Cold War. In its struggle against apartheid, the African National Congress had a network of offices across Europe and training camps in a number of African countries. Both leftist insurgent groups and counterinsurgent states drew on transnational ties during the 1970s and 1980s in Latin America. Revolutionary uprisings spread across Eastern Europe and the states of the former Soviet Union beginning in the late 1980s, and revolution spread from France to several European and Latin American countries in 1848.

Despite its evident importance in both contemporary and historical cases, scholars have only recently analyzed systematically the role of the transnational in civil conflict. The reasons for the neglect are diverse. One reason was the division of labor between comparative politics scholars, who tended to focus on domestic politics at the expense of international influences, and international relations scholars whose work on transnational politics focused on the diffusion of international norms or economic policies but paid little attention to transnational aspects of civil conflict (see also Checkel, this volume). Another challenge that quantitative scholars confronted was the difficulty of building databases that adequately capture transnational influences, often covert. Scholars immersed in single case studies or regional comparisons often shrank from framing their findings as generalizations that could be tested in other settings.

Beginning less than a decade ago, scholars have increasingly documented the role of transnational dynamics on civil conflict – on conflict onset, duration, and sometimes its attenuation. The literature is diverse, ranging from quantitative analysis of new data sets that include variables for refugees, insurgent bases, transnational ethnic groups, various forms of intervention by states, to careful qualitative analysis of individual cases of transnational politics undergirding civil conflict. The chapters in this volume are exemplary works of the latter type, pushing forward the frontiers of our understanding of transnational conflict dynamics through their identification of relevant causal mechanisms, their careful assessment of the evidence for those mechanisms as well as rival explanations (in some cases including original data gathered through field research), and their articulation (sometimes implicit) of the conditions under which those mechanisms are likely to shape conflict and its aftermath.

In this chapter, I assess the state of the literature on transnational dynamics of civil conflict with particular attention to the contributions of this volume. I also discuss the volume's methodological advances and challenges, focusing on process tracing as a technique to identify causal mechanisms and to demonstrate their effect. I begin with a discussion of the recent literature on the transnational diffusion of policy, as it in some ways sets the standard for the study of diffusion. That discussion also lays the groundwork for an assessment of the contributions of this volume to our understanding of conflict as well as to the broader literature. I emphasize the recent move to study how diffusion of a policy depends on the partisan composition of the government considering its adoption, as well as on its political (not merely policy) consequences where it was adopted earlier.

I then review the recent quantitative literature, similarly emphasizing work that shows how the risk of conflict depends on the ethnic composition of the state (in particular, whether large ethnic groups are excluded from political power) as well as of its neighbors. Next, I assess this volume's contributions to our understanding of civil conflict, diffusion, and qualitative methods. Finally, in the conclusion, I identify promising research topics arising from this volume.

Diffusion: a metaphor, an outcome, a process?

Imagine that the trees spread out across a broad swathe of rolling grassland all shriveled up and quickly died, with those further to the south dying first and those to the north last. We might say that a drought had spread, or diffused, across the area from south to north, as evidenced by the sequence and location of dead trees. What precisely would be the causal mechanisms behind the diffusion of drought? It might be the case that the trees died independently as rains failed first in the south and later in the north. Tree death "diffused" across the landscape, but in this case, the "diffusion" of the drought is a metaphor as there was in fact no interdependence between the trees associated with their death. Or perhaps the trees died because a pest spread from tree to tree beginning in the south, killing trees as it went. In this case, the material cause of tree death itself diffused across tree borders.

A more difficult case would be if a very water-intensive crop was planted beyond the southern border, depleting underground water there. The roots of the trees along the southern border tried to make up for decreased water supply by drawing water from under their neighbors just to the north, depleting some of their water. Each group of trees tried to adjust by taking water from farther north, with the result that all gradually shriveled as none could get enough. In this case, an absence of sufficient water spread as in the first case, but there is an interdependence between the trees that causes the drought to spread as in the second case.

I begin this way to contrast diffusion as a mere *metaphor* – in which some outcome "spreads" but without interdependence between the units – with diffusion as a *process* – in which the outcome in one unit occurs because it occurred in another: they are interdependent in some way. Is a geographical cluster of conflict-riven states a result of diffusion, or is it merely the case that domestic factors that make conflict more likely were equally high across the region with no "spillover" between one conflict to the next? To distinguish the *diffusion* of an outcome from its mere spread, it is necessary to specify the causal mechanism whereby the interdependence of units results in similarity of outcome.[1] In this section, I illustrate these challenges through a discussion of policy diffusion, the social science literature that has most explicitly addressed them.

The causal mechanisms underlying diffusion of policy are generally understood as falling into four categories: emulation, learning, coercion, and competition (Dobbin et al. 2007). In *emulation*, policy-makers adopt a policy innovation not because they believe it the best for their country but because they strive to emulate early adopters or take the advice of policy experts, thereby signaling their conformity, modernity, or innovator status. Interdependence in this instance is socially constructed: policy-makers willingly emulate global policy innovators (or perhaps they emulate innovations among their peers) with no consideration for whether the policy is appropriate for their polity.

In *learning*, policy-makers evaluate the new policy – its likely costs and benefits in their setting – and adopt it as the policy more likely to bring about the desired outcome. It is the assessed efficacy of the policy rather than mere copying that distinguishes learning from emulation. Learning may be rational in that the policy-maker carefully evaluates all sources and options for the polity's own circumstances (and prior beliefs are not so strong as to undermine Bayesian updating, Meseguer 2006). Or it may be boundedly rational in which some sources are weighed more heavily than others for reasons that are not rational. Chile's pension privatization policy, for example, was copied across much of the Southern Cone, despite differences in welfare systems (Weyland 2007).

Similarly, revolution diffused across much of Europe and Latin America in 1848 through the mechanism of boundedly rational learning, according to Weyland (2009): opposition members across many countries learned from the French example that revolution was possible but did not adequately account for their distinct circumstances

---

[1] For a helpful formulation of varying degrees of interdependence, see Franzese and Hays (2008, 752–754).

(except in extreme cases, which showed that learning was rational, not merely emulation). Jeff Checkel (2001) points out that a stronger form of learning – "complex learning" – occurs when policy-makers come to be persuaded through principled debate; indeed, in some cases learning may lead to the development of new interests, norms, or identities rather than merely a more informed cost benefit calculation.

In *coercion*, policy-makers face incentives that compel them to adopt the new policy because their choice has been limited by the conditions imposed by strong states. Or coercive power takes the form of promoting hegemonic ideas such that deviation is difficult to imagine.

In *competition*, policy-makers adopt a policy innovation because their rivals have done so (or will do so soon) and thus they must as well to remain competitive. As in coercion, policy-makers respond to incentives but choice is not constrained in principle, despite there being only one outcome – adoption – that is rational in the competitive circumstances.

Bearing in mind the example of the pest spreading across the grasslands to infect trees, *migration* is a fifth category that is very relevant for transnational conflict dynamics, as we will see: a policy is adopted in a new jurisdiction because an agent moves to the new polity and carries the policy along (Franzese and Hays 2008).

Despite the articulation of distinct causal mechanisms underlying diffusion, in much of the literature, the causal mechanism is theorized and the spread of an outcome is demonstrated, but without showing that the particular mechanism was, in fact, the operative cause (Dobbin et al. 2007, 463). Gilardi (2010, 650) emphasizes the accumulating evidence that policies do in fact diffuse, but goes on to argue:

On the other hand, the literature has been less successful in unpacking diffusion empirically, that is, in identifying specific diffusion mechanisms. Policies diffuse, but why? There is agreement that competition, learning, and social emulation are the main drivers of diffusion, but empirical evidence usually is ambiguous and unable to discriminate convincingly among these different explanations. Learning has been a particularly elusive hypothesis.

While more recent literature attempts to show that a particular diffusion mechanism is at work, interpretation is complicated by the overlap between mechanisms. In both emulation and bounded learning, for example, policy-makers adopt policies that may be inappropriate for their polity, but do so for different reasons that may be difficult to observe (Meseguer and Gilardi 2009, 530–531).

The challenges are theoretical, conceptual, and methodological. Meseguer and Gilardi (2009, 531–533; see also Gilardi 2010) point out that the literature makes broadly homogenizing assumptions that all actors respond in the same way to the same things, implying an underlying theory of diffusion in which the mechanisms (each itself sufficient) are additive causal factors. Moreover, they argue, it neglects the possibility that policy-makers assess the likely *political* consequences of policies, as well as their likely outcome. The underlying problem is the absence of a theory of diffusion with hypotheses specifying the conditions under which each mechanism is likely to be causally important. Methodologically, if the adoption of some policy in country B after witnessing its adoption in country A depends on particular characteristics of country A and/or B, standard (non-dyadic) quantitative approaches to analyzing diffusion from A to B will likely fail to isolate the relevant, *dyadic* effect (Franzese and Hays 2008; Gilardi 2010).

Gilardi's "Who learns from what in the policy diffusion process?" (2010) addresses several of these concerns, highlighting the salience of political consequences as well as policy outcomes in a model in which policy-makers learn from others but what they learn is conditional on their ideology. Policy-makers are not equally sensitive to new information about the likely effects of policy change, he argues, and they learn from both policy and political consequences of reform. Prior beliefs (which reflect ideological positions) shape the interpretation of new evidence, and therefore differently positioned policy-makers react differently to the same evidence. In his analysis of unemployment benefits (specifically, the replacement rate, which is the share of the salary a worker receives through unemployment insurance after losing his or her job) in 18 OECD countries, Gilardi demonstrates the importance of the inclusion of these political considerations: policy and political outcomes in other countries do not affect policy decisions per se, but do so in interaction with the partisan composition of the government (2010, 658). Thus the proper question is "Who learns from what …?" (the article's title), and learning is more complicated than usually recognized (2010, 661).

What is "learned" may thus be distinct from what was taught, depending on conditions in the "learning" country. Acharya (2004) argues that norm diffusion involves the *localization* of the norm, by which he means the adaptation of the norm so that it is sufficiently congruent with local norms (see also Checkel 1999). The degree of localization may vary across countries, across issues within the same country, and also over time as when a norm's initial acceptance (as a localized norm) leads to the later displacement of the local norm by the global norm. Based on field research in four countries, a team of researchers lead by Peggy Levitt and Sally Merry (2009) found that global ideas about women's rights were appropriated and deployed very differently in Peru, China, India, and the US. Localization or what they term vernacularization – the process of appropriating and locally adopting globally generated ideas and strategies – thus differs across countries. Vernaculizers face two dilemmas, the need to *resonate* with existing culture but also to advocate effectively for *change*. The appearance of macro similarity in the adoption of a global "package" of ideas and norms masks differences in interpretation on the ground.

Thus, researchers analyzing the patterns and consequences of policy diffusion – even in the case of their formal adoption by countries with stable institutions – face significant theoretical, methodological, and empirical challenges. Policy scholars have nonetheless advanced this research agenda through a mix of careful qualitative studies that isolate particular mechanisms (Checkel 2001; Weyland 2007, 2009); conceptual clarification that political consequences as well as policy outcomes may diffuse, conditional on the politics of the policy-maker (Gilardi 2010); the development of methods to capture such conditional diffusion; and the construction of new data sets.

Creating adequate conceptual tools, methodological approaches, and data to address the challenges discussed above is more demanding still for scholars studying the transnational dynamics of civil conflict. In such settings, actors and processes may be covert, data often unavailable or imprecise, institutions unstable and contested, interviews with knowledgeable insiders possible only in some settings (and often only for one party to the conflict), and dissimulation of goals and tactics a strategic imperative for many actors.

Transnational dynamics of civil conflict: recent quantitative literature

Despite these difficulties, the quantitative literature on civil wars has recently taken up the challenge of analyzing transnational conflict dynamics. While the importance of transnational actors and spillover effects was a prominent theme in earlier qualitative literature, quantitative analysis of the significance and substantive effect of transnational factors has surged in the past half decade or so (see also Checkel, this volume). The dependent variable in this literature is usually the risk of conflict onset, conflict duration, or the risk of renewed conflict after war's end. Similarly to the policy diffusion literature, advances have depended on the development of new data sets that capture key variables at the relevant unit of analysis and statistical approaches that look at interdependence through a dyadic modeling lens. Moreover, just as the diffusion of policy depends on the partisan composition of the government, many of the findings demonstrate the importance of the ethnic configuration (not ethnic diversity) of the state and its neighbors in transnational dynamics.

Transnational influences are significant in conflict onset, according to a variety of studies. In their exhaustive exploration of the sensitivity of empirical analysis of civil war onset to variation in data set and model specification, Hegre and Sambanis (2006) found that contiguity to a neighboring state in conflict was a robust predictor of conflict. Gleditsch (2007) found that the effect on the risk of civil conflict onset due to transnational factors was at least as large as domestic factors. Salehyan (2007, 238–239) showed that civil war in a neighboring country increases the risk of conflict onset by 85 percent. Moreover, civil wars with outside involvement tend to last longer, result in more deaths, and are more fatal (Salehyan, Gleditsch, and Cunningham 2011, 710).

The empirical demonstration that civil conflict spreads does not, however, show that it *diffuses*. The observed regional clustering of conflict might be due simply to a regional clustering of domestic factors that enhance the risk of conflict. In these studies, the authors controlled for domestic factors and thus the finding is that conflict, in fact, diffuses rather than merely spreads.

What then are the mechanisms of transnational diffusion of conflict? In principle, any of the mechanisms discussed above may underlie the diffusion of conflict. Prospective insurgents may emulate those in another country (whether or not the circumstances are propitious); they may assess the costs and benefits of embarking on a similar struggle and learn that the circumstances are propitious; they may be coerced into rebellion (perhaps because of threats to family members across the border). Incentives for conflict may increase because conflict across the border sharpens perception of grievances at home or because economic externalities (decreased trade or growth) weaken the state. Citizens or insurgents themselves may cross borders, bringing with them grievances and perhaps organizational and technological skills that deepen conflict in the host state.[2]

Although demonstrating that a particular mechanism is responsible for conflict diffusion is challenging compared to doing so for policy diffusion, scholars have nonetheless made several advances in systematically analyzing cross-national patterns.

Ethnic links across state borders have received perhaps the most sustained scholarly attention. Gleditsch (2007) found that such links predicted that conflict in one state raised the risk of conflict in neighbors that were also home to the ethnic group, and raised it more the less democratic the neighbor and the less the integration of trade between the countries. Buhaug and Gleditsch (2008) refined this finding to show that transnational ethnic ties between a group in a separatist conflict in one contributed to the emergence of a separatist conflict in the second.

The nature of the causal mechanism underlying such "ethnic links" was not, however, well specified. The existence of ethnic links indicated the presence of an ethnic group that spans both sides of a border between one state in conflict and another whose increased risk of conflict is the subject of study. Yet conflict erupts in few states compared to the number of states that share an ethnic group with another. For example, Russians in the many states that emerged after the end of the Soviet Union did not rebel against their new governments (Cederman, Gleditsch, Salehyan, and Wucherpfennig, forthcoming).

More recent work has built on the literature assessing the risk of conflict as a result of the domestic configuration of ethnic groups, with results that clearly establish the importance of ethnic politics for civil conflict. The key move is threefold. First, research designs are dyadic, focusing on the interaction between the challenger (a rebel organization in some cases, an ethnic group in others) and the state, with key variables coded at the group level. This is an essential step away from the mismatch between theories based on analysis of relations between a challenger and the state and empirical tests that relied on inappropriate

---

[2] Salehyan (2008) found that 55 percent of rebel groups conduct operations in other states.

country-level aggregate measures (Buhaug and Rod 2006; Cunningham, Gleditsch, and Saleyhan 2009; Blattman and Miguel 2010; Cederman, Wimmer, and Min 2010).

Second, analysis of ethnic conflict does not focus on ethnicity per se (for example, ethnic diversity as measured by linguistic diversity) but on the ethnic configuration of power, which includes measures for the degree of political inclusion for all politically relevant ethnic groups. This has now been compiled in an "Ethnic Power Relations" (EPR) database (Cederman, Wimmer, and Min 2010). Third, analysis of conflict increasingly relies on measures of the attributes of rebel groups, rather than inadequate proxies, drawing on the "Non-State Actor" (NSA) data set (Cunningham, Gleditsch, and Salehyan 2009).

In a seminal contribution based on the EPR data set, Cederman, Wimmer, and Min (2010) show that the risk of conflict between a particular ethnic group and the state increases with the degree of the group's exclusion from state power (especially if it experienced a loss of power in the recent past), its size, and the experience of past conflict. The effect is significant and substantial, and relevant in about half of post-World War II conflicts. Thus it is not ethnic diversity per se but exclusion from power that leads to conflict. Wucherpfennig, Metternich, Cederman, and Gleditsch (2012) linked rebel groups in the NSA data set with ethnic groups in the EPR data sets and found that civil wars in which rebel organizations recruit from and fight on behalf of excluded ethnic groups last longer than other civil conflicts. Ethnic exclusion leads to strong collective solidarity (in part through everyday humiliation of the excluded) and therefore high tolerance for risk on the part of combatants, and greater legitimacy among civilians. The state is reluctant to compromise, both because of its perceived ethnic superiority and the fear that compromise would lead other excluded groups to rebel.

As these studies have reinstated the importance of ethnicity in the domestic political dynamics that lead to civil war, others have established the salience *of transnational* ethnic links for the emergence of conflict. In a dyadic analysis of states and ethnic groups in Eurasia and North Africa, Cederman, Girardin, and Gleditsch (2009) found that while the mere presence of ethnic kin in a neighboring state had no significant effect on the risk of conflict (even when those kin were in power), the probability of conflict rose sharply (a large and significant effect) when the excluded minority was large (in the first state).

However, this finding draws upon the coding of ethnic groups in the *Atlas Narodov*, a coding of ethnic groups based only on language (not, for example, religion) in the 1960s that includes politically irrelevant groups and is thus a poor proxy for conflict-relevant ethnicity.

In a forthcoming paper, Cederman, Gleditsch, Salehyan, and Wucherpfennig use the EPR data set with a new transnational extension coding the existence (and attributes) of ethnic kin across the border. They show that the presence of ethnic kin across the border has a strongly significant and large, *curvilinear* effect on the probability of conflict. The risk of conflict increases as the number of ethnic kin increases but only to a certain point, after which it declines – the result, they argue, of the incumbent's strategically negotiating (and thereby avoiding conflict) with groups that have powerful kin across the border. The transborder effect is limited to groups that are *excluded* in the neighboring state. Stateless groups such as the Kurds are more likely to launch armed conflict: "Thus, the pernicious effect of political exclusion has a tendency to spill over state borders" (26).

While these findings clarify the conditions under which transborder ethnic groups contribute to conflict, the precise nature of the contribution of co-ethnics in the other state is not clear. How precisely does the presence of co-ethnics contribute to conflict but only when the group is a large, excluded minority? Do the neighbors support conflict but only when they weigh the prospective costs as outweighed by the benefits given the size of their excluded co-ethnics? Are the neighbors *mobilized* into such support by rebel agents? If so, is their decision better captured as emulation or bounded learning, rather than rational learning? Might they be coerced by threats against family across the border?

Sometimes such transborder ties are constructed by conflict, or the threat of conflict, as when civilians flee conflict in one state across the borders of another. The presence of refugees may contribute to conflict in the host state for various reasons, according to Salehyan and Gleditsch (2006). With refugees may come rebels, arms, and supply networks; in addition, a large presence of refugees may threaten the ethnic balance in the host state, or impose externalities on the host, for example, as when competition for scarce resources increases. In their statistical analysis, they confirmed that the presence of refugees led to a significant and substantial increase in risk of conflict in the host country (controlling for both domestic risk factors in the host and the presence of conflict in neighboring states). However, other studies have failed to confirm this finding. Buhaug and Gleditsch (2008) found that refugees have no effect on the risk of conflict in the host in general. When they disaggregated the dependent variable into conflicts over territory versus conflicts over control of the center, they found that the presence of refugees did affect both, but in opposite directions. Focusing on the effect of refugees on conflict in their state of origin (not the host), Salehyan (2007) found that their presence affected the duration but not the onset of conflict, and did so only when they were present in unstable states hostile to their state of origin.

Thus, the causal mechanism linking the presence of refugees to increased conflict remains insufficiently articulated in the quantitative literature. A distinct mechanism is the presence of rebel bases across the border. Salehyan (2007) found that it strongly increased the duration of conflict in the state of origin. Moreover, Salehyan (2008) found that the presence of rebel bases in one country strongly increases the risk of inter-state conflict between the host state and the rebels' state of origin, particularly when the two states are long-standing rivals.

Another configuration linking state actors to conflict actors is the support for insurgents by an external state. In their dyadic analysis of which rebel groups get such external support, Salehyan, Gleditsch, and Cunningham (2011) found that groups were more likely to receive military or financial support from the host state if either there was a transnational constituency or audience (a social group sympathetic on either ethnic or ideological grounds with the rebels) in the host state, or the host state was a long-standing rival of the conflict state. The effect was stronger in the case of territorial conflicts and when the non-host state itself receives external assistance (presumably from a third state). Such support tends not to go, however, to rebel groups that are either quite strong or weak compared to the enemy state.

As may be evident, most of these studies assess the correlation between conflict diffusion and the conditions hypothesized to contribute to that diffusion, rather than the process of diffusion itself. To increase the support for the claim that the hypothesized mechanism indeed underlies the empirical finding, scholars sometimes complement the quantitative analysis with qualitative evidence. For example, in an appendix, Salehyan, Gleditsch, and Cunningham (2011) report the results of their analysis of case narratives and confirm that, in 80.3 percent of the cases, the expected states (those with transnational constituencies or rivals) were in fact the ones providing rebel support. To address endogeneity issues, some authors explicitly test the reverse hypotheses – for example, in Salehyan's study of rebel bases (2008), that foreign ties predict rebel strength, rather than the reverse – to rule out inverse causality, or more minimally lag the left-hand side variables.

Despite these significant advances in the analysis of the transnational diffusion of conflict, the precise causal mechanisms underlying diffusion are not yet adequately clear. The findings often identify the conditions under which diffusion is likely (the presence of transborder ethnic ties, for example), without demonstrating precisely what mechanism drives the effect across borders. While new data sets of theoretically relevant variables mark a significant advance over earlier proxies, this literature remains largely driven by structural configurations and deploys better-specified but as-yet inadequate proxies, such as demographic size as a measure of mobilizational capacity. The *process* of conflict diffusion is difficult to observe much less capture in a cross-national database. The challenge is to identify not only the relevant conditions but also to specify *how* particular configurations of actors affect the dynamics of conflict. This is where the chapters of this volume make their most important contribution, to which we now turn.

The contributions of this volume

This volume contributes to our understanding of the transnational dimension of conflict through a focus on causal mechanisms, the specification of their observable implications, and a careful tracing of the evidence for those mechanisms in the available data. In short, the chapters focus on *how* transnational factors have causal effect. The challenges to doing so are compounded by the covert nature of many of the transnational networks and flows, the difficulty in accessing key insiders, and in many cases the fact that the views of powerful actors dominate existing narrative accounts of conflicts. In light of these challenges, essential to the persuasiveness of this type of research is the identification of rival mechanisms and their observable implications, and tracing the competing evidence for those mechanisms. In the following assessment, I first highlight the authors' contributions to our understanding of the transnational dynamics of civil conflicts, focusing on transnational mobilization and transnational insurgents, then turn to the lessons for the analysis of diffusion and qualitative methods.

The transnational mobilization of support

In her chapter on diasporas and civil conflict, Adamson identifies three mechanisms whereby diasporas may be mobilized in support of armed actors in their homeland, and two whereby that mobilization shapes a conflict's course. The first of the three mobilization mechanisms is *transnational brokerage*: conflict entrepreneurs link diaspora networks with conflict actor networks. In the case of Kurdish migrants from Turkey in Germany, some entrepreneurs were migrants who drew on their personal ties to conflict actors. Others were PKK activists who traveled between Turkey or Syria and Europe for the purpose of building support for the Kurdish armed struggle. These brokers engaged in a variety of activities to further the cause of Kurdish separatism.

These conflict entrepreneurs engaged in *strategic framing*, the second mechanism, promoting Kurdish language and culture to strengthen Kurdish over Turkish (or German) identity using transnational frames such as kinship and duty. The framing was effective, she argues, because many migrants were doubly marginalized: as Turkish immigrants they were denied German citizenship; as Kurds they were also marginalized in Turkey. As a result, the frame of resistance resonated in the diaspora, a core requirement for effective transnational mobilization. The PKK came to dominate Kurdish politics in Europe through a process of *ethnic outbidding*, the third mechanism. As a result of their double marginalization, the radical politics of the PKK came to be seen as more legitimate than the more moderate approaches of their rivals.

The mobilization was very effective in both generating significant resources for the PKK and in advocating for Kurdish interests in Europe, the two mechanisms – *lobbying-persuasion* and *resource mobilization* – whereby Adamson argues that diaspora mobilization can affect the conflict. On the former, PKK activists in the diaspora built civil society organizations to lobby European governments through both informal civic activities, such as cultural festivals, and formal institutional politics, such as developing a government in exile to facilitate the lobbying of politicians and building ties to leftist parties. Such initiatives often focused on Turkey's human rights violations. Regarding resource mobilization, the PKK developed covert networks to collect donations, extort "taxes," and recruit militants, getting these resources to Damascus and into Turkey through a variety of channels.

This analysis illuminates the mechanisms underlying the findings in the quantitative literature about the role of transnational ethnic ties. Kurds are an excluded, sizeable minority in Turkey, and so confirm the results of Cederman, Girardin, and Gleditsch (2009) discussed above. Such ties did not play a role in and of themselves, however; essential was a process of active mobilization by political entrepreneurs who set out to do just that – despite the lack of a common border. Mobilization along militant lines was thus the result of political agency by entrepreneurs, not something given by the fact of ethnic ties. Moreover, the recognition of such ties was itself a result of political agency, as many migrants from southeast Turkey who thought of themselves as Turks discovered their "Kurdishness" as a result of and through the process of mobilization. Thus Adamson's analysis shows *how* those ties played a role in both the mobilization of the diaspora and its effect back in Turkey. The mobilization follows the "boomerang" pattern of transnational activism laid out by Keck and Sikkink (1998), but with the difference that it originates with an insurgent rather than a civic organization.The case also raises further questions. The success of mobilization in Europe appears to depend critically on democratic practice there. Activists developed civil society organizations and also covert networks that engaged in a very wide range of activities, taking full advantage of associational freedoms and often appealing to human rights and self-governance global norms. Moreover, the rhetoric of campaigns often played on the complicated geopolitics between Europe and Turkey, a NATO member aspiring to European Union membership. The patterns of mobilization of the Salvadoran diaspora in the United States in support of Salvadoran insurgents follows strikingly similar patterns (Perla 2008), with a similar mix of overt and covert tactics and the leverage of human rights abuses by a state allied with the US. To what extent does successful mobilization in the diaspora depend on such democratic space? On the geopolitical issues of the day?

In his analysis of the demobilization of child soldiers by the separatist movement of southern Sudan – the Sudan People's Liberation Army (SPLA) – Hamberg also focuses on the process of transnational mobilization, but in a case with a distinct configuration of actors. In this instance, the transnational ties were originally between Christian congregations in southern Sudan and evangelical Christian organizations in the US. In light of increasing human rights abuses of civilians by the SPLA, the New Sudan Council of Churches both strengthened transnational ties to co-religionists in order to indirectly pressure the insurgent group from the US and also pressed the SPLA directly. In a context of increasing support from not only US civil society but also nationally prominent politicians, the SPLA announced that it would demobilize its child soldiers, and proceeded to do so over the ensuing months and years.

The insurgents were not responding to "naming and shaming," as in the usual model of transnational advocacy, Hamberg argues. He points out that naming and shaming campaigns were not particularly targeted at the SPLA and that, when they did mention Sudan, were focused on the government. Such campaigns thus do not explain why the SPLA was the only active rebel group to demobilize child soldiers. The SPLA, he suggests, responded to promises of concrete support, a "modified boomerang" model.

This case raises several questions about transnational mobilization by co-religionists in the context of civil conflict. While other cases of such mobilization have certainly occurred – perhaps most well documented in the mobilization of progressive religious congregations in the US by their counterparts in Central America during the 1980s (Smith 1996) – such campaigns have generally targeted governments rather than rebel groups. Under what conditions do religious networks attempt to mobilize transnationally to affect the behavior of rebel groups? And under what conditions does such mobilization succeed? Hamberg himself emphasizes the domestic attempt by the Council of Churches to directly influence the SPLA (thereby modifying the boomerang), which may suggest that this particular pattern may be most likely in the case of separatist conflicts based on a religious cleavage. But the analysis leaves other questions unanswered. Why was the culmination of the campaign the demobilization of child soldiers rather than some other change of SPLA policy? To what extent was demobilization a core demand of the Council, and to what extent was it a positive side effect of a broader campaign for negotiations to end the war? Moreover, to what extent was the learning by US Christians about the situation in southern Sudan shaped by their south Sudanese counterparts, and therefore likely to have been boundedly rational? How were the ties between the groups established in the first place? Were the US groups driven only by sympathy for their co-religionists in Sudan or did the opportunity to influence US policy more broadly also play a role? How were the transnational religious contacts initiated? What precisely were the relations between the south Sudanese congregations and the SPLA, and how did they change as a result of the former's transnational ties?

Transnational insurgents

In her analysis of the role of transnational insurgents in Chechnya, Bakke focuses on domestic, rather than transnational, mobilization. After documenting the role of Arab and other transnational insurgents in the founding of training camps, mosques, and schools, and sometimes advising key Chechen commanders, Bakke analyzes their effect on the mobilization of Chechens. She identifies three possible mechanisms: Transnational insurgents might cause shifts in framing, tactics, or resource mobilization. She argues that the increasingly Islamic (as opposed to nationalist) framing of the Chechen rebellion is best explained by the influence of the transnational insurgents. She is more skeptical about their influence on the radicalization of tactics by the rebels (attacks on civilian targets outside of Chechnya, kidnaping, and suicide attacks), but on balance suggests that transnational insurgents likely played a role in this area as well, as there was no precedent for suicide attacks in Chechen tradition. Transnational flows of financial resources as well as recruits clearly contributed to the funding of training camps, schools, and mosques (and thereby contributed to shifts in framing and tactics).

Bakke carefully traces the limits of the role of transnational insurgents as well as their contribution. At least initially, their influence was dependent on domestic "gatekeepers," whose permission was necessary for their presence. Moreover, she traces the domestic roots of some of the radical tactics such as kidnaping and attacks on civilians to raise the cost of occupation, showing that only in the adoption of suicide attacks was the influence of the transnationals indisputable. Finally, given that the significant financial flows laid out incentives for adopting an Islamist framing, she acknowledges that the shift in framing may have been strategic emulation rather than genuine learning.

Bakke's analysis illuminates the mechanisms whereby such transnational insurgents may affect conflict dynamics. The ability to channel resources, both material and ideational, appears to have been essential to the growing ties between the transnational insurgents and Chechen rebels. Yet ideational resources were controversial within the Chechen movement. Indeed, the later split in that movement indicates their resonance with domestic culture was only partial. The influence on Chechen mobilization was clearest in the shift in framing (if genuine and not strategic emulation) towards an Islamist justification, raising once again the role of broadly similar religious culture in the success of transnational mobilization in this case as well as in southern Sudan. Would they have been as effective in shifting tactics if from a different global religion? If transnational mobilization had been limited to ideational resources, would the transnational insurgents have been as effective? To what extent was the shift in framing from Chechen nationalism to Islamist jihad contested within insurgent organizations?

Harpviken and Lischer analyze a distinct pattern of transnational movement, focusing on refugee militants who engage in violence on return to their home countries. With both the return of Rwandan refugees from Uganda in 1990–1994 and Afghan refugees from Pakistan in 1992, they analyze a "transnational complex," or a history of interaction before the return between the refugees and various actors in their host countries. They discern three central mechanisms that lead to refugee militancy on return. The first is *socialization*. In both cases, many refugees were deeply socialized toward militancy during exile as they were often socially isolated in conditions of great uncertainty. The internalization and habituation to militancy in each case included battlefield socialization (fighting with Ugandan rebels for many Rwandan refugees and in trips to fight in the homeland for Afghans in Pakistan). The second is *resource control*. In Pakistan, particular political organizations (or their armed wings) controlled resources and founded both secular and religious schools as well as military training camps. On return, the urgent need to access resources to rebuild livelihoods reinforced ties to such organizations, which were often the only access to land or to state resources in the fragile and uncertain post-conflict conditions. The third is *security entrapment*. On return, many refugees faced escalating security threats as competition for access to resources increased, with the result that many sought protection with a familiar militarized group.

These mechanisms also account for local support for the resurgent Taliban after the US invasion in 2001. Most returned refugees did not support the Taliban after the US invasion, but as collateral damage from US attacks accumulated (combined with the inability of the

Afghan government to deliver on anything from basic services to security), they rejoined the Taliban as the best way to address their security dilemma. (The authors also show that Hutu extremists, after being forced from Rwanda into the eastern Democratic Republic of Congo [DRC], attempted to build institutions to socialize the mainly Hutu refugees through their control of resources, but those efforts were cut short when Rwanda invaded and forced many to return to Rwanda, where they were put in camps to re-socialize them.) Harpviken and Lischer thus identify a distinct mechanism underlying the connection between refugees and conflict – one not discussed in any detail in the quantitative literature – namely, the return of militant refugees. Their analysis suggests that returnee violence – the dark side of refugee agency – is most likely when refugees are socialized by militant groups in exile, particularly if it includes battlefield socialization, and when they rely on armed groups for protection or access to resources on return. However, the analysis does not explore the conditions under which the return will be as a coherent, effective militarized organization, as in Rwanda, rather than a disparate set of factions, as in Afghanistan in 1992 (but not after 2001). Whether or not the three mechanisms account for this divergence is not clear.

Schmitz analyzes the case where a rebel group itself became transnational. The Lord's Resistance Army is a hard case for showing transnational influences, for the reasons he points out but also because the group appears to have engaged in little mobilization of the diaspora or built an overt transnational network of any kind. On the other hand, the group itself has been based in a series of distinct countries, moving from its origins in Uganda to southern Sudan, then to northeastern DRC via Uganda, and then to the Central African Republic. Schmitz argues that even in this case, transnational mechanisms had an important but not necessarily overwhelming role in shaping the course of the conflict.

Like Bakke, Schmitz analyzes transnational influences in terms of shifts in framing, tactics, and resources. He traces the origins of the group's ideology to the transnational influence of Christian missions, lending a messianic cadence to its beliefs. While in southern Sudan, where the group engaged in operations with Sudanese government forces (and pro-government militias), it widened its repertoire to include mutilation of supposed collaborators. In response to increasing criticism from human rights groups and the Acholi diaspora, the group shifted both its repertoire (with mutilation nearly disappearing) and framing (shifting away from religious to more secular, human rights focused rhetoric). Resource mobilization had long been transnational for the LRA, with access to bases and financial resources from Khartoum as part of its policy of arming the group as a proxy force against the SPLA. Despite these transnational links, Schmitz is careful to point out that the influence of diaspora politics is much less than in the Kurdish case analyzed by Adamson.

Schmitz analyzes the international prosecution of armed group leaders as a distinct causal mechanism shaping transnational conflict dynamics. In his analysis of the failure of peace negotiations, Schmitz emphasizes the negative effects of the indictment of LRA leaders by the International Criminal Court (originally, on the government of Uganda's invitation). He interprets international prosecution as a form of non-relational diffusion, arguing that – in the absence of the personal ties of relational diffusion – it may create sharp disincentives for conflict termination.

The case appears to be a compelling instance of the arming of an insurgency (and allowing base camps) by a rival state, in this case Sudan. But as is perhaps inevitable in this hard-to-document case, Schmitz' analysis begs more questions than the available evidence can address. Was Sudan's target the government of a rival state, or its own insurgent group? The evidence appears to support the latter given the record of activity in Sudan that Schmitz presents. Under what conditions will a state arm the insurgents of a rival state as a proxy against its own insurgents? Was the widening of the LRA's repertoire after going on operations with Sudanese forces an instance of emulation, as he argues, of bounded learning, or perhaps of coercive learning in response to conditioning of aid from Sudan in some way? Emulation or bounded learning appears equally plausible given the limited evidence. Under what perhaps implicit conditions did the government of Sudan arm the LRA, and what precisely undermined that relationship?

On transnational diffusion

The chapters thus contribute to our understanding of the causal mechanisms underlying transnational diffusion by showing *how* the dynamics of conflict in one country are shaped by dynamics in another. The mechanisms include most of those analyzed in the policy diffusion literature (emulation, learning, and shifting incentives) and in the quantitative literature (the presence of transnational ethnic ties, refugees, and rebel bases) and thus add to our understanding of the "dark side" of transnational politics under which it is not positive global norms but conflict dynamics that shape the behavior of conflict actors. Moreover, the chapters also identify new mechanisms of transnational diffusion and demonstrate their importance for understanding conflict dynamics.

More specifically, one theme of the volume is the extent to which migration is an essential mechanism of diffusion, a mechanism little emphasized in the policy literature. In Chechnya, transnational insurgents brought a variety of material and ideational resources to separatist rebels. In Europe, PKK members founded civil society organizations as well as covert networks. In both Rwanda and Afghanistan in the early 1990s, militant refugees returning from exile engaged in battles for control of their homeland state as well as for control of territory and resources. In Sudan, the DRC, and the Central African Republic as well as Uganda, the LRA carried out its repertoire of violence, particularly looting and abductions. The LRA case also points to the importance of a multiplicity of state borders for an insurgent group seeking refuge.

A second, broad mechanism is the mobilization of external populations. As Adamson demonstrates in her chapter on the Kurdish/Turkish civil conflict – and in contrast to the quantitative literature which generally treats diasporas as unitary actors predisposed to become active in conflicts – diasporas must be actively mobilized through the usual contentious politics mechanisms of framing, tactical innovation, and resource mobilization. Hamberg's chapter shows that non-diasporic, external groups may be mobilized as well, particularly religious networks in support of actors fighting against discrimination and violence targeted at members of that religion. The chapter demonstrates the importance of personal contact for such mobilization, between representatives of the two religious networks but also between the politicians lobbied by each one. Mobilization in this case led to a lessening of conflict both in the form of child soldier demobilization and arguably in the form of increased international support for a negotiated resolution of the decades-long conflict.

Similarly, if refugee populations are to actively shape the conflict in their homeland, they must be mobilized, as Harpviken and Lischer show.

The conditions are, however, fairly stringent, according to their analysis. Militant groups must control sufficient resources in exile (to monopolize institutions through which they can effectively socialize the refugee population) and also on return (to enforce group loyalty through the control of scarce resources), and the returnees must face a security trap (and thus redouble their allegiance to the militant group). Nome and Weidmann's agent-based model confirms the efficacy of brokerage by transnational norm entrepreneurs as a mechanism for mobilizing transnational populations. The model focuses on the role of such brokers in laying the groundwork for mobilization through changes in the repertoire of imagined social identities. In circumstances where signals from the homeland are noisy (likely the case from a country in conflict), brokerage is significantly more effective in diffusing the new, though latent, social identify. That identity could then become active (and thus mobilizeable) under conditions of not unreasonably high receptivity among the diaspora. The cases of the actively mobilized Kurdish and minimally mobilized Acholi diaspora (the ethnic group on which the LRA originally drew) appear to be positive and negative instances of this mechanism.

The model also raises the question of mobilization of a diaspora in support of the state rather than the insurgency, as nothing in the model presumes the brokers are rebels. Hector Perla Jr., (2005; 2009) demonstrated just such a pattern – which he terms the "signal flare" mechanism – in the case of Sandinista Nicaragua mobilizing Nicaraguans in the US to oppose US policy in Central America, particularly US support for the *contra* insurgents.

The chapters thus contribute to research on transnational contentious politics through the identification and demonstration of the causal force (under certain conditions) of the mechanisms highlighted in that literature. Tarrow (2005) identifies three classes of transnational diffusion mechanisms: relational (diffusion through personal ties), mediated (through the brokering of a mutual contact), and non-relational (through impersonal means such as learning from publications or news reports). Bakke emphasizes the importance of relational diffusion (personal ties between insurgent leaders and a Chechen commander) early in her Chechen case. Transnational brokers, as Adamson demonstrates, were essential to the mobilization of the Kurdish diaspora in Europe.

The role of non-relational diffusion through global media of innovations in framing, tactics, and resource mobilization, which may occur alongside relational and brokered diffusion, is much more difficult to assess. To what extent did jihadist videos available via DVDs and the internet (specifically, those not distributed by the schools, mosques, and camps founded by the transnational insurgents themselves) also influence the shift toward Islamist framing from that of Chechen nationalism in Bakke's study? The chapters thus deepen our understanding of transnational diffusion by disaggregating that overly broad concept into several analytically distinct mechanisms – and sometimes disaggregating those, as when mobilization of a diaspora is understood as a composite mechanism made up of the contentious politics mechanisms of framing, tactical innovation, and resource mobilization. As noted by Checkel (this volume), the proper level of disaggregation is given by the state of the literature. One measure of this volume's advances in the understanding of diffusion is the disaggregation of mechanisms along with the (often implicit) statement of when each is likely.

On method

To address the challenging task of identifying causal mechanisms that shape transnational conflict dynamics, the chapters engage in process tracing (with the exception of the chapter by Nome and Weidmann to which I return below). Process tracing involves a commitment to showing *how* a result was brought about. To persuasively show that a particular mechanism was in fact the "how" that brought about the result in the difficult setting of transnational conflict dynamics, an author must identify a plausible mechanism and its observable implications; tell a compelling, well-evidenced narrative documenting that those observable implications in fact occurred (subject to the limitations and bias of the relevant data), and also show that the observable implications of rival mechanisms do not occur after "relentlessly" (Bennett, this volume) pursuing that data.

In working with incomplete, indeed sometimes fragmentary, data, the assessment of the likely bias in the source is, of course, crucial. Moreover, arguments based on process tracing should account for important turning points in the sequence of events (Bennett, this volume). Given the limitations of data, it may emerge that while no "smoking gun" was found, the explanation based on that mechanism gains plausibility if alternatives are not supported (or are significantly less well supported).

Hamberg's chapter stands out for his careful construction of a difficult argument despite the lack of a smoking gun, which in his case would have been direct confirmation that in fact the SPLA demobilized child soldiers in exchange for support from US political actors. No such datum was forthcoming, but Hamberg persuasively shows that arguments based on rival mechanisms – the SPLA no longer needed child soldiers, that NGO or UN naming and shaming campaigns calling for demobilization of child soldiers had made their retention untenable, among others – are unpersuasive. Bakke also carefully weighs the evidence for the domestic origins of the shifts in framing, tactics, and resources she documented, reaching a nuanced judgment that the influence of transnational insurgents varied across those three issues. Schmitz discusses the authenticity of manifestos supposedly put out by the LRA, concluding that, while it was not possible to attribute authorship to particular group leaders, the documents nonetheless reflected the organization's views at the time. Harpviken and Lischer take advantage of the additional analytic leverage available through the comparison of two cases of refugees who engaged in violence on their return. The divergent ways refugees were socialized in exile (Afghans largely residing in camps controlled by militant factions and immersed in institutions for military and political socialization; Rwandans living in isolation without such immediate dominance of everyday lives), allowed the authors to focus on particular aspects of exile socialization, and argue for the causal centrality of these common factors. For example, the role of battlefield socialization is persuasive in part because it was present in both cases. The authors also leveraged internal comparison to some degree, comparing those Afghan factions who fought for Kabul in 1992 with those who did not, the return of Afghan refugees in 1992 and after 2001, and the return of Rwandan Tutsi refugees from 1990 to 1994 with the coerced return of Rwandan Hutu refugees after 1996.

Nome and Weidmann in their chapter demonstrate how agent-based modeling complements both process tracing and quantitative analysis. After noting that quantitative studies usually only capture the conditions that are said to result in diffusion or the fact of outcome (but not the process), they model two mechanisms whereby transnational diffusion of social identity might occur. They are able to show through their analysis of simulations that one mechanism (brokerage in the form of a transnational norm entrepreneur, followed by social adaptation) more consistently results in successful diffusion than the other (adaptation across country borders). They are careful to label the result a confirmation of the one mechanism as a "candidate explanation" subject to further empirical testing.

The chapter shows how the method forces its practitioners to clearly lay out the logic of the mechanism in the form of the rules that the agents follow (with some degree of error) and nonetheless produces results that are not obvious beforehand. In particular, drawing on the logic of the brokerage-followed-by-adaptation mechanism, Nome and Weidmann show that a change of social identity on the part of both young Chechens and young Kurds would have been likely, not simply the shift in framing traced by Bakke in Chechnya nor the promotion of new cultural tropes by PKK activists in Europe, as discussed by Adamson.

Process tracing as conducted in this volume thus demonstrates the power of the method when deployed with careful assessments of rival mechanisms. The chapters also demonstrate how the method is complementary to quantitative analysis (Sambanis 2004; George and Bennett 2005; Gerring 2007b) and agent-based modeling (Nome and Weidmann, this volume), confirming some mechanisms discussed in the quantitative literature, identifying new ones, and fleshing out the actors, motives, alliances, and the intended and unintended consequences of their actions.

Conclusion: a research agenda

How might the above contributions to our understanding of transnational conflict dynamics, transnational diffusion, and qualitative method be further leveraged to advance that understanding still more deeply? Moving from the identification of causal mechanisms towards a theory of transnational conflict dynamics depends on the specification of scope conditions in the form of hypotheses and then the aggregation of distinct hypotheses into a coherent theory. Such a task is far beyond what this chapter can achieve. In what follows, I take up a more feasible task, suggesting aspects of the research agenda implied by this volume's essays. Just as scholars of policy diffusion are beginning to study how learning is conditional on the politics of both source and innovating country – the who-learns-what-from-whom approach mentioned above – one promising way forward for students of transnational conflict dynamics is to interrogate more carefully the conditions under which diasporas are mobilized, coalitions constructed, and resources dispersed.

We saw above that the successful mobilization of the Kurdish diaspora in Europe was in part due to the democratic nature of European governance (particularly freedom of association). Moreover, that mobilization leveraged (more or less successfully at different times) both the global normative discourse of human rights and also the geopolitical ties between Europe and Turkey. This suggests the following hypothesis:

The more democratic is the host state and the more allied it is with the origin state, the more likely is mobilization of support in the diaspora by insurgents.

It also begs further questions. Under what conditions will the state itself attempt to mobilize support in the diaspora? And when do contending efforts to mobilize the diaspora arise, with one group of transnational entrepreneurs attempting to mobilize the diaspora in favor of one group (perhaps the insurgents) and another in favor of another group (a rival non-state group, or perhaps the state itself)?

As discussed in the chapter by Adamson, the PKK emerged as the dominant force in the Kurdish diaspora because its more radical message resonated more deeply with the doubly marginalized Kurds in Germany than that of its moderate rivals. This suggests the following hypothesis:

The more democratic is the host state and the marginalized are members of the diaspora in the state of origin, the more likely is mobilization of the diaspora (perhaps by contending actors).

However, the mobilization of Nicaraguan diaspora in the US by the Sandinista government (Perla 2005; 2008) suggests that such mobilization might also be likely when the states are themselves in conflict, leading to the more complex hypothesis:

The more democratic is the host state and the more conflictual are the host and origin states, the more likely mobilization of the diaspora will occur by the state of orgin.

Another question raised by the chapters on southern Sudan and Chechnya is the role of a common religion in the building of transnational alliances. Would the transnational insurgents have been as welcome in Chechnya if Islam had not been a shared religion (notwithstanding the many differences between the Salafi approach to Islamist thought and that of Chechen Muslims)? Similarly, the alliance between southern Sudanese Christian churches and evangelical networks in the US appears to have depended to a large degree on a shared Christian faith, framed as under attack in southern Sudan. Are conflicts along the lines of a religious cleavage between two world religions particularly likely to draw in transnational allies, either for mitigating conflict as in this case, or for stoking it, as in the former? This suggests the following hypothesis:

Transnational mobilization of allies is more likely in the case of conflicts along the lines of a religious (or ethnic) cleavage than where that cleavage is absent.

Note that both these conflicts are separatist conflicts, so one might argue more specifically that: transnational mobilization of allies is more likely in the case of separatist conflicts along the lines of a religious cleavage.

The volume's emphasis on migration as a mechanism of transnational diffusion (one nearly absent in the literature on policy diffusion) similarly suggests research questions and hypotheses. Are the mechanisms identified in the Rwandan and Afghan cases of refugee militants relevant for other instances of refugee militancy? This leads to the following hypothesis:

Where militant groups control schools in exile and promote military training, refugees themselves participate in military excursions, and on return such groups control access to livelihood and security, refugees are more likely to participate in violence.

Raised but not fully answered in the Rwandan/Afghan comparison is an additional research question: given the conditions for refugee militancy, what are the further conditions for the emergence of a coherent, unitary organization in exile (versus a variety of factions)?

The agent-based model of transnational diffusion of social identity suggested that transnational norm entrepreneurs are more efficient in such diffusion than mere social adaptation given that the "signal" coming from a conflict-ridden country is likely complex (noisy) and assuming that the receptivity on the part of the diaspora population to the new identity is not too low. As a candidate explanation, the implications call for further research on cases where mobilization of a diaspora occurred – and also where it did not despite efforts of either type. More generally, the chapter highlights the usefulness of agent-based modeling in clarifying the logic of causal mechanisms through precisely stipulating this logic and simulating the consequences. The comparison of two candidate mechanisms in the same modeling framework in the chapter is particularly useful.

The analysis of the diffusion of violent tactics – for example, suicide terrorism into Chechnya – suggests that a broader study of the diffusion of distinct patterns of insurgent violence would be a timely research initiative, complementing the many studies on terrorism. Ideally, an investigation would document and analyze the conditions for the transnational diffusion of targeting patterns and of forms of violence (massacres as retaliation, disappearances, particular forms of torture, etc.) as well as the underlying mechanisms, including migration of combatants, emulation, learning from peer organizations or from media, coercion, and competition. Although it is more difficult to gather data on non-lethal than lethal injuries, scholars and activists increasingly collect data on torture, sexual violence, abduction, and other types of violence (Hafner-Burton and Ron 2009). Additionally, disaggregated data about the pattern of attacks is increasingly available, as in the recently released Uppsala Conflict Data Program – Georeferenced Event Dataset, which covers Africa (see Sundberg, Lindgren, and Padskocimaite 2010).

While the chapters largely focus on transnational dynamics – that is, relations across borders between non-state actors and between non-state actors and states – the empirical reality of transnational mechanisms linking insurgencies and external states to another state's insurgency raises the issue of the contribution of state-to-state relations to transnational dynamics of conflict. It is likely that an adequate understanding of transnational dynamics will be impossible without an understanding of state-to-state innovation, many times in response to transnational developments – a crucial analytic move increasingly seen in the broader transnational politics literature as well (Orenstein and Schmitz 2006).

More broadly still, further development and testing of the mechanisms underlying transnational conflict dynamics will likely come from analysis of a broader range of cases, particularly those from the Cold War era, including national liberation movements, revolutionary armed struggles, and the transnational dynamics of states opposing both.

Bibliography

Abdelal, R., Y. M. Herrera, A. I. Johnston, & R. McDermott, 2009. "Identity as a Variable." In R. Abdelal, Y. M. Herrera, A. I. Johnston, & R. McDermott (eds.), *Measuring Identity: A Guide for Social Scientists.* Cambridge University Press.

Acharya, Amitaev. 2004. "How Ideas Spread: Whose Norms Matter? Norm Localization and Institutional Change in Asian Regionalism." *International Organization.* 58 (2), 239–275.

Achverina, Vera & Simon Reich. 2009. "No Place to Hide: Refugees, Displaced Persons, and Child Soldier Recruits." In Scott Gates & Simon Reich (eds.), *Child Soldiers in the Age of Fractured States.* Pittsburg University Press.

Adam, Jeroen, Bruno De Cordier, Kristof Titeca, & Koen Vlassenroot. 2007. "In the Name of the Father? Christian Militantism in Tripura, Northern Uganda, and Ambon." *Studies in Conflict & Terrorism.* 30, 963–983.

Adamson, Fiona B. 2002. "Mobilizing for the Transformation of Home: Politicized Identities and Transnational Practices." In Nadje al-Ali & Khalid Koser (eds.), *New Approaches to Migration? Transnational Communities and the Transformation of Home.* London: Routledge, 155–168.

2004. "Displacement, Diaspora Mobilization, and Transnational Cycles of Political Violence." In John Tirman (ed.), *Maze of Fear: Migration and Security after 9/11.* New York: New Press, 45–58.

2005. "Globalization, Transnational Political Mobilization, and Networks of Violence." *Cambridge Review of International Affairs.* 18 (1) April, 35–53.

2006. "Crossing Borders: International Migration and National Security." *International Security.* 31 (1) Summer, 165–199.

2012. "Constructing the Diaspora: Diaspora Identity Politics and Transnational Social Movements." In Terrence Lyons & Peter Mandaville (eds.), *Globalization and Diaspora: Politics from Afar.* London: Hurst and Co., 25–42.

Adamson, Fiona B. & Madeleine Demetriou. 2007. "Rethinking the Boundaries Between 'State' and 'National Identity:' Incorporating Diasporas into IR Theorizing." *European Journal of International Relations.* 13 (4) December, 489–526.

Adelman, Howard. 2002. "Refugee Repatriation." In Stephen John Stedman, Donald Rotchild, & Elizabeth M. Cousens (eds.), *Ending Civil Wars: The Implementation of Peace Agreements.* Boulder, CO: Lynne Rienner, 273–302.

Adler, Emanuel. 2002. "Constructivism and International Relations." In Walter Carlsnaes, Thomas Risse, & Beth Simmons (eds.), *Handbook of International Relations.* London: Sage Publications, 95–118.

Akgündüz, Ahmet. 1993. "Labour Migration from Turkey to Western Europe (1960–1974): An Analytical Review." *Capital and Class.* 51, 153–194.

Allen, Tim. 2005. *War and Justice in Northern Uganda: An Assessment of the International Criminal Court's Intervention.* London: Crisis States Research Centre/London School of Economics.

2006. *Trial Justice. The International Criminal Court and the Lord's Resistance Army.* London: Zed Books.

Allen, Tim and Mareike Schomerus. 2006. *A Hard Homecoming: Lessons Learned from the Reception Center Process on Effective Interventions for Former "Abductees" in Northern Uganda.* Washington DC/Kampala: USAID/UNICEF.

Allen, Tim and Koen Vlassenroot (eds.). 2010. *The Lord's Resistance Army: Myth and Reality.* London: Zed Books.

Ames, Barry. 2009. "Methodological Problems in the Study of Child Soldiers." In Scott Gates and Simon Reich (eds.), *Child Soldiers in the Age of Fractured States.* Pittsburg University Press.

Amnesty International. 1991. *Sudan: Human Rights Violations during the Military Government's Second Year in Power.* London: Amnesty International.

1997. *"Breaking God's Commands:" The Destruction of Childhood by the Lord's Resistance Army.* London: Amnesty International.

1999. *Uganda. Breaking the Circle: Protecting Human Rights in the Northern War Zone.* London: Amnesty International.

Amstutz, J. Bruce. 1986. *Afghanistan: The First Five Years of Soviet Occupation.* Washington DC: National Defense University Press.

Anderson, Benedict. 1998. "Long-Distance Nationalism." In Benedict Anderson, *The Spectre of Comparisons: Nationalism, Southeast Asia, and the World.* London: Verso, 58–74.

Andvig, Jens Christopher and Scott Gates. 2009. "Recruiting Children for Armed Conflict." In Scott Gates & Simon Reich (eds.), *Child Soldiers in the Age of Fractured States.* Pittsburg University Press.

Angousteres, Aline and Valerie Pascal. 1996. "Diasporas et financement des conflits." In F. Jean & J.-C. Ruffin (eds.), *Economie des Guerres Civiles*. Paris: Hachette.

Annan, Jeannie, Christopher Blattman, Dyan Mazurana, & Khristopher Carlson. 2009. "Women and Girls at War: 'Wives,' Mothers and Fighters in the Lord's Resistance Army." Mimeo. New Haven: Department of Political Science, Yale University (October).

Arusha Peace Agreement. 1993. "Arusha Peace Agreement: Protocol of Agreement between the Government of the Republic of Rwanda and the Rwandese Patriotic Front on the Repatriation of Rwandese Refugees and the Resettlement of Displaced Persons."

Autesserre, Severine. 2009. "Hobbes and the Congo: Frames, Local Violence and International Intervention." *International Organization*. 63 (2), 249–280.

Baiev, Khassan. 2003. *The Oath: A Surgeon Under Fire*. London: Simon & Schuster.

Baltrusaitis, Daniel. 2009. *Coalition Politics and the Iraq War: Determinants of Choice*. Boulder, CO: Lynne Reiner.

Barfield, Thomas J. 2010. *Afghanistan: A Cultural and Political History*. Princeton University Press.

Barkey, Henri J. & Graham E. Fuller. 1998. *Turkey's Kurdish Question*. Oxford: Rowman and Littlefield.

Barnett, Michael. 1999. "Culture, Strategy and Foreign Policy Change: Israel's Road to Oslo." *European Journal of International Relations*. 5 (1), 5–36.

Beah, Ishmael. 2007a. "The Making, and Unmaking, of a Child Soldier." *New York Times*. January 14.

  2007b. *A Long Way Gone: Memoirs of a Boy Soldier*. New York: Farrar, Straus and Giroux.

Behrend, Heike. 1999. *Alice Lakwena & the Holy Spirits: War in Northern Uganda, 1985–97*. Oxford: James Curry.

Beissinger, Mark. 2002. *Nationalist Mobilization and the Collapse of the Soviet State*. New York: Cambridge University Press.

Belz, Mindy. 2001. "More than a Warlord." *World Magazine*. July 21.

Benford, Robert D. 1993. "Frame Disputes within the Nuclear Disarmament Movement." *Social Forces*. 71 (3), 677–701.

Benford, Robert D. & David A. Snow. 2000. "Framing Processes and Social Movements: An Overview and Assessment." *Annual Review of Sociology*. 26, 611–639.

Bennett, Andrew. 2003. "A Lakatosian Reading of Lakatos: What Can we Salvage from the Hard Core?" In Colin Elman & Miriam Elman (eds.),

Progress in International Relations Theory: Appraising the Field. Cambridge, MA: MIT Press, 455–494.

2008. "Process Tracing: A Bayesian Approach." In Janet Box-Steffensmeier, Henry Brady, & David Collier (eds.), *Oxford Handbook of Political Methodology.* Oxford University Press.

Bennett, Andrew & Jeffrey T. Checkel (eds.). Forthcoming. *Process Tracing in the Social Sciences: From Metaphor to Analytic Tool.*

Bennett, Andrew, & Colin Elman. 2006. "Qualitative Research: Recent Developments in Case Study Methods." *Annual Review of Political Science.* 9, 455–476.

2007. "Case Study Methods in the International Relations Subfield." *Comparative Political Studies.* 40 (2), 170–195.

Bennett, Andrew & Alexander George. 2005. *Case Studies and Theory Development in the Social Sciences.* Cambridge, MA: MIT Press.

Bennett, Andrew, Joseph Lepgold, & Danny Unger. 1994. "Burden-sharing in the Persian Gulf War." *International Organization.* 48, 39–75.

Bevan, James. 2007. "The Myth of Madness: Cold Rationality and 'Resource' Plunder by the Lord's Resistance Army." *Civil Wars.* 9, 343–358.

Bhaskar, Roy. 1975. *A Realist Theory of Science.* Leeds Books.

Biswas, Bidisha. 2004. "Nationalism by Proxy: A Comparison of Social Movements Among Diasporic Sikhs and Hindus." *Nationalism and Ethnic Politics.* 10 (2), 269–295.

Black, Richard. 2006. "Return of Refugees: Retrospect and Prospect." In Michael Dumper (ed.), *Palestinian Refugee Repatriation: Global Perspectives.* London: Routledge, 23–40.

Blattman, Christopher. 2007. "The Causes of Child Soldiering: Theory and Evidence from Northern Uganda." Paper presented at the Annual Convention of the International Studies Association, Chicago (March).

Blattmann, Christopher & Jeannie Annan. 2010. "On the Nature and Causes of LRA Abduction: What the Abductees Say." In Tim Allen & Koen Vlassenroot (eds.), *The Lord's Resistance Army: Myth and Reality.* London: Zed Books, 132–155.

Blattman, Christopher & Edward Miguel. 2010. "Civil war." *Journal of Economic Literature.* 48 (1), 3–57.

Bob, Clifford. 2005. *The Marketing of Rebellion: Insurgents, Media and International Activism.* New York: Cambridge University Press.

Bobrovnikov, Vladimir. 2001. "Al-Azhar and Shari'a Courts in Twentieth-Century Caucasus." *Middle Eastern Studies.* 37 (4), 1–24.

Borchgrevink, Kaja. 2010. "Religious Education in Afghanistan and Trans-border Religious Networks." PRIO Paper. Peace Research Institute Oslo.

Boutroue, Joel. 1998. "Missed Opportunities: The Role of the International Community in the Return of the Rwandan Refugees from Eastern Zaire: July 1994–December 1996." Cambridge, MA: Center for International Studies, MIT and UNHCR.

Brady, Henry. 2008. "Causation and Explanation in Social Science." In Janet Box-Steffensmeier, Henry Brady, & David Collier (eds.), *The Oxford Handbook of Political Methodology*. Oxford University Press, 217–270.

Branch, Adam. 2007. "Uganda's Civil War and the Politics of ICC Intervention." *Ethics & International Affairs*. 21, 179–198.

Brinkerhoff, Jennifer. 2006. "Digital Diasporas and Conflict Prevention: The Case of Somalinet.com." *Review of International Studies*. 32 (1), 25–47.

Brown, Elijah, M. 2008. "The Road to Peace: The Role of the Southern Sudanese Church in Communal Stabilization and National Resolution." Ph.D. Dissertation, University of Edinburgh. www.era.lib.ed.ac.uk/bitstream/1842/3260/1/EM%20Brown%20PhD%20thesis%2008.pdf. (Accessed July 11, 2010)

Brownback, Sam. 1999. "Brownback Presses for Food Aid to Suffering Victims in Sudan." News Release. http://brownback.senate.gov/press-app/record.cfm?id=175969. (Accessed July 26, 2010)

2007. *From Power to Purpose*. Nashville: Thomas Nelson.

Brubaker, Rogers. 1996. *Nationalism Reframed: Nationhood and the National Question in the New Europe*. Cambridge University Press.

2005. "The 'Diaspora' Diaspora." *Ethnic and Racial Studies*. 28 (1), 1–19.

Brubaker, Rogers & David D. Laitin. 1998. "Ethnic and Nationalist Violence." *Annual Review of Sociology*. 24, 423–452.

Bruce, John. 2007. "Drawing a Line Under the Crisis: Reconciling Returnee Land Access and Security in Post-conflict Rwanda." In Humanitarian Policy Group Working Paper. London: Overseas Development Institute.

Bruinessen, Martin van. 1998. "Shifting National and Ethnic Identities: The Kurds in Turkey and the European Diaspora." *Journal of Muslim Minority Affairs*. 18 (1), 39–51.

Buhaug, Halvard & Scott Gates. 2002. "The Geography of Civil War." *Journal of Peace Research*. 39 (4), 417–433.

Buhaug, Halvard & Kristian Skrede Gleditsch. 2008. "Contagion or Confusion? Why Conflicts Cluster in Space." *International Studies Quarterly*. 52, 214–233.

Buhaug, Halvard & Jan Ketil Rød. 2006. "Local Determinants of African Civil Wars, 1970–2001." *Political Geography*. 25 (3), 315–335.

Bundesamt für Verfassungsschutz. 1996. *Die Arbeiterpartei Kurdistans (PKK) – Strukturen, Ziele, Aktivitaeten.* Cologne: Bundesamt für Verfassungsschutz.

Burt, Ronald S. 2005. *Brokerage and Closure: An Introduction to Social Capital.* Oxford University Press.

Busby, Joshua William. 2007. "Bono Made Jesse Helms Cry: Jubilee 2000, Debt Relief, and Moral Action in International Politics." *International Studies Quarterly.* 51 (2), 247–275.

Byman, Daniel, Peter Chalk, Bruce Hoffman, William Rosenau, & David Brannan. 2001. *Trends in Outside Support for Insurgent Movements.* Santa Monica: Rand.

Capie, David. 2008. "Localization as Resistance: The Contested Diffusion of Small Arms Norms in Southeast Asia." *Security Dialogue.* 39, 637–658.

Caporaso, James. 2009. "Is There a Quantitative-Qualitative Divide in Comparative Politics? The Case of Process Tracing." In Todd Landman & Neil Robinson (eds.), *The Sage Handbook of Comparative Politics.* London: Sage Publications.

Carpenter, R. Charli. 2007. "Setting the Advocacy Agenda: Theorizing Issue Emergence and Nonemergence in Transnational Advocacy Networks." *International Studies Quarterly.* 51 (1), 99–120.

Cederman, Lars-Erik. 2001. "Agent-Based Modeling in Political Science." *The Political Methodologist: Newsletter of the Political Methodology Section of the American Political Science Association.* 10 (1), 16–22.

2003. "Modeling the Size of Wars: From Billiard Balls to Sandpiles." *American Political Science Review.* 97 (1), 135–150.

Cederman, Lars-Erik, Kristian Skrede Gleditsch, Idean Salehyan, & Julian Wucherpfennig. Forthcoming. "Transborder Ethnic Kin and Civil War." *International Organization.*

Cederman, Lars-Erik, Luc Girardin, & Kristian Skrede Gleditsch. 2009. "Ethnonationalist Triads: Assessing the Influence of Kin Groups on Civil War." *World Politics.* 61 (3), 403–437.

Cederman, Lars-Erik, Andreas Wimmer, & Brian Min. 2010. "Why do Ethnic Groups Rebel? New Data and Analysis." *World Politics.* 62 (1), 87–119.

Centlivres, Pierre & Micheline Centlivres-Demont. 1988. "The Afghan Refugees in Pakistan: A Nation in Exile." *Current Sociology.* 36 (2), 71–92.

Chabal, Patrick & Jean-Pascal Daloz. 1999. *Africa Works: Disorder as Political Instrument.* Oxford/Bloomington: James Currey/Indiana University Press.

Chandra, Kanchan. 2005. "Ethnic Parties and Democratic Stability." *Perspectives on Politics*. 3 (2), 235–252.

Checkel, Jeffrey T. 1997. *Ideas and International Political Change: Soviet/ Russian Behavior and the End of the Cold War*. New Haven: Yale University Press.

1999. "Norms, Institutions, and National Identity in Contemporary Europe." *International Studies Quarterly*. 43 (1), 83–114.

2001. "Why Comply? Social Learning and European Identity Change." *International Organization*. 55 (3), 553–588.

2003. "'Going Native' in Europe? Theorizing Social Interaction in European Institutions." *Comparative Political Studies*. 36 (1)–(2), 209–231.

2005. "International Institutions and Socialization in Europe: Introduction and Framework." *International Organization*. 59 (4), 801–826.

2006. "Tracing Causal Mechanisms." *International Studies Review*. 8 (2), 362–370.

2007. *International Institutions and Socialization in Europe*. Cambridge University Press.

2008a. "Process Tracing." In Audie Klotz & Deepa Prakash (eds.), *Qualitative Methods in International Relations: A Pluralist Guide*. New York: Palgrave Macmillan, 114–130.

2008b. "Bridging the Gap? Connecting Qualitative and Quantitative Methods in the Study of Civil War (Symposium)." *Qualitative Methods: Newsletter of the American Political Science Association Organized Section for Qualitative and Multi-Method Research*. 6 (1), 13–29.

2010. Review of Idean Salehyan, *Rebels Without Borders: Transnational Insurgencies in World Politics*. *Perspectives on Politics*. 8 (4), 1275–1276.

2011. "The Social Dynamics of Civil War: Insights from Constructivist Theory." Simons Papers in Security and Development, No.10. Vancouver: School for International Studies, Simon Fraser University (March).

Chernoff, Fred. 2002. "Scientific Realism as a Meta-Theory of International Relations." *International Studies Quarterly*. 46 (2), 189–207.

2007. "Critical Realism, Scientific Realism, and International Relations Theory." *Millenium: Journal of International Studies*. 35 (2), 399–407.

Civil Georgia. 2003. "Security Ministry Unveils Classified Details on Pankisi." January 20. www.civil.ge/eng/article.php?id=3033. (Accessed June 22, 2010)

Cline, Lawrence E. 2003. "Spirits and the Cross: Religiously Based Violent Movements in Uganda." *Small Wars & Insurgencies*. 14, 113–130.

Coalition to Stop the Use of Child Soldiers. 2001. "Child Soldiers: Global Report 2001." www.child-soldiers.org/global_report_reader.php?id=280. (Accessed May 2, 2010)

2008. "Child Soldiers: Global Report 2008." www.childsoldiersglobalreport. org/files/country_pdfs/FINAL_2008_Global_Report.pdf. (Accessed October 7, 2008)

Cochrane, Feargal. 2012. "Mediating the Diaspora Space: Charting the Changing Nature of Irish-America in the Global Age." In Terence Lyons & Peter Mandaville (eds.), *Politics from Afar: Transnational Diasporas and Networks.* London: Hurst, 117–138.

Cohen, Dara Kay. 2010. "Explaining Sexual Violence During Civil War." Ph.D. Dissertation, Stanford University.

Cohen, Robin. 1997. *Global Diasporas: An Introduction.* London: UCL Press.

Coleman, James S. 1986. "Social Theory, Social Research, and a Theory of Action." *The American Journal of Sociology.* 91, 1309–1335.

Collier, David. 2011. "Understanding Process Tracing." *PS: Political Science and Politics.* 44, 823–830.

Collier, Paul. 2000. "Economic Causes of Civil Conflict and Their Implications for Policy." Washington, DC: World Bank Working Paper.

Collier, Paul & Anke Hoeffler. 1998. "On Economic Causes of Civil War." *Oxford Economic Papers.* 50 (4), 563–573.

2004. "Greed and Grievance in Civil War." *Oxford Economic Papers.* 56 (4).

Conciliation Resources. 2006. *Coming Home. Understanding Why Commanders of the Lord's Resistance Army Choose to Return to Civilian Life.* London: Conciliation Resources/Quaker Peace & Social Justice.

2010. *Initiatives to End the Violence in Northern Uganda: 2002–2009 and the Juba Peace Process.* Vol. 11, *Accord: An International Review of Peace Initiatives.* London: Conciliation Resources.

Cooley, Alexander & James Ron. 2002. "The NGO Scramble: Organizational Insecurity and the Political Economy of Transnational Action." *International Security.* 27 (1), 5–39.

Cunningham, David, Kristian Gleditsch, & Idean Salehyan. 2006. "Transnational Linkages and Civil War Interactions." Paper presented at the Annual Convention of the American Political Science Association, Philadelphia (September).

2009. "It Takes Two: a Dyadic Analysis of Civil War Duration and Outcome." *Journal of Conflict Resolution.* 53 (4), 570–597.

Cunningham, Kathleen Gallagher. 2011. "Divide and Conquer or Divide and Concede: How Do States Respond to Internally Divided Separatists?" *American Political Science Review.* 105 (2), 275–297.

Cunningham, Kathleen, Kristin M. Bakke, & Lee J. M. Seymour. 2012. "Shirts Today, Skins Tomorrow: Dual Contests and the Effects of Fragmentation in Self-Determination Conflicts." *Journal of Conflict Resolution.* 56 (1), 67–93.

Dalman, Metin & Ismail Tabak. 1995. *Avrupa'da Insan Ticareti ve PKK*. Istanbul: Turk Alman Basin Ajansi.

Danforth, Loring M. 1995. *The Macedonian Conflict: Ethnic Nationalism in a Transnational World*. Princeton University Press.

Davidson, Jason. 2011. *America's Allies and War: Kosovo, Afghanistan, and Iraq*. New York: Palgrave Macmillan.

de Temmermann, Els. 2001. *Aboke Girls. Children Abducted in Northern Uganda*. Kampala: Fountain Press.

della Porta, Donatella. 1996. "Social Movements and the State: Thoughts on the Policing of Protest." In Doug McAdam, John D. McCarthy, & Mayer N. Zald (eds.), *Comparative Perspectives on Social Movements: Political Opportunities, Mobilizing Structures, and Cultural Framings*. New York: Cambridge University Press, 62–92.

della Porta, Donatella & Sidney Tarrow. 2004. "Transnational Processes and Social Activism: An Introduction." In Sidney Tarrow & Donnatella della Porta (eds.), *Transnational Protest and Global Activism*. Lanham: Rowman and Littlefield.

Dobbin, Frank, Beth Simmons, & Geoffrey Garrett. 2007. "The Global Diffusion of Public Policies: Social Construction, Coercion, Competition, or Learning?" *Annual Review of Sociology*. 33, 449–472.

Dolan, Chris. 2009. *Social Torture: The Case of Northern Uganda, 1986–2006*. New York: Berghahn Books.

Doom, Ruddy & Koen Vlassenroot. 1999. "Kony's Message: A New *Koine*? The Lord's Resistance Army in Northern Uganda." *African Affairs*. 98, 5–36.

Dorronsoro, Gilles. 2005. *Revolution Unending: Afghanistan, 1979 to the Present*. New York: Columbia University Press.

Dudayev, Umalt. 2004. "Chechnya's Homemade Weapons Fuel War." *Caucasus Reporting Service*, April 15.

Dufoix, Stephane. 2008. *Diasporas*. Berkeley: University of California Press.

Dunlop, John B. 1998. *Russia Confronts Chechnya: Roots of a Separatist Conflict*. New York: Cambridge University Press.

Earl, Jennifer. 2008. "An Admirable Call to Improve, But Not Fundamentally Change, Our Collective Methodological Practices." *Qualitative Sociology*. 31 (4), 355–359.

Egadu, Samuel Richard. 2009. *Uganda Probes Alleged Supplies to LRA*. Washington, DC: Institute for War & Peace Reporting.

Ehrenreich, Rosa. 1998. "The Stories We Must Tell: Ugandan Children and the Atrocities of the Lord's Resistance Army." *Africa Today*. 45, 79–102.

Eccarius-Kelly, Vera. 1999. "Inter-Community Ethnic Conflict in Post-Unification Germany: the Kurdish Conundrum." Paper prepared for the 39th International Studies Association Annual Meeting. Washington, DC (February).

Elkins, Z., & B. Simmons. 2005. "On Waves, Clusters, and Diffusion: A Conceptual Framework." *Annals of the American Academy of Political and Social Science.* 598 (1), 33–51.

Elman, Colin. 2005. "Explanatory Typologies in Qualitative Studies of International Politics." *International Organization.* 59, 293–326.

Elman, Colin & Miriam Elman. 2003. "Introduction," and "Lessons From Lakatos." In Colin Elman & Miriam Elman (eds.), *Progress in International Relations Theory: Appraising the Field.* Cambridge, MA: MIT Press, 1–70.

Elster, Jon. 1998. "A Plea for Mechanisms." In Peter Hedstroem & Richard Swedberg (eds.), *Social Mechanisms: An Analytical Approach to Social Theory.* Cambridge University Press, 45–73.

Entessar, Nader. 1992. *Kurdish Ethnonationalism.* Boulder, CO: Lynne Rienner.

Epstein, J. M., & R. Axtell. 1996. *Growing Artificial Societies: Social Science from the Bottom Up.* Washington, DC: Brookings Institution Press.

Evangelista, Matthew. 1995. "The Paradox of State Strength: Transnational Relations, Domestic Structures, and Security Policy in Russia and the Soviet Union." *International Organization.* 49 (1), 1–38.

1999. *Unarmed Forces: The Transnational Movement to End the Cold War.* Ithaca, NY: Cornell University Press.

2002. *The Chechen Wars: Will Russia Go the Way of the Soviet Union?* Washington, DC: Brookings Institution Press.

Fair, Christine C. 2005. "Diaspora Involvement in Insurgencies: Insights from the Khalistan and Tamil Eelam Movements." *Nationalism and Ethnic Politics.* 11 (1), 125–156.

2009. *The Madrasa Challenge: Militancy and Religious Education in Pakistan.* Washington, DC: United States Institute of Peace.

Falleti, Tulia & Julia Lynch. 2009. "Context and Causal Mechanisms in Political Analysis." *Comparative Political Studies.* 42 (9), 1143–1166.

Farmar, Sam. 2006. "Uganda Rebel Leader Breaks Silence." *BBC Newsnight,* June 28.

Fearon, James & David Laitin. 2003. "Ethnicity, Insurgency and Civil War." *American Political Science Review.* 97 (1), 75–90.

Fielden, Matthew B. 1998. "The Geopolitics of Aid: The Provision and Termination of Aid to Afghan Refugees in North-West Frontier Province, Pakistan." *Political Geography.* 17 (4), 459–487.

Finnemore, Martha & Kathryn Sikkink. 1998. "International Norm Dynamics and Political Change." *International Organization.* 52, 887–917.

Finnström, Sverker. 2008. *Living With Bad Surroundings: War, History, and Everyday Moments in Northern Uganda*. Durham: Duke University Press.

Forsberg, E. 2008. "Polarization and Ethnic Conflict in a Widened Strategic Setting." *Journal of Peace Research*. 45 (2), 283–300.

Fortna, Virginia Page. 2004. "Interstate Peacekeeping: Causal Mechanisms and Empirical Effects." *World Politics*. 56 (4), 481–519.

Franco, Claudio. 2009. "The Tehrik-e Taliban Pakistan." In Antonio Giustozzi (ed.), *Decoding the New Taliban: Insights from the Afghan Field*. New York: Columbia University Press, 269–291.

Franzese, Robert & Jud Hays. 2008. "Interdependence in Comparative Politics: Substance, Theory, Empirics, Substance." *Comparative Political Studies*. 41 (4/5), 742–780.

Friedman, Milton. 1953. "The Methodology of Positive Economics." Reprinted in Uskali Maki (ed.), *The Methodology of Positive Economics: Reflections on the Milton Friedman Legacy*. Cambridge University Press (2009). 3–44.

Frist, William, H. 2009. *A Heart to Serve: The Passion to Bring Health, Hope and Healing*. Nashville, TN: Center Street Publishing.

Fujii, Lee Ann. 2009. *Killing Neighbors: Webs of Violence in Rwanda*. Ithaca, NY: Cornell University Press.

2010. "Shades of Truth and Lies: Interpreting Testimonies of War and Violence." *Journal of Peace Research*. 47 (2), 231–241.

Gagnon, V. P. Jr. 1994. "Ethnic Nationalism and International Conflict: The Case of Serbia." *International Security*. 19 (3), 130–166.

Gall, Carlotta & Thomas de Waal. 1998. *Chechnya: Calamity in the Caucasus*. New York University Press.

Gammer, Moshe. 2005. "Between Mecca and Moscow: Islam, Politics, and Political Islam in Chechnya and Daghestan." *Middle Eastern Studies*. 41 (6), 833–848.

2006. *The Lone Wolf and the Bear: Three Centuries of Chechen Defiance of Russian Rule*. Pittsburg University Press.

Gamson, William A. 1975. *The Strategy of Social Protest*. Homewood: The Dorsey Press.

Gates, Scott. 2002. "Recruitment and Allegiance: The Microfoundations of Rebellion." *Journal of Conflict Resolution*. 46 (1), 111–130.

2008. "Mixing it Up: The Role of Theory in Mixed-Methods Research." *Qualitative Methods: Newsletter of the American Political Science Association Organized Section for Qualitative and Multi-Method Research*. 6 (1), 27–29.

2011. "The Dynamics of Group Allegiance." Memo prepared for a workshop on "The Social Dynamics of Civil War." Peace Research Institute Oslo, Centre for the Study of Civil War (February).

Gates, Scott & Simon Reich (eds). 2009. *Child Soldiers in the Age of Fractured States*. Pittsburg University Press.

George, Alexander. 1993. *Bridging the Gap: Theory and Practice in Foreign Policy*. Washington, DC: United States Institute of Peace Press.

George, Alexander & Andrew Bennett. 2005. *Case Studies and Theory Development in the Social Sciences*. Cambridge, MA: The MIT Press.

German, Tracey C. 2003. *Russia's Chechen War*. New York: Routledge Curzon.

Gerring, John. 2007a. *Case Study Research: Principles and Practices*. Cambridge University Press.

2007b. "The Mechanismic Worldview: Thinking Inside the Box." *British Journal of Political Science*. 38, 161–179.

Gerring, John & Paul Barresi. 2003. "Putting Ordinary Language to Work: A Min-Max Strategy of Concept Formation in the Social Sciences." *Journal of Theoretical Politics*. 15 (2), 20–32.

Gersony, Robert 1997. *The Anguish of Northern Uganda. Results of a Field-based Assessment of the Civil Conflicts in Northern Uganda*. Kampala: USAID Mission.

Gheciu, Alexandra. 2005. "Security Institutions as Agents of Socialization? NATO and Post-Cold War Central and Eastern Europe." *International Organization*. 59 (4), 973–1012.

Giddens, Anthony. 1984. *The Constitution of Society: Outline of a Theory of Structuration*. Cambridge: Polity Press.

Gilardi, Fabrizio. 2010. "Who Learns from What in Policy Diffusion Processes." *American Journal of Political Science*. 54 (3), 650–666.

Giugni, Marco. 1999. "How Social Movements Matter: Past Research, Present Problems, Future Developments." In Marco Giugni, Doug McAdam, & Charles Tilly (eds.), *How Social Movements Matter*. University of Minnesota Press, xiii–xxxiii.

Giuliano, Elise. 2000. "Who Determines the Self in the Politics of Self-Determination? Identity and Preference Formation in Tatarstan's Nationalist Mobilization." *Comparative Politics*. 32, 295–316.

Giustozzi, Antonio. 2007. *Koran, Kalashnikov, Laptop: The Neo-Taliban Insurgency in Afghanistan*. London: Hurst.

2009. *Empires of Mud: Wars and Warlords in Afghanistan*. London: Hurst & Co.

Gleditsch, Kristian Skrede. 2002. *All International Politics is Local: The Diffusion of Conflict, Integration, and Democratization.* Ann Arbor: University of Michigan Press.

2007. "Transnational Dimensions of Civil War." *Journal of Peace Research.* 44 (3), 293–309.

Gleditsch, Kristian Skrede and Idean Salehyan. 2006. "Refugees and the Spread of Civil War." *International Organization.* 60 (2), 335–366.

Goddard, Stacie. 2007. "When Position is Power: Entrepreneurs, Networks and International Politics." Paper prepared for delivery at the Annual Convention of the American Political Science Association, Chicago.

Goertz, Gary & James Mahoney. 2004. "The Possibility Principle: Choosing Negative Cases in Comparative Research." *American Political Science Review.* 98 (4), 653–659.

Goffman, Erving. 1974. *Frame Analysis: An Essay on the Organization of Experience.* London: Harper and Row.

Goldstone, Jack. 2002. "Population and Security: How Demographic Change can Lead to Violent Conflict." *Columbia Journal of International Affairs* 56, 245–263.

Goodwin, Jeff. 2001. *No Other Way Out: States and Revolutionary Movements 1945–1991.* New York: Cambridge University Press.

Gopal, Anand. 2010. "The Battle for Afghanistan." Washington, DC: New America Foundation.

Griswold, Eliza. 2008. "The Man for a New Sudan." *New York Times Magazine.* June 15. www.nytimes.com/2008/06/15/magazine/15SUDAN-t.html? pagewanted=all. (Accessed May 15, 2010)

Gunaratna, Rohan. 2001. "Dynamics of Contemporary Terrorist and Guerrilla Campaigns: International and Domestic Factors Facilitating and Inhibiting PKK, LTTE, ETA, FARC, GIA and MTA to Escalate and De-escalate Violence." Paper Prepared for the Workshop, "Trajectories of Terrorist Violence in Europe" at the Minda de Gunzburg Center for European Studies, Harvard University.

Gunter, Michael. 1990. *The Kurds in Turkey: A Political Dilemma.* Boulder, CO: Westview Press.

Gusterson, Hugh. 2008. "Ethnographic Research." In Audie Klotz & Deepa Prakash (eds.), *Qualitative Methods in International Relations: A Pluralist Guide.* New York: Palgrave Macmillan, 93–113.

Haas, Peter. 1992. "Introduction: Epistemic Communities and International Policy Coordination." *International Organization.* 46 (1), 1–35.

Hafner-Burton, Emily. 2008. "Sticks and Stones: Naming and Shaming the Human Rights Enforcement Problem." *International Organization.* 62 (4), 689–716.

2009. *Forced to be Good: Why Trade Agreements Boost Human Rights.* Ithaca, NY: Cornell University Press.

Hafner-Burton, Emily & James Ron. 2009. "Seeing Double: Human Rights Impact through Qualitative and Quantitative Eyes." *World Politics.* 61 (2), 360–401.

Haider, Ziad. 2005. "Sino-Pakistan Relations and Xinjiang's Uighurs: Politics, Trade, and Islam along the Karakoram Highway." *Asian Survey.* 45, 522–545.

Hall, Peter. 2003. "Aligning Ontology & Methodology in Comparative Politics." In James Mahoney & Dietrich Rueschemeyer (eds.), *Comparative Historical Analysis in the Social Sciences.* Cambridge University Press, 373–406.

Harpviken, Kristian Berg. 1996. "Political Mobilization among the Hazara of Afghanistan: 1978–1992." University of Oslo, Department of Sociology.

1997. "Transcending Traditionalism: The Emergence of Non-State Military Formations in Afghanistan." *Journal of Peace Research.* 34 (3), 271–287.

2009. *Social Networks and Migration in Wartime Afghanistan.* Houndmills: Palgrave Macmillan.

2010. "The Return of the Refugee Warrior: Migration and Armed Resistance in Herat." In Ceri Oeppen & Angela Schlenkhoff (eds.), *Beyond the 'Wild Tribes': Understanding Modern Afghanistan and Its Diaspora.* London: Hurst, 121–137.

Hassanpour, Amir. 1998. "Satellite Footprints as National Borders: MED-TV and the Extraterritoriality of State Sovereignty." *Journal of Muslim Minority Affairs.* 18 (1), 53–72.

Hedström, P. & R. Swedberg (eds.). 1998. *Social Mechanisms: An Analytical Approach to Social Theory.* New York: Cambridge University Press.

Hegghammer, Thomas. 2010. "The Rise of Muslim Foreign Fighters: Islam and the Globalization of Jihad." *International Security.* 35 (3), 53–94.

Hegre, Håvard & Nicholas Sambanis. 2006. "Sensitivity Analysis of Empirical Results on Civil War Onset." *Journal of Conflict Resolution.* 50 (4), 508–535.

Helfer, Hans-Ulrich. 1988. *Arbeiterpartei Kurdistans (PKK) – Organisation – Aktivitaeten in der Schweiz.* Zurich: Presdok.

Hempel, Carl & P. Oppenheim. 1948. "Studies in the Logic of Explanation." Philosophy of Science 15: 135–175. Reprinted in Carl Hempel. [1965]. *Aspects of Scientific Explanation and Other Essays in the Philosophy of Science.* New York: Free Press, 245–290.

Henkin, Yagil. 2006. "From Tactical Terrorism to Holy War: The Evolution of Chechen Terrorism." *Central Asian Survey*. 25 (1), 193–203.

Hertzke, Allen D. 2004. *Freeing God's Children: The Unlikely Alliance for Global Human Rights*. New York: Rowman & Littlefield.

Hill, S. & D. Rothchild. 1986. "The Contagion of Political Conflict in Africa and the World." *Journal of Conflict Resolution*. 30 (4), 716–735.

Hironaka, Ann. 2005. *Neverending Wars: The International Community, Weak States, and the Perpetuation of Civil War*. Cambridge, MA: Harvard University Press.

Ho, Enseng. 2004. "Empire Through Diasporic Eyes: A View from the Other Boat." *Comparative Studies in Society and History*. 46 (2), 17–44.

Hockenos, Paul. 2003. *Homeland Calling: Exile Patriotism and the Balkan Wars*. Ithaca, NY: Cornell University Press.

Hoffmann, Matthew. 2008. "Agent-based Modeling." In Audie Klotz & Deepa Prakash (eds.), *Qualitative Methods in International Relations: A Pluralist Guide*. New York: Palgrave Macmillan, 187–210.

Hopf, Ted. 2007. "The Limits of Interpreting Evidence." In Mark Lichbach & Ned Lebow (eds.), *Theory and Evidence in Comparative Politics and International Relations*. New York: Palgrave Macmillan, 55–86.

Horowitz, Donald. 1985. *Ethnic Groups in Conflict*. University of California Press.

Hughes, James. 2007. *Chechnya: From Nationalism to Jihad*. University of Pennsylvania Press.

Human Rights Watch. 1994. "Sudan: The Lost Boys." New York: Human Rights Watch.

1996. "Children in Combat." New York: Human Rights Watch.

1997. "The Scars of Death. Children Abducted by the Lord's Resistance Army in Uganda." New York: Human Rights Watch.

2005. "Uprooted and Forgotten: Impunity and Human Rights Abuses in Northern Uganda." New York: Human Rights Watch.

2006. "Sudan: Regional Government Pays Ugandan Rebels not to Attack." New York: Human Rights Watch.

Humphreys, Macartan, & Jeremy M. Weinstein. 2006. "Handling and Manhandling Civilians in Civil War." *American Political Science Review*. 100 (3), 429–447.

2007. "Demobilization and Reintegration." *Journal of Conflict Resolution*. 51 (4), 531–567.

Huntington, Samuel P. 1996. *The Clash of Civilizations and the Remaking of World Order*. New York: Simon and Schuster.

1997. "The Erosion of American National Interest." *Foreign Affairs*. 76 (5), 28–49.

Imset, Ismet G. 1992. *The PKK: A Report on Separatist Violence in Turkey*. Ankara: Turkish Daily News Publications.

International Crisis Group. 2002. "God, Oil and Country: Changing the Logic of War in Sudan." ICG Africa Report no. 39. www.crisisgroup.org/library/documents/report_archive/A400534_28012002.pdf. (Accessed February 19, 2008)

2003. "Afghanistan: The Problem of Pashtun Alienation." ICG Asia Report. Brussels/Kabul: International Crisis Group.

2004. "Northern Uganda: Understanding and Solving the Conflict." ICG Africa Report no.77. Brussels/Nairobi: International Crisis Group.

2010. "LRA: A Regional Strategy Beyond Killing Kony." ICG Africa Report no. 157. Brussels/Nairobi: International Crisis Group.

Izady, Mehrdad. 1992. *The Kurds: A Concise History*. London: Taylor and Francis.

Jackson, Paul. 2002. "The March of the Lord's Resistance Army. Greed or Grievance in Northern Uganda?" *Small Wars & Insurgencies*. 13, 29–52.

James, Paul & R. R. Sharma. 2006. "Transnational Conflict: A Critical Introduction." In Paul James & R. R. Sharma (eds.), *Globalization and Violence: vol. IV, Transnational Conflict*. London: Sage, ix–xxxiv.

Jamestown Foundation. 1995. "Prism Interview: 'We Set Off For Budennovsk with a One-Way Ticket'." *Prism*. October 20.

1996. "Peer Criticizes Performance of Chechen Commander Raduyev." *Monitor*. January 26.

2006. "Basayev Issues Statement; Umarov Gives Interview." *Chechnya Weekly*. April 20.

2007. "Chechens Weigh In on the 'Caucasus Emirate' Idea." *North Caucasus Analysis*. November 8.

Jenne, Erin. 2007. *Ethnic Bargaining: The Paradox of Minority Empowerment*. Ithaca, NY: Cornell University Press.

Johnson, Douglas, H. 1989. "The Structuring of a Legacy: Military Slavery in Northeast Africa." *Ethnohistory*. 36 (1), 72–88.

1992. "Recruitment and Entrapment in Private Slave Armies: The Structure of Zara'ib in the Southern Sudan." *Slavery & Abolition*. 13 (1), 162–173.

2003. *The Root Causes of Sudan's Civil Wars*. Indiana University Press.

Johnson, James. 2006. "Consequences of Positivism: A Pragmatist Assessment." *Comparative Political Studies*. 39 (2), 224–252.

Johnson, Scott. 2009. "Hard Target. The Hunt for Africa's Last Warlord." *Newsweek*. May 16.

Johnston, Alastair Iain. 2001. "Treating International Institutions as Social Environments." *International Studies Quarterly* 45/4: 487–516.

2005. "Conclusions and Extensions: Toward Mid-Range Theorizing and Beyond Europe." *International Organization*. 59 (4), 1013–1044.

2008. *Social States: China in International Institutions, 1980–2000*. Princeton University Press.

Justice and Peace Commission of the Archdiocese of Gulu. 2008. "Northern Situation Now." *Justice and Peace News*. 8, 2–4.

Kaldor, Mary. 1999. *New and Old Wars: Organized Violence in a Global Era*. Stanford University Press.

Kalyvas, Stathis. 2003. "The Ontology of 'Political Violence': Action and Identity in Civil Wars." *Perspectives on Politics*. 1, 475–494.

2006. *The Logic of Violence in Civil War*. Cambridge University Press.

2007. Review of Jeremy Weinstein, *Inside Rebellion: The Politics of Insurgent Violence*, in *Comparative Political Studies*. 40 (9), 1146–1151.

2008. "Ethnic Defection in Civil War." *Comparative Political Studies*. 41 (8), 1043–1068.

Kalyvas, Stathis & Laia Balcells. 2010. "International System and Technologies of Rebellion: How the End of the Cold War Shaped Internal Conflict." *American Political Science Review*. 104 (3), 415–429.

Kastner, Philipp. 2007. "ICC in Darfur: Savior or Spoiler?" *ILSA Journal of International & Comparative Law*. 14, 145–188.

Katzenstein, Peter, and Nobuo Okawara. 2002. "Japan, Asian-Pacific Security, and the Case for Analytical Eclecticism." *International Security*. 26 (3), 153–185.

Katzenstein, Peter & Rudra Sil. 2008. "Eclectic Theorizing in the Study and Practice of International Relations." In Christian Reus-Smit and Duncan Snidal (eds.), *The Oxford Handbook of International Relations*. New York: Oxford University Press, 109–130.

Katzenstein, Suzanne & Jack Snyder. 2009. "Expediency of Angels." *The National Interest*. March–April, 58–65.

Keck, Margaret & Kathryn Sikkink. 1998. *Activists Beyond Borders: Advocacy Networks in International Politics*. Ithaca, NY: Cornell University Press.

Keohane, Robert and Joseph Nye (eds.). 1972. *Transnational Relations and World Politics*. Harvard University Press.

Khagram, Sanjeev, James V. Riker & Kathryn Sikkink (eds.). 2002. *Restructuring World Politics: Transnational Social Movements, Networks, and Norms*. Minneapolis: University of Minnesota Press.

King, Charles. 2004. "The Micropolitics of Social Violence (A Review Essay)." *World Politics*. 56 (3), 431–455.

2008. *The Ghost of Freedom: A History of the Caucasus*. New York: Oxford University Press.

King, Charles & Neil J. Melvin. 2000. "Diaspora Politics: Ethnic Linkages, Foreign Policy, and Security in Eurasia." *International Security*. 24 (3), 108–138.

King, Gary, Robert Keohane, & Sidney Verba. 1994. *Designing Social Inquiry*. Princeton University Press.

Kinzer, Stephen. 2008. *A Thousand Hills: Rwanda's Rebirth and the Man Who Dreamed It*. New Jersey: John Wiley.

Klotz, Audie. 1995. *Norms in International Relations: The Struggle Against Apartheid*. Ithaca, NY: Cornell University Press.

Koinova, Maria. 2009. "Diasporas and Democratization in the Post-Communist World." *Communist and Post-Communist Studies*. 42, 41–64.

2010. "Diasporas and Secessionist Conflicts: The Mobilization of the Armenian, Albanian and Chechen Diasporas. *Ethnic and Racial Studies*. 34 (2), 333–356.

Kuehn, David & Ingo Rohlfing. 2009. "Does It, Really? Measurement Error and Omitted Variables in Multi-Method Research." *Qualitative Methods: Newsletter of the American Political Science Association Organized Section for Qualitative and Multi-Method Research*. 7 (2), 18–22.

Kuhn, Thomas. 1962. *The Structure of Scientific Revolutions*. University of Chicago Press.

Kuperman, Alan J. 2004. "Provoking Genocide: A Revised History of the Rwandan Patriotic Front." *Journal of Genocide Research*. 6 (1), 61–84.

Kuran, T. 1998. "Ethnic Dissimilation and Its International Diffusion." In D. A. Lake & D. Rothchild (eds.), *The International Spread of Ethnic Conflict: Fear, Diffusion, and Escalation*. Princeton University Press, 35–60.

Kurki, Milja. 2008. *Causation in International Relations: Reclaiming Causal Analysis*. Cambridge University Press.

Kydd, Andrew & Barbara Walter. 2006. "Strategies of Terrorism." *International Security*. 31 (1), 49–80.

Lakatos, Imre. 1970. "Falsification and the Methodology of Scientific Research Programmes." In Imre Lakatos & A. Musgrave (eds.), *Criticism and the Growth of Knowledge*. Cambridge, NY: Cambridge University Press, 91–196.

Landesamt für Verfassungsschutz Berlin. 1994. *Auslaenderextremismus in Berlin*. Berlin: Landesamt für Verfassungsschutz.

Lawrence, Adria. 2010. "Triggering Nationalist Violence: Competition and Conflict in Uprisings against Colonial Rule." *International Security*. 35 (2), 88–122.

Leggewie, C. 1996. "How Turks Became Kurds, Not Germans." *Dissent*. 43, 79–83.

Leiby, Michele. 2009a. "Digging in the Archives: The Promise and Perils of Primary Documents." *Politics & Society*. 37 (1), 75–100.

2009b. "Wartime Sexual Violence in Guatemala and Peru." *International Studies Quarterly*. 53 (2), 445–468.

Lemarchand, René. 2001. "Exclusion, Marginalization and Political Mobilization: The Road to Hell in the Great Lakes." *CAS Africa Papers*. Centre of African Studies, University of Copenhagen.

Levitt, Peggy & Sally Merry. 2009. "Vernacularization on the Ground: Local uses of Global Women's Rights in Peru, China, India and the United States." *Global Networks*. 9 (4), 441–461.

Levy, Marc, Oran Young, & Michael Zuern. 1995. "The Study of International Regimes." *European Journal of International Relations*. 1 (3), 267–330.

Lewis, Jeffrey. 2005. "The Janus Face of Brussels: Socialization and Everyday Decision Making in the European Union." *International Organization*. 59 (4), 937–972.

Lichbach, Mark I. 1994. "What Makes Rational Peasants Revolutionary? Dilemma, Paradox, and Irony in Peasant Collective Action." *World Politics*. 46 (3), 383–418.

1998. *The Rebels' Dilemma: Economics, Cognition, and Society*. Ann Arbor, University of Michigan Press.

2008. "Modeling Mechanisms of Contention: MTT's Positivist Constructivism." *Qualitative Sociology*. 31 (4), 345–354.

Lischer, Sarah Kenyon. 2003. "Collateral Damage: Humanitarian Assistance as a Cause of Conflict." *International Security*. 28 (1), 79–109.

2005. *Dangerous Sanctuaries: Refugee Camps, Civil Wars and the Dilemmas of Humanitarian Aid*. Ithaca, NY: Cornell University Press.

Loescher, Gil. 1992. *Refugee Movements and International Security*. London: International Institute for Strategic Studies.

Lynch, Marc. 2002. "Why Engage? China and the Logic of Communicative Engagement." *European Journal of International Relations*. 8 (2), 187–230.

Lyon, Alynna J. & Emek M. Ucarer. 2001. "Mobilizing Ethnic Conflict: Kurdish Separatism in Germany and the PKK." *Ethnic and Racial Studies*. 24 (6), 925–948.

Lyons, Terrence. 2006. "Diasporas and Homeland Conflict." In Miles Kahler & Barbara Walter (eds.), *Territoriality and Conflict in an Era of Globalization*. New York: Cambridge University Press, 111–131.

Mahoney, James. 2000. "Path Dependence in Historical Sociology." *Theory and Society*. 29 (4), 507–538.

2001. "Review – Beyond Correlational Analysis: Recent Innovations in Theory and Method." *Sociological Forum.* 16 (3), 575–593.

Malet, David. 2007. "'The More Irregular the Service': Transnational Identity Communities and the Foreign Fighter." Paper presented at the annual meeting of the American Political Science Association, Chicago, September.

2010. "Why Foreign Fighters? Historical Perspectives and Solutions." *Orbis.* 54 (1), 97–114.

2011. "The Foreign Fighter Project." http://davidmalet.com/The_Foreign_ Fighter_Project.php. (Accessed September 7, 2010)

Maliniak, Daniel, Amy Oakes, Susan Peterson, & Michael Tierney. 2011. "International Relations in the US Academy," *International Studies Quarterly*, 437–464.

Malkki, Lisa. 1995. "Refugees and Exile: From 'Refugee Studies' to the National Order of Things." *Annual Review of Anthropology.* 24, 495–523.

Mamdani, Mahmood. 1984. *Imperialism and Fascism in Uganda.* Trenton, NJ: Africa World Press.

2001. *When Victims Become Killers: Colonialism, Nativism, and the Genocide in Rwanda.* Princeton University Press.

Mantilla, Giovanni. 2009. "Emerging International Human Rights Norms for Transnational Corporations." *Global Governance.* 15, 279–298.

March, James & Johan Olsen. 1984. "The New Institutionalism: Organizational Factors in Political Life." *American Political Science Review.* 78 (3), 734–749.

Marcus, Aliza. 1993. "Turkey's Kurds After the Gulf War: A Report from the Southeast." In Gerard Chaliand (ed.), *A People Without a Country: The Kurds and Kurdistan.* London: Zed Press.

Markides, Kyriacos C. 1977. *The Rise and Fall of the Cyprus Republic.* New Haven, Conn.: Yale University Press.

Mathias, Charles, Jr. 1981. "Ethnic Groups and Foreign Policy." *Foreign Affairs.* 59, 975–998.

Mayntz, Renate. 2004. "Mechanisms in the Analysis of Macro-Social Phenomena." *Philosophy of the Social Sciences.* 34 (2), 237–259.

McAdam, Doug. 1983. "Tactical Innovation and the Pace of Insurgency." *American Sociological Review.* 48 (6), 735–754.

McAdam, Doug, John D. McCarthy, & Mayer N. Zald (eds.). 1996. *Comparative Perspectives on Social Movements: Political Opportunities, Mobilizing Structures, and Cultural Framings.* New York: Cambridge University Press.

McAdam, Doug & Sidney Tarrow. 2005. "Scale Shift and Transnational Contention." In Sidney Tarrow & Donnatella della Porta (eds.),

Transnational Protest and Global Activism. Lanham, MD: Rowman and Littlefield, 121–150.

McAdam, Doug, Sidney Tarrow, & Charles Tilly. 1996. "To Map Contentious Politics." *Mobilization: An International Journal.* 1 (1), 17–34.

2001. *Dynamics of Contention.* Cambridge University Press.

2008. "Methods for Measuring Mechanisms of Contention." *Qualitative Sociology.* 31 (4), 307–331.

McCarthy, John D. & Mayer N. Zald. 1977. "Resource Mobilization and Social Movements: A Partial Theory." *American Journal of Sociology.* 82 (6), 1212–1241.

McDowall, David. 1996. *A Modern History of the Kurds.* London: IB Tauris.

McGrory, Mary. 2001. "Suddenly, Sudan." *Washington Post.* March 11.

McKeown, Timothy. 1999. "Case Studies and the Statistical Worldview: Review of King, Keohane and Verba's *Designing Social Inquiry: Scientific Inference in Qualitative Research.*" *International Organization.* 53 (1), 161–190.

Meseguer, Covadonga. 2006. "Rational Learning and Bounded Learning in the Diffusion of Policy Innovation." *Rationality and Society.* 18 (1), 35–66.

Meseguer, Covadonga & Fabrizio Gilardi. 2009. "What is New in the Study of Policy Diffusion?" *Review of International Political Economy.* 16 (3), 527–543.

Meyer, David S. & Nancy Whittier. 1994. "Social Movement Spillover." *Social Problems.* 41 (2), 277–298.

Mgbako, Chi. 2005. "Ingando Solidarity Camps: Reconciliation and Political Indoctrination in Post-Genocide Rwanda." *Harvard Human Rights Journal.* 18, 201–224.

Miliband, David. 2009. "The Army Alone cannot Defeat this Taliban Insurgency." *The Independent.*

Minear, Larry, & Randolph C. Kent. 1998. "Rwanda's Internally Displaced: A Conundrum Within a Conundrum." In Roberta Cohen & Francis M. Deng (eds.), *The Forsaken People: Case Studies of the Internally Displaced.* Washington, DC: The Brookings Institution, 57–95.

Moghaddam, Sippi Azerbaijani, Mirwais Wardak, Idrees Zaman, & Annabel Taylor. 2008. "Afghan Hearts, Afghan Minds: Exploring Afghan Perceptions of Civil-Military Relations." Kabul: European Network of NGOs in Afghanistan (ENNA) and the British and Irish Agencies Afghanistan Group (BAAG).

Moore, Cerwyn. 2007. "The Radicalisation of the Chechen Separatist Movement – Myth or Reality?" *Prague Watchdog.* May 16.

Moore, Cerwyn, & Paul Tumelty. 2008. "Foreign Fighters and the Case of Chechnya: A Critical Assessment." *Studies in Conflict and Terrorism.* 31, 412–43.

——. 2009. "Assessing the Unholy Alliances in Chechnya: From Communism and Nationalism to Islamism and Salafism." *Journal of Communist Studies and Transition Politics.* 25 (1), 73–94.

Moravcsik, Andrew. 1993. "Introduction – Integrating International and Domestic Theories of International Bargaining." In Peter Evans, Harold Jacobson, & Robert Putnam (eds.), *Double-Edged Diplomacy: International Bargaining and Domestic Politics.* Berkeley: University of California Press.

Murphy, Paul J. 2004. *The Wolves of Islam: Russia and the Faces of Chechen Terror.* Dulles, VA: Brassey's.

Museveni, Yoweri Kaguta. 1992. *What is Africa's Problem?* Kampala: NRM Publications.

Muzaev, Timur. 1997. "Chechenskaja Respublika Ichkerija" [The Chechen Republic of Ichkeria], Political Monitoring, Institute for Humanitarian and Political Studies (IGPI), October. http://igpi.ru/monitoring/north_caucas. (Accessed May 3, 2011)

——. 1998a. "Chechenskaja Respublika Ichkerija" [The Chechen Republic of Ichkeria], Political Monitoring, Institute for Humanitarian and Political Studies (IGPI), January. http://igpi.ru/monitoring/north_caucas. (Accessed May 3, 2011)

——. 1998b. "Chechenskaja Respublika Ichkerija" [The Chechen Republic of Ichkeria], Political Monitoring, Institute for Humanitarian and Political Studies (IGPI), April. http://igpi.ru/monitoring/north_caucas. (Accessed May 3, 2011)

——. 1998c. "Chechenskaja Respublika Ichkerija" [The Chechen Republic of Ichkeria], Political Monitoring, Institute for Humanitarian and Political Studies (IGPI), June. http://igpi.ru/monitoring/north_caucas. (Accessed May 3, 2011)

——. 1998d. "Chechenskaja Respublika Ichkerija" [The Chechen Republic of Ichkeria], Political Monitoring, Institute for Humanitarian and Political Studies (IGPI), November. http://igpi.ru/monitoring/north_caucas. (Accessed May 3, 2011)

——. 1998e. "Chechenskaja Respublika Ichkerija" [The Chechen Republic of Ichkeria], Political Monitoring, Institute for Humanitarian and Political Studies (IGPI), December. http://igpi.ru/monitoring/north_caucas. (Accessed May 3, 2011)

——. 1999a. "Chechenskaja Respublika Ichkerija" [The Chechen Republic of Ichkeria], Political Monitoring, Institute for Humanitarian and Political

Studies (IGPI), February. http://igpi.ru/monitoring/north_caucas. (Accessed May 3, 2011.

1999b. "Chechenskaja Respublika Ichkerija" [The Chechen Republic of Ichkeria], Political Monitoring, Institute for Humanitarian and Political Studies (IGPI), April. http://igpi.ru/monitoring/north_caucas. (Accessed May 3, 2011)

1999c. "Chechenskaja Respublika Ichkerija" [The Chechen Republic of Ichkeria], Political Monitoring, Institute for Humanitarian and Political Studies (IGPI), May. http://igpi.ru/monitoring/north_caucas. (Accessed May 3, 2011)

1999d. "Chechenskaja Respublika Ichkerija" [The Chechen Republic of Ichkeria], Political Monitoring, Institute for Humanitarian and Political Studies (IGPI), June. http://igpi.ru/monitoring/north_caucas. (Accessed May 3, 2011)

1999e. "Chechenskaja Respublika Ichkerija" [The Chechen Republic of Ichkeria], Political Monitoring, Institute for Humanitarian and Political Studies (IGPI), July. http://igpi.ru/monitoring/north_caucas. (Accessed May 3, 2011)

Neu, Joyce. 2002. "Restoring Relations Between Uganda and Sudan: The Carter Center Process." *Accord. Protracted Conflict, Elusive Peace.* 11, 46–51.

Neumann, Iver. 2008. "Discourse Analysis." In Audie Klotz & Deepa Prakash (eds.), *Qualitative Methods in International Relations: A Pluralist Guide.* New York: Palgrave Macmillan, 61–77.

Nivat, Anne. 2001. *Chienne de Guerre: A Woman Reporter Behind the Lines of War in Chechnya.* New York: Public Affairs.

2005. "The Black Widows: Chechen Women Join the Fight for Independence – and Allah." *Studies in Conflict and Terrorism.* 28 (5), 413–419.

Nixon, Hamish. 2011. *"Prospects for Durable Peace in Afghanistan: A Review of the Literature (draft)."* Bergen/Oslo/Washington, DC: Chr. Michelsen Institute/Peace Research Institute Oslo/United States Institute of Peace.

Nye, Joesph S., & Robert O. Keohane. 1971. "Transnational Relations and World Politics: An Introduction." *International Organization.* 25 (3), 329–349.

Obama, Barack. 2011. Letter from the President to the Speaker of the House of Representatives and the President Pro Tempore of the Senate regarding the Lord's Resistance Army (October 14). Washington, DC: The White House.

Obita, James Alfred. 1997. "A Case for National Reconciliation, Peace, Democracy, and Economic Prosperity for all Ugandans." The official presentation of the Lord's Resistance Movement/Army (LRA/M). Kacoke Madit Conference. University of London.

O'Kadameri, Billie. 2002. "LRA/Government Negotiations 1993–4." *Accord: Protracted Conflict, Elusive Peace.* 11, 34–41.

Okiror, Samuel. 2007. "Museveni Wants LRA Warrants - For Now." *ACR Issue 123.* Washington, DC: Institute for War & Peace Reporting.

Olson, Mancur. 1965. *The Logic of Collective Action.* Cambridge, MA: Harvard University Press.

Olson, Mancur & Richard Zeckhauser. 1966. "An Economic Theory of Alliances." *The Review of Economics and Statistics.* 48 (3), 266–279.

Omara-Otunnu, Amii. 1987. *Politics and the Military in Uganda, 1890–1985.* New York: St. Martin's Press.

1992. "The Struggle for Democracy in Uganda." *The Journal of Modern African Studies.* 30, 443–463.

O'Neill, Bard E. 2001. *Insurgency & Terrorism: Inside Modern Revolutionary Warfare.* New York: Brassey's.

Orenstein, Mitchell & Hans Peter Schmitz. 2006. "The New Transnationalism and Comparative Politics." *Comparative Politics.* 38 (4), 479–500.

Østergaard-Nielsen, Eva. 2001. "Transnational Political Practices and the Receiving State: Turks and Kurds in Germany and the Netherlands." *Global Networks: A Journal of Transnational Affairs.* 1 (3), 261–282.

2003. *Transnational Politics: Turks and Kurds in Germany.* London: Routledge.

Otim, Michael & Marieke Wierda. 2010. *Uganda. Impact of the Rome Statute and the International Criminal Court.* New York: International Center for Transitional Justice.

Padgett, John F. & Christopher K. Ansell. 1993. "Robust Action and the Rise of the Medici, 1400–1434." *American Journal of Sociology.* 98 (6), 1259–1319.

Payne, Rodger A. 2001. "Persuasion, Frames and Norm Construction." *European Journal of International Relations.* 7, 37–61.

Pearlman, Wendy. 2009. "Spoiling Inside and Out: Internal Political Contestation and the Middle East Peace Process." *International Security.* 33 (3), 79–109.

Perla, Hector, Jr. 2005. "Revolutionary Deterrence: The Sandinista Response to Reagan's Coercive Policy Against Nicaragua, Lessons Toward a Theory of Asymmetric Conflict." Ph.D. dissertation, University of California, Los Angeles.

2008. "Grassroots Mobilization Against US Military Intervention in El Salvador." *Socialism and Democracy.* 22 (3), 143–159.

2009. "Heirs of Sandino: The Nicaraguan Revolution and the US-Nicaragua Solidarity Movement." *Latin American Perspectives.* 36 (6), 80–100.

Pichardo, Nelson A. 1988. "Resource Mobilization: An Analysis of Conflicting Theoretical Variations." *Sociological Quarterly.* 29 (1), 97–110.

Pickvance, Christopher J. 1999. "Democratization and the Decline of Social Movements: The Effects of Regime Change on Collective Action in Eastern Europe, Southern Europe, and Latin America." *Sociology.* 33 (2), 353–372.

Piven, Frances Fox & Richard A. Cloward. 1979. *Poor People's Movements: Why They Succeed, How They Fail.* New York: Vintage Books.

Policzer, Pablo. 2006. "Human Rights Beyond the State." *Journal of Human Rights.* 5 (2), 215–233.

Politkovskaya, Anna. 2001. *A Dirty War: A Russian Reporter in Chechnya.* London: The Harvill Press.

2003. *A Small Corner of Hell: Dispatches from Chechnya.* University of Chicago Press.

Popkin, Samuel. 1988. "Political Entrepreneurs and Peasant Movements in Vietnam." In Michael Taylor (ed.), *Rationality and Revolution.* New York: Cambridge University Press, 9–62.

Powell, Bill. 1996. "A Religious War?" *Newsweek.* October 14.

Power, Samantha. 2004. "Dying in Darfur." *The New Yorker.* August 30.

Press, Robert, M. 1989. "Sudan Rebels Court US Congressmen." *Christian Science Monitor.* April 3.

Price, Richard. 1998. "Reversing the Gunsights: Transnational Civil Society Targets Land Mines." *International Organization.* 52 (3), 613–644.

Prunier, Gerard. 1998. "The Rwandan Patriotic Front." In Christopher Clapham (ed.), *African Guerillas.* Oxford: James Currey, 119–133.

2004. "Rebel Movements and Proxy Warfare: Uganda, Sudan and the Congo (1986–1999)." *African Affairs.* 103, 359–383.

Purdeková, Andrea. 2008. "Repatriation and Reconciliation in Divided Societies: The Case of Rwanda's 'Ingando'." Refugee Studies Centre Working Papers.

Quinn-Judge, Paul. 2004. "Russia's Most Wanted." *Time.* October 17.

Rabushka, Alvin & Kenneth Shepsle. 1972. *Politics in Plural Societies: A Theory in Democratic Instability.* Columbus, Ohio: Charles E. Merrill.

Radnitz, Scott. 2006. "Look Who's Talking! Islamic Discourse in the Chechen Wars." *Nationalities Papers.* 34 (2), 237–256.

Rapoport, David C. 2003. "The Four Waves of Rebel Terror and September 11." In Charles W. Kegley, Jr. (ed.), *The New Global Terrorism: Characteristics, Causes, Controls.* Upper Saddle River: Prentice Hall, 36–59.

Rasanayagam, Angelo. 2003. *Afghanistan: A Modern History.* London: I.B. Tauris.

Rashid, Ahmed. 2008. *Descent into Chaos: How the War against Islamic Extremism is being Lost in Pakistan, Afghanistan and Central Asia.* London: Allen Lane.

Rastegar, Farshad. 1991. "Education and Revolutionary Political Mobilization: Schooling Versus Uprootedness as Determinants of Islamic Political Activism Among Afghan Refugee Students in Pakistan." Ph.D. dissertation, University of California, Los Angeles.

Rein, Martin & Donald A. Schoen. 1996. "Frame-Critical Policy Analysis and Frame-Reflective Policy Practice." *Knowledge and Policy.* 9, 85–104.

Reno, William 2009. "The Evolution of Warfare in Africa." *Afrika Focus.* 22, 7–19.

Republic of Rwanda. National Unity and Reconciliation Commission (NURC). 2008. "The Causes of Violence after the 1994 Genocide in Rwanda." Kigali, Rwanda: Premier Consulting Group.

Reuter, John. 2004. "Chechnya's Suicide Bombers: Desperate, Devout, or Deceived?" Report presented by the American Committee for Peace in Chechnya and the Jamestown Foundation.

Risse, Thomas. 2000. "'Let's Argue!': Communicative Action in World Politics." *International Organization.* 54 (1), 1–40.

   2002. "Transnational Actors and World Politics." In Walter Carlsnaes, Thomas Risse, & Beth Simmons (eds.), *Handbook of International Relations.* London: Sage Publications, 255–274.

Risse, Thomas, Stephen Ropp, & Kathryn Sikkink (eds.). 1999a. *The Power of Human Rights: International Norms and Domestic Change.* Cambridge University Press.

Risse, Thomas & Kathryn Sikkink. 1999b. "The Socialization of International Human Rights Norms into Domestic Practices. Introduction." In Thomas Risse, Stephen Ropp, & Kathryn Sikkink (eds.), *The Power of Human Rights: International Rights and Domestic Change.* Cambridge University Press, 1–38.

Risse-Kappen, Thomas (ed.). 1995a. *Bringing Transnational Relations Back In: Non-State Actors, Domestic Structures and International Institutions.* Cambridge University Press.

   1995b. "Bringing Transnational Relations Back In: Introduction." In Thomas Risse-Kappen (ed.), *Bringing Transnational Relations Back In: Non-State Actors, Domestic Structures and International Institutions,* Cambridge University Press, 3–33.

Rizvi, Gowher. 1990. "The Afghan Refugees: Hostages in the Struggle for Power." *Journal of Refugee Studies.* 3 (3), 144–161.

Rolandsen, Øystein, H. 2005. *Guerilla Government: Political Changes in Southern Sudan during the 1990s.* Uppsala: Nordic African Institute.

Romano, David. 2006. *The Kurdish Nationalist Movement: Opportunity, Mobilization and Identity*. Cambridge University Press.

Rotberg, Robert I. (ed.). 2004. *When States Fail: Causes and Consequences*. Princeton University Press.

Roy, Olivier. 1986. *Islam and Resistance in Afghanistan*. Cambridge University Press.

    1989. "Afghanistan: War as a Factor of Entry into Politics." *Central Asian Survey*. 8 (4), 43–62.

    1995. *Afghanistan: From Holy War to Civil War*. Princeton, NJ: Darwin Press.

Rubin, Barnett R. 1991. "Afghanistan: Political Exiles in Search of a State." In Y. Shain (ed.), *Governments-in-Exile in Contemporary World Politics*. New York: Routledge, 69–91.

    2002. *The Fragmentation of Afghanistan*. New Haven, Conn.: Yale University Press.

Ruggie, John. 1998. "What Makes the World Hang Together? Neo-Utilitarianism and the Social Constructivist Challenge." *International Organization*. 52, 855–885.

Rushton, Simon. 2008. "The UN Secretary-General and Norm Entrepreneurship: Boutros Boutros-Ghali and Democracy Promotion." *Global Governance*. 14, 95–110.

Sageman, Marc. 2004. *Understanding Terror Networks*. University of Pennsylvania Press.

Saideman, Stephen, 2001. *The Ties that Divide: Ethnic Politics, Foreign Policy, and International Politics*. New York: Columbia University Press.

    2002. "Discrimination in International Relations: Analyzing External Support for Ethnic Groups." *Journal of Peace Research*. 39 (1), 27–50.

Salehyan, Idean. 2007. "Transnational Rebels: Neighboring States as Sanctuary for Rebel Groups." *World Politics*. 59 (2), 217–242.

    2008. "No Shelter Here: Rebel Sanctuaries and International Conflict." *Journal of Politics*. 70 (1), 54–66.

    2009. *Rebels without Borders: Transnational Insurgencies in World Politics*. Ithaca, NY: Cornell University Press.

    2010. "The Delegation of War to Rebel Organizations." *The Journal of Conflict Resolution*. 54 (3), 493–515.

Salehyan, Idean & Kristian Skrede Gleditsch. 2006. "Refugees and the Spread of Civil War." *International Organization*. 60, 335–366.

Salehyan, Idean, Kristian Skrede Gleditsch, & David E. Cunningham. 2011. "Explaining External Support for Insurgent Groups." *International Organization*. 65, 709–744.

Salmon, Wesley. 1990. *Four Decades of Scientific Explanation*. University of Minnesota Press.

Sambanis, Nicholas. 2004. "Using Case Studies to Expand Economic Models of Civil War." *Perspectives on Politics*. 2 (2), 259–280.

Saurugger, Sabine. 2010. "The Social Construction of the Participatory Turn: The Emergence of a Norm in the European Union." *European Journal of Political Research*. 49, 471–495.

Sayan, Giyas & Rüdiger Lötzer. 1998. *Kurden in Berlin*. Berlin: Kurdische Gemeinde zu Berlin e.V.

Schatz, Edward (ed.). 2009. *Political Ethnography: What Immersion Contributes to the Study of Power*. University of Chicago Press.

Schimmelfennig, Frank. 2005. "Strategic Calculation and International Socialization: Membership Incentives, Party Constellations and Sustained Compliance in Central and Eastern Europe." *International Organization*. 59 (4), 827–860.

Schmitz, Hans Peter. 2004. "Transnational NGOs as Agents of Change: Towards Understanding Their Governance, Leadership and Effectiveness." Washington, DC: National Science Foundation, Grant SES-0527679 (2005–2008).

2006. *Transnational Mobilization and Domestic Regime Change: Africa in Comparative Perspective*. New York: Palgrave Macmillan.

Schöch, Rüdiger. 2008. "Afghan Refugees in Pakistan during the 1980s: Cold War Politics and Registration Practice." *New Issues in Refugee Research*. Geneva: UN High Commissioner for Refugees.

Schomerus, Mareike. 2007. "The Lord's Resistance Army in Sudan: A History and Overview." *HSBA Working Papers*. Geneva: Small Arms Survey/Graduate Institute of International Studies.

2008. "International Involvement for Peacemaking in Northern Uganda." In Aaron Griffiths & Catherine Barnes (eds.), *Accord. Powers of Persuasion. Incentives, Sanctions, and Conditionality in Peacemaking*. London: Conciliation Resources, 92–96.

Schomerus, Mareike & Kennedy Tumutegyereize. 2009. *After Operation Lightning Thunder. Protecting Communities and Building Peace*. London: Conciliation Resources.

Schroen, Gary C. 2005. *First In: An Insider's Account of How the CIA Spearheaded the War on Terror in Afghanistan*. New York: Ballantine Books.

Shahrani, M. Nazif. 1995. "Afghanistan's Muhajirin (Muslim 'Refugee - Warriors'): Politics of Mistrust and Distrust of Politics." In E. Valentine Daniel & John Chr. Knudsen (eds.), *Mistrusting Refugees*. Berkeley: University of California Press, 187–206.

Shain, Yossi. 1999. *Marketing the American Creed Abroad: Diasporas in the US and Their Homelands*. New York: Cambridge University Press.

2002. "The Role of Diasporas in Conflict Perpetuation and Resolution." *SAIS Review*. 22 (2), 115–144.

Shain, Yossi & Ravinatha P. Aryasinha. 2006. "Spoilers or Catalysts? The Role of Diasporas in Peace Processes." In Edward Newman & Oliver Richmond (eds.), *Challenges to Peacebuilding: Managing Spoilers During Conflict Resolution*. Tokyo: United Nations University Press.

Shain, Yossi & Aharon Barth. 2003. "Diasporas and International Relations Theory." *International Organization*. 57 (3).

Shea, Nina. 1998. "A War on Religion." *Wall Street Journal*. July 31.

Sheehy, Ann. 1991. "Power Struggle in Checheno-Ingushetia." RFE-RL Report on the USSR. November 15.

Sheffer, Gabriel. 2003. *Diaspora Politics: At Home Abroad*. Cambridge University Press.

Shlapentokh, Dmitry. 2008. "The Rise of the Chechen Emirate?" *Middle East Quarterly*. 15 (3), 49–56.

Sil, Rudra & Peter Katzenstein. 2010a. "Analytic Eclecticism in the Study of World Politics: Reconfiguring Problems and Mechanisms across Research Traditions." *Perspectives on Politics* 8 (2): 411–431.

2010b. *Beyond Paradigms: Analytical Eclecticism in the Study of World Politics*. New York: Palgrave Macmillan.

Simmons, Beth, Frank Dobbin, & Geoffrey Garrett. 2006. "Introduction: The International Diffusion of Liberalism." *International Organization*. 60 (4): 781–810.

Singer, David J. 1961. "The Level-of-Analysis Problem in International Relations." *World Politics*. 14 (1), 77–92.

Singer, Peter W. 2004. "Talk is Cheap: Getting Serious About Preventing Child Soldiers." *Cornell International Law Journal*. 37 (3), 561–586.

2006. *Children at War*. Berkeley: University of California Press.

Smirnov, Andrei. 2007a. "Umarov Trying to Increase Financial Support from the Middle East." *Chechnya Weekly*. October 25.

2007a. "Will the Rebels Declare the 'Caucasian Emirate'?" *Chechnya Weekly*. November 1.

2007b. "The Caucasian Emirate: A Not so New Idea." *Chechnya Weekly*. November 8.

2007c. "Astemirov Takes Credit for Idea of Caucasian Emirate." *Chechnya Weekly*. November 29.

2007d. "Is the Caucasian Emirate Threat a Threat to the Western World?" *Chechnya Weekly*. December 6.

Smith, Christian. 1996. *Resisting Reagan: the US Central America Peace Movement*. University of Chicago Press.

Smith, Hazel & Paul Stares (eds.). 2007. *Diasporas in Conflict: Peace-Makers or Peace-Wreckers?* Tokyo: United Nations University Press.

Smith, Tony. 2001. *Foreign Attachments: The Power of Ethnic Groups in the Making of American Foreign Policy.* Cambridge, MA: Harvard University Press.

Snow, David A. & Robert D. Benford. 1992. "Master Frames and Cycles of Protest." In Aldon Norris & Carol M. Mueller (eds.), *Frontiers in Social Movement Theory.* New Haven, Conn.: Yale University Press. 133–155.

Snow, David, E. Burke Rochford, Jr., Steven K. Worden, & Robert D. Benford. 1986. "Frame Alignment Processes, Micromobilization and Movement Participation." *American Sociological Review.* 51, 464–481.

Sokirianskaia, Ekaterina. 2010. "Governing Fragmented Societies: State-Building and Political Integration in Chechnya and Ingushetia (1991–2009)." Ph.D. dissertation. Department of Political Science, Central European University, Budapest.

Speckhard, Anne & Khapta Ahkmedova. 2006. "The Making of a Martyr: Chechen Suicide Terrorism." *Studies in Conflict and Terrorism.* 29 (5), 429–492.

Staggenborg, Suzanne. 2008. "Seeing Mechanisms in Action." *Qualitative Sociology.* 31 (4), 341–344.

Staniland, Paul. 2005. "Defeating Transnational Insurgencies: The Best Offence is a Good Fence." *The Washington Quarterly.* 29 (1), 21–40.

Stark, Rodney & William Sims Bainbridge. 1980. "Networks of Faith: Interpersonal Bonds and Recruitment to Cults and Sects." *The American Journal of Sociology.* 85 (6), 1376–1395.

Stedman, Stephen John & Fred Tanner (eds.). 2003. *Refugee Manipulation: War Politics and the Abuse of Human Suffering.* Washington, DC: Brookings Institution Press.

Stein, Gottfried. 1994. *Endkampf um Kurdistan? Die PKK, die Tuerkei und Deutschland.* Munich: Bonn Aktuell.

Stenersen, Anne. 2009. "Are the Afghan Taliban Involved in International Terrorism?" *CTC Sentinel.* 2 (9), 1–5.

Suhrke, Astri & Frank Klink. 1987. "Contrasting Patterns of Asian Refugee Movements: The Vietnamese and Afghan Syndromes." In James T. Fawcett & Benjamin V. Carino (eds.), *Pacific Bridges: The New Immigration from Asia and the Pacific Islands.* New York: Center for Migration Studies, 85–102.

Sundberg, Ralph, Mathilda Lindgren, & Ausra Padskocimaite. 2010. *UCDP GED Codebook Version 1.0–2011.* Department of Peace and Conflict Research, Uppsala University.

Symposium. 2006. "Diffusion of Liberalism." *International Organization.* 60 (4), 781–934.

2007a. "Symposium: Multi-Method Work – Dispatches from the Front Lines." *Qualitative Methods: Newsletter of the American Political Science Association Organized Section on Qualitative Methods.* 5 (1), 9–27.

2007b. "John Gerring, *Case Study Research: Principles and Practices* (Cambridge, 2007)." *Qualitative Methods: Newsletter of the American Political Science Association Organized Section for Qualitative and Multi-Method Research.* 5 (2), 2–15.

2008. "McAdam, Tarrow and Tilly's 'Measuring Mechanisms of Contention'." *Qualitative Sociology.* 31 (4) 333–354.

Tarrow, Sidney. 1998. *Power in Movement: Social Movements and Contentious Politics*, 2nd edition. New York: Cambridge University Press.

2001. "Transnational Politics: Contention and Institutions in International Politics." *Annual Review of Political Science.* 4, 1–20.

2005. *The New Transnational Activism.* New York: Cambridge University Press.

2007. "Inside Insurgencies: Politics and Violence in an Age of Civil War" (Book Review Essay). *Perspectives on Politics.* 5 (3), 587–600.

2010. "Dynamics of Diffusion: Mechanisms, Institutions, and Scale Shift." In Rebecca Givan, Kenneth Roberts, & Sarah Soule (eds.), *The Diffusion of Social Movements: Actors, Mechanisms, and Political Effects.* Cambridge University Press.

Tarrow, Sidney & Donnatella della Porta. 2004. "Conclusion: 'Globalization', Complex Internationalism, and Transnational Contention." In Sidney Tarrow & Donnatella della Porta (eds.), *Transnational Protest and Global Activism.* Lanham, MD: Rowman and Littlefield.

Terry, Fiona. 2002. *Condemned to Repeat: The Paradox of Humanitarian Action.* Ithaca, NY: Cornell University Press.

Thomson, Susan. 2011. "Reeducation for Reconciliation: Participant Observations on the Ingando." In Scott Straus & Lars Waldorf (eds.), *Remaking Rwanda: State Building and Human Rights after Mass Violence.* Madison: University of Wisconsin Press, 331–339.

Tilly, Charles. 1978. *From Mobilization to Revolution.* Massachusetts: Addison-Wesley.

Tishkov, Valery. 2004. *Chechnya: Life in a War-Torn Society.* Berkeley: University of California Press.

Toft, Monica Duffy. 2007. "Getting Religion? The Puzzling Case of Islam and Civil War." *International Security.* 31 (4), 97–131.

Tuathail, Gearóid Ó. 2009. "Placing Blame: Making Sense of Beslan." *Political Geography.* 28 (1), 4–15.

Tucker, R. W., C. B. Keely, & L.Wrigley (eds.). 1990. *Immigration and US Foreign Policy*. Boulder, CO: Westview Press.

Tumelty, Paul. 2006. "The Rise and Fall of Foreign Fighters in Chechnya." *Terrorism Monitor*. January 26.

Turkish Democracy Foundation. 1997. Fact Book on PKK Terrorism. Ankara.

UN. 1993. "Situation of Human Rights in the Sudan." Note by the Secretary-General. http://daccess-dds-ny.un.org/doc/UNDOC/GEN/N94/408/18/pdf/N9440818.pdf?OpenElement. (Accessed May 25, 2010)

UN General Assembly. 1997. The Rights of the Child. 51st Session. Resolution 51/77. http://daccess-dds-ny.un.org/doc/UNDOC/GEN/N97/768/37/PDF/N9776837.pdf?OpenElement. (Accessed May 20, 2010)

UNHCR. 2001. *The State of the World's Refugees: Fifty Years of Humanitarian Action*. Oxford University Press.

2002. "External Evaluation of the UNHCR Shelter Program in Rwanda 1994–1999." RLSS Mission Report 2000/3. Geneva, Switzerland: UNHCR.

2003. "UNHCR Assisted Voluntary Repatriation to Afghanistan – Report from Daily Encashment Centres." Kabul: United Nations High Commissioner for Refugees.

2010a. "2009 Global Trends: Refugees, Asylum-seekers, Returnees, Internally Displaced and Stateless Persons." Geneva: United Nations High Commissioner for Refugees.

2010b. "Democratic Republic of the Congo, 1993–2003: Report of the Mapping Exercise on Human Rights Violations." New York: UNHCR.

UNICEF. 2000. "Sudan Rebels give UNICEF a guarantee on child soldiers", UNICEF press release. www.unicef.org/newsline/00prslpa.htm. (Accessed July 17, 2010)

2001a. "UNICEF airlifts over 2,500 demobilized child soldiers out of Sudan combat zone", UNICEF Press Release. www.unicef.org/newsline/01pr22.htm. (Accessed July 17, 2010)

2001b. "UNICEF Returns Former Child Soldiers Home", UNICEF Press Release. www.unicef.org/newsline/01pr71.htm. (Accessed July 17, 2010)

UN Security Council. 1999. "On the Children and Armed Conflict." *Resolution* 1261. http://daccess-dds-ny.un.org/doc/UNDOC/GEN/N99/248/59/PDF/N9924859.pdf?OpenElement.

2000. "On the Children and Armed Conflict." Resolution 1314. http://daccess-dds-ny.un.org/doc/UNDOC/GEN/N00/604/03/PDF/N0060403.pdf?OpenElement. (Accessed May 20, 2010)

2001. "On Children and Armed Conflict." Resolution 1379. http://dac-cess-dds-ny.un.org/doc/UNDOC/GEN/N01/651/10/PDF/N0165110. pdf?OpenElement. (Accessed May 20, 2010)

2003. "Children and Armed Conflict." Resolution 1460. http://daccess-dds-ny.un.org/doc/UNDOC/GEN/N03/231/16/PDF/N0323116.pdf? OpenElement. (Accessed May 20, 2010)

2004. "Children and Armed Conflict." Resolution 1539. http://daccess-dds-ny.un.org/doc/UNDOC/GEN/N04/318/63/PDF/N0431863.pdf? OpenElement. (Accessed May 20, 2010)

2005. "Children and Armed Conflict." Resolution 1612. http://daccess-dds-ny.un.org/doc/UNDOC/GEN/N05/439/59/PDF/N0543959.pdf? OpenElement. (Accessed May 20, 2010)

United States Department of State, Office for the Coordinator for Counter-terrorism. 2010. "Designation of Caucasus Emirates Leader Doku Umarov." June 23. www.state.gov/s/ct/rls/other/des/143564.htm. (Accessed July 5, 2010)

Uslaner, Eric M. 1991. "A Tower of Babel on Foreign Policy?" In Allan J. Cigler & A.Burdett (eds.), *Loomis Interest Group Politics*. Washington, DC: Congressional Quarterly Inc.

US Senate. 2000. Committee on Foreign Relations. US Commission on International Religious Freedom: Findings on Russia, China and Sudan; and Religious Persecutions in the World. 106th Cong., 2d sess., May 16.

Ustinova, Mara. 2004. *The Chechen Conflict in the Eyes of Prominent Chechen Intellectuals: An Oral History Approach*. Moscow: Institute for Ethnology and Anthropology, Russian Academy of Sciences.

Van Acker, Frank. 2004. "Uganda and the Lord's Resistance Army: The New Order no one Ordered." *African Affairs*. 103, 335–357.

van Bijlert, Martine. 2009. "Unruly Commanders and Violent Power Struggles: Taliban Networks in Uruzgan." In Antonio Giustozzi (ed.), *Decoding the New Taliban: Insights from the Afghan Field*, New York: Columbia University Press, 155–178.

van der Meeren, Rachel. 1996. "Three Decades in Exile: Rwandan Refugees 1960–1990." *Journal of Refugee Studies*. 9(3), 252–267.

Van Evera, Stephen. 1997. *Guide to Methods for Students of Political Science*. Ithaca, NY: Cornell University Press.

Van Hear, Nicholas. 1998. *New Diasporas: The Mass Exodus, Dispersal and Regrouping of Migrant Communities*. London: UCL Press.

2002. "Sustaining Societies Under Strain: Remittances as a form of Trans-national Exchange in Sri Lanka and Ghana." In Nadje al-Ali & Khalid

Koser (eds.), *New Approaches to Migration? Transnational Communities and the Transformation of Home.* London: Routledge, 202–223.

van Linschoten, Alex Strick, & Felix Kuehn. 2011. "Separating the Taliban from Al-Qaeda: The Core of Success in Afghanistan." CIC Study. Center on International Cooperation, New York University.

Vatchagaev, Mairbek. 2007. "The Dagestani Jamaat (Part 1)." *North Caucasus Analysis.* December 13.

Vidino, Lorenzo. 2005. "How Chechnya Became a Breeding Ground for Terror." *Middle East Quarterly.* 7 (3), 57–66.

Vinci, Anthony. 2007. "Existential Motivations in the Lord's Resistance Army's Continuing Conflict." *Studies in Conflict & Terrorism.* 30, 337–352.

Vinjamuri, Leslie. 2010. "Deterrence, Democracy, and the Pursuit of International Justice." *Ethics & International Affairs.* 24, 191–211.

Waislamah News Network. 2002. *The Life and Times of Khattab.* www. maktabah.net/store/Products/ViewProductDetails.aspx?ProductID=29048 &ID=0. (Accessed September 29, 2009)

Waldorf, Lars. 2009. *"Transitional Justice and DDR: The Case of Rwanda."* New York: International Center for Transitional Justice.

Walhbeck, Östen. 1999. *Kurdish Diasporas: A Comparative Study.* London: MacMillan.

Walter, Barbara F. 2003. "The Critical Barrier to Civil War Settlement." *International Organization.* 51 (3), 335–364.

Waltz, Kenneth. 1979. *Theory of International Politics.* Reading, MA: Addison-Wesley.

Ware, Robert Bruce. 2005. "A Multitude of Evils: Mythology and Political Failure in Chechnya." In Richard Sakwa (ed.), *Chechnya: From Past to Future.* London: Anthem Press, 79–116.

Watts, Nicole, F. 2004. "Institutionalizing Virtual Kurdistan West: Pro-Kurdish Politics in Western Europe." In Joel Migdal (ed.), *Boundaries and Belonging: States and Societies in the Struggle to Shape Identities and Local Practice.* Cambridge University Press,

Weidmann, Nils B. 2007. "From Sparks to Prairie Fires: Spatial Mechanisms of Group Mobilization." Paper presented at the Annual Convention of the American Political Science Association, Chicago.

Weil, Martin. 1974. "Can the Blacks Do for Africa what the Jews Did for Israel?" *Foreign Policy.* 15, 109–130.

Weiner, Myron. 1992. "Security, Stability and International Migration." *International Security.* 17(3), 91–126.

1996. "Bad Neighbors, Bad Neighborhoods." *International Security.* 21 (1), 5–42.

Weinstein, Jeremy. 2007. *Inside Rebellion: The Politics of Insurgent Violence*. New York: Cambridge University Press.

Wendt, Alexander. 1992. "Anarchy is What States Make of It: The Social Construction of Power Politics." *International Organization*. 46 (2), 391–425.

1999. *Social Theory of International Politics*. Cambridge University Press.

Weyland, Kurt. 2007. *Bounded Rationality and Policy Diffusion: Social Sector Reform in Latin America*. Princeton University Press.

2009. "The Diffusion of Revolution: '1848' in Europe and Latin America." *International Organization*. 63, 391–423.

White, Paul J. 2001. *Primitive Rebels or Revolutionary Modernizers? The Kurdish National Movement in Turkey*. London: Zed Books.

Wight, Colin. 2002. "Philosophy of Science and International Relations." In Walter Carlsnaes, Thomas Risse, & Beth Simmons (eds.), *Handbook of International Relations*. London: Sage Publications, 23–51.

2006. *Agents, Structures and International Relations: Politics as Ontology*. Cambridge University Press.

2007. "A Manifesto for Scientific Realism in IR: Assuming the Can-Opener Won't Work!" *Millenium: Journal of International Studies*. 35 (2), 379–398.

Wilhelmsen, Julie. 2004. *When Separatists Become Islamists: The Case of Chechnya*. Kjeller, Norway: The Norwegian Defence Research Establishment.

Williams, Brian Glyn. 2000. "Commemorating 'The Deportation': The Role of Memorialization and Collective Memory in the 1994–96 Chechen War." *Memory and History*. 12 (1), 101–134.

2003. "Shattering the Al-Qaeda-Chechen Myth (Part II)." *Chechnya Weekly*. November 6.

2005a. "The 'Chechen Arabs': An Introduction to the Real Al-Qaeda Terrorists from Chechnya." *Terrorism Monitor*. May 5.

2005b. "Turkish Volunteers in Chechnya." *Terrorism Monitor*. April 6.

2007. "Allah's Foot Soldiers An Assessment of the Role of Foreign Fighters and Al-Qa'ida in the Chechen Insurgency." In Moshe Gammer (ed.), *Ethno-Nationalism, Islam and the State in the Caucasus: Post-Soviet Disorder*. London: Routledge, 156–178.

Williams, Paul D. 2007. "From Non-Intervention to Non-Indifference: The Origins and Development of the African Union's Security Culture." *African Affairs*. 106, 253–279.

Wolf, Frank, R. 2001. "Op-Ed: Peace In Sudan Needs To Be International Priority." http://wolf.house.gov/index.cfm?sectionid=34&sectiontree=6,34 &itemid=483. (Accessed July 20, 2010)

Wood, Elisabeth Jean. 2003. *Insurgent Collective Action and Civil War in El Salvador*. New York: Cambridge University Press.

    2008. "The Social Processes of Civil War: The Wartime Transformation of Social Networks." *Annual Review of Political Science*. 11, 539–561.

    2009. "Armed Groups and Sexual Violence: When is Wartime Rape Rare?" *Politics and Society*. 37 (1), 131–162.

    2010. "Sexual Violence During War: Variation and Accountability." In Alette Smeulers & Elies van Sliedregt (eds.), *Collective Crimes and International Criminal Justice: An Interdisciplinary Approach*. Antwerp: Intersentia, 295–322.

Woodward, Peter. 2006. *US Foreign Policy and the Horn of Africa*. Burlington, VT: Ashgate.

Wucherpfennig, Julian, Nils Metternich, Lars-Erik Cederman, & Kristian Skrede Gleditsch. 2012. "Ethnicity, the State, and the Duration of Civil War." *World Politics*. 64 (1), 79–115.

Yousaf, Mohammad & Mark Adkin. 1992. *The Bear Trap: Afghanistan's Untold Story*. Lahore: Jang.

Zahab, Mariam Abou & Olivier Roy. 2004. *Islamic Networks: The Pakistan-Afghan Connection*. London: C. Hurst.

Zolberg, Aristide, Astri Suhrke, & Sergio Aguayo. 1986. "International Factors in the Formation of Refugee Movements." *International Migration Review*. 20 (2), 151–169.

    1989. *Escape from Violence: Conflict and the Refugee Crisis in the Developing World*. New York: Oxford University Press.

Zürcher, Christoph. 2007. *The Post-Soviet Wars: Rebellion, Ethnic Conflict, and Nationhood in the Caucasus*. New York University Press.

Index

Abdelal, R., 173, 179
abductions, 120, 123–4, 126, 128,
  134–9, 141–2, 144, 147, 251, 258
  See also hostage-taking; kidnapping
Abdulkhadzhie, Aslambek, 55
Abkhazia, 46
Abu Walid al-Ghamdi, 50, 57
accountability, 65, 131, 135, 145, 165
  "accountability and reconciliation",
  145
Acharya, Amitaev, 195, 236
Acholi, 124–5, 127–30, 133, 136–7,
  140, 144, 147
  diaspora, 123, 138–9, 249, 252
  See also Lord's Resistance Army;
  Uganda
Achverina, Vera, 153
Adamson, Fiona, 123, 200, 217,
  219–20, 223, 225, 244–5, 250–2,
  255–6
adaptation, social, 14–15, 122, 218–19,
  255
  and appropriateness, 179
  and entrepreneurship, 173–201, 220,
  257
  and Sudan, 147
  defined, 174, 179
  vs. emulation, 179
Afghanistan
  Hezb-e Islami, 99, 101–3
  Jamiat-e Islami, 99, 103–4
  Junbesh-e Milli, 101
  Kabul, 101, 103, 106, 254
  Kandahar, 104
  Northern Alliance, 104
  Operation Enduring Freedom, 106
  People's Democratic Party of
  Afghanistan, 97, 101, 103
African Union, 180
agency, 4, 16, 23

collective, 68
  of refugees, 119, 249
  political, 89, 245
  vs. structure, 178
agenda-setting, 84
agent-based modeling, 11, 15, 17, 20,
  22, 174–5, 178, 181–4, 188, 195,
  217, 220, 252, 254–5, 257–8
Aguayo, Sergio, 96
aid, 106–7, 126, 141, 161, 225, 250
  emergency, 119
  food, 108
  humanitarian, 60, 98, 110, 113, 139,
  161, 164
  military, 171
  refugee, 98
  See also NGOs
Al Jazeera, 56
al-Qaeda, 65, 106, 231
  See also terrorism
Algeria, 86
alienation, 38, 193, 220
allegiance/loyalty, 25, 94, 102–3,
  116–17, 119, 252
alliances, 33, 177, 222, 255
  and security dilemma, 222
  burden-sharing, 222
  transnational mobilization of, 256–7
Amin, Idi, 110, 127–8, 136
amnesty, 124, 130–2, 142–4, 146, 217
Amnesty International, 126, 167
analytic eclecticism, 11, 21, 212–13
Andvig, Jens Christopher, 153
appropriateness, social, 38–9, 174, 178,
  180, 185, 192–3, 215
  "logic of appropriateness", 214
  and free-riding, 214
  and norm entrepreneurs, 180–1
  and scientific realism, 209
  and social adaptation, 179, 185